# HERMENEUTICS AND THE CHURCH

READING THE SCRIPTURES

Gary A. Anderson, Matthew Levering, and Robert Louis Wilken
*series editors*

JAMES A. ANDREWS

# HERMENEUTICS
## AND THE CHURCH

## IN DIALOGUE WITH AUGUSTINE

*University of Notre Dame Press*

*Notre Dame, Indiana*

Library of Congress Cataloging-in-Publication Data

Andrews, James A.
Hermeneutics and the church : in dialogue with Augustine / James A. Andrews.
p. cm. — (Reading the Scriptures)
Includes bibliographical references (p.    ) and index.
ISBN 978-0-268-02041-5 (pbk.) — ISBN 978-0-268-07475-3 (e-book)
1. Augustine, Saint, Bishop of Hippo. De doctrina Christiana. 2. Bible—Criticism,
interpretation, etc.—History—Early church, ca. 30–600. 3. Theology—History—
Early church, ca. 30-600. I. Title.
BR65.A6552A53  2012
230'.14—dc23
2012024893

TO CHRIS

# Contents

# Acknowledgments

This book has taken some five years to finish, but the questions behind it have concerned me for much longer. In my first homiletics course, I could not figure out how to bridge the gap between the biblical exegesis I had learned and the sermon I had to preach on Acts 22:3–11. Only after writing two outlines and one disregarded draft did I discover Calvin's commentary. This, I remember thinking, is how one interprets the Bible. I know many have similar experiences, and that, in and of itself, is reason enough for the hermeneutical investigation that follows.

For various reasons, I graduated seminary feeling unprepared for ordained ministry and decided to pursue further academic study. Perhaps, I thought, I would fit better in the academy than in the church, and I was unprepared for what actually happened: through a detailed study of Augustine and his hermeneutics, I find myself on the other side of a Ph.D. pursuing the possibility of ordination once more. As with any academic book, attention to a small, theoretical area can lead to much larger, practical conclusions, but these are not necessarily drawn in the text itself. This interaction between academic and practical concerns informs the entire project—even when it is not immediately obvious—and, for that reason, it seems appropriate to take a moment to acknowledge all those whose influence can be felt in the pages that follow.

The initial draft of this book was my doctoral thesis, finished at King's College, University of Aberdeen, under the supervision of Francis Watson. I am grateful to him for many things, not the least of which is that he encouraged me to pursue a topic in which I was very interested—Augustine and hermeneutics—rather than a New Testament one I thought was vaguely intriguing. I cannot over-emphasize how delightful it was to work with such an enthusiastic supervisor.

Theology at Aberdeen is a serious occupation, and while there I soaked in things of which I was unconscious until beginning to teach theology myself. Phil Ziegler offered numerous comments on the thesis manuscript in the months before I submitted it, and he deserves thanks for his careful theological eye and insightful com-ments. I am particularly grateful for the numerous conversations I had with Matthew Edwards, Darren Sarisky, and Don Wood. In addition, I could not have had a better set of Ph.D. examiners—John Webster and Lewis Ayres—to whom I am indebted for their careful engagement with my ideas and their helpful suggestions to improve the work for publication.

The book began at Aberdeen, but it has benefited from a much wider network of people, all of whom deserve mention. I met with both of my primary interlocutors—Werner Jeanrond and Stephen Fowl—and both were kind enough to spend an hour or so talking with me. I have learned a good deal from engaging with their ideas. Several of the discussions and concepts of this book were explored in an earlier article, "Why Theological Hermeneutics Needs Rheto-ric" (*International Journal of Systematic Theology* 12 [2010]: 184–200), and I am grateful to Stephen Fowl for thoughtfully responding to it when I sent it to him. I am also grateful to Carol Harrison, who read a draft of the initial two chapters and offered helpful comments.

I began working at the University of St. Andrews after complet-ing my Ph.D., and while there I have been fortunate to work with Karla Pollmann on the After Augustine project. Karla kindly met with me and discussed aspects of her own work, while reading por-tions of my initial manuscript and giving helpful comments. She was kind enough to read the first two chapters once I revised them, and, once more, she offered invaluable remarks that strengthened the material.

I also had the opportunity to work in St. Mary's College, St. Andrews, as an associate lecturer of theology, and my thinking has benefited from conversations with Ivor Davidson, Mark Elliott, Gavin Hopps, Alan Torrance, and Tom Wright. I am particularly grateful to the College for the provision of an office, even outside of term time, where I managed to revise the Ph.D. thesis and turn it into the present book. I am thankful for my students, who asked questions and reminded me why one works on a Ph.D. to begin with. Thanks also go to Debbie Smith, Susan Millar, and Margot Clement for their ever-friendly assistance.

I am grateful to the University of Notre Dame Press, particularly to Matthew Levering, Chuck Van Hof, Rebecca DeBoer, Josh Messner, and to my peer reviewers, whose reports helped me clarify potentially obscure portions of the argument. I must also gratefully acknowledge two bodies that funded the initial research: the College of Arts and Social Sciences at the University of Aberdeen and the Overseas Research Scholarship Awards Scheme.

More people impact academic work than those whose influence can be discerned within the pages. Two particular former teachers helped me along the way, neither of whom will likely agree with the conclusions I draw but who nonetheless deserve my sincerest thanks: Bruce Winter and Professor Joachim Schaper. Likewise, one's academic work would suffer without continual interaction with friends and family. There are too many friends to name, but I would particularly like to thank Joseph Hammond, Kristin Lindfield-Ott, Phill Pass, Sarah Schell, and Paul and Amber Warhurst (and Ruby and Margot).

I owe much to my family. Erin Chandler read the original draft in its entirety, offering many helpful editorial comments. In more ways than one, the following would have been impossible without Randal and Janice Chandler. Many complain about their in-laws, but I have nothing to say to mine but "thank you." My father has always been fascinated by what I am writing, and his constant interest has been a source of encouragement. Throughout my academic studies, my mother did not fail to ring at least once a week. Her support is unwavering, and for that, I am grateful.

Finally, I am most thankful to my wife, Chris. Though she has her own research to do, she only rarely complains that I talk about my own more than I should, and she reminds me that there is more to life than study. She even patiently read the initial manuscript and offered suggestions. Her reserves of faith and strength are astounding, and she has taught me a great deal. I am grateful for our last nine years, and I look forward to the future. I dedicate this book to her.

Still, coming full circle, I owe one final statement of thanks. When working on Augustine, one cannot help but be impressed by just how important the church is for his theology and, as the following pages will demonstrate, for his hermeneutics. As I said above, I began the investigation to answer my own questions about how one connects biblical interpretation to theology, and while I worked on Augustine, I attended All Saints' Church, St. Andrews. My gratitude to this wonderful congregation goes well beyond any practical thanks I can express here. While there, I was privileged to hear the skillful sermons of Fr. Jonathan Mason. Eventually, I was preaching regularly, once more highlighting the questions that informed this project's inception. Hearing Jonathan's sermons and preaching myself reinforced the conclusions I drew when researching and writing the book. If scripture is an instrument in the divine economy of salvation, established to engender the double love of God and neighbor, the church is indispensable for biblical interpretation and, by extension, for theology. When I think about the conclusions of this investigation, I know they could have been drawn simply by reading *De doctrina* closely, but the actual process was more complex. Seeing how scripture is integrated into the worship at All Saints'—from the weekly sung eucharist to the Stations of the Cross to the Easter Vigil—made it easier to see what Augustine was doing in the pages of his book and easier to put the conclusions of my book into practice.

# Abbreviations

## WORKS BY AUGUSTINE

In the following pages, I use the abbreviations from the *Augustinus-Lexikon*, ed. Cornelius Mayer (Würzburg: Schwabe, 1986 –).[1] Unless otherwise noted, the translations are my own. The bibliography contains the critical editions of the texts as well as English translations.

| | |
|---|---|
| *agon.* | *De agone christiano* |
| *c. ep. Man.* | *Contra epistulam Manichaei quam vocant fundamenti* |
| *c. ep. Pel.* | *Contra duas epistulas Pelagianorum* |
| *c. Faust.* | *Contra Faustum* |
| *cat. rud.* | *De catechizandis rudibus* |
| *civ.* | *De civitate dei* |
| *conf.* | *Confessiones* |
| *Cresc.* | *Contra Cresconium* |
| *doctr. chr.* | *De doctrina christiana* |
| *en. Ps.* | *Enarrationes in Psalmos* |
| *ench.* | *Enchiridion ad Laurentum de fide spe et caritate* |
| *ep.* | *Epistulae* |
| *ep. Rm. inch.* | *Epistulae ad Romanos inchoata expositio liber unus* |
| *exp. Gal.* | *Expositio epistulae ad Galatas* |
| *Gn. adv. Man.* | *De Genesi adversus Manichaeos* |
| *Gn. litt.* | *De Genesi ad litteram* |

---

[1] I use a "v" for the consonantal "u."

| | |
|---|---|
| *Gn. litt. inp.* | *De Genesi ad litteram liber unus inperfectus* |
| *gr. et lib. arb.* | *De gratia et libero arbitrio* |
| *gr. et pecc. or.* | *De gratia Christi et de peccato originali* |
| *Io. ev. tr.* | *In Iohannis evangelium tractatus* |
| *mag.* | *De magistro* |
| *nat. et gr.* | *De natura et gratia* |
| *nupt. et conc.* | *De nuptiis et concupiscentia* |
| *ord.* | *De ordine* |
| *pecc. mer.* | *De peccatorum meritis et remissione et de baptismo parvulorum* |
| *retr.* | *Retractiones* |
| *s. dom. m.* | *De sermone Domini in monte* |
| *Simpl.* | *De diversis quaestionibus ad Simplicianum* |
| *spir. et litt.* | *De spiritu et littera* |
| *trin.* | *De trinitate* |
| *util. cred.* | *De utilitate credendi* |

## WORKS BY OTHER ANCIENT AUTHORS

| | |
|---|---|
| *LR* | Tyconius, *Liber Regularum* |
| *Orat.* | Cicero, *Orator* |

## OTHER ABBREVIATIONS

| | |
|---|---|
| *BA* | *Bibliothèque Augustinienne* |
| CCL | Corpus Christianorum Series Latina (Turnhout: Brepols, 1953–) |
| CD | Karl Barth, *Church Dogmatics*. Edited by G. W. Bromiley and T. F. Torrance. 4 vols. 12 parts. Edinburgh: T&T Clark, 1936–1977. |
| CSEL | Corpus Scriptorum Ecclesiasticorum Latinorum (Vienna: Tempsky, 1865–) |
| FC | The Fathers of the Church |
| LCC | Library of Christian Classics |

| | |
|---|---|
| LXX | Septuagint |
| MT | Masoretic Text |
| NPNF | Nicene and Post-Nicene Fathers |
| WSA | The Works of Saint Augustine: A Translation for the Twenty-First Century |

# Introduction

Scriptural interpretation is an enduring concern of the church and will remain so until the eschaton. There is no shortage of methodologies on offer and, for that reason, it might seem out of place for another book to be written that argues for a certain form of appropriate interpretive practice. Likewise, engaging with Augustine is one of the oldest forms of Christian thought. There is, again, no shortage of research on this Church Father, and it might seem pointless to publish yet another book examining his ideas. Nonetheless, because scriptural interpretation is of utmost importance, theological hermeneutics will always remain a topic worthwhile to reconsider. And because Augustine is one of the preeminent saints of the church, a dialogue with his ideas on scriptural interpretation will never be out of place or outmoded. The church is, after all, the fellowship of the saints in the power of the Spirit. Those who have gone before us still speak to us, and we would do well to listen. And not only that: we would also do well to ask questions.

What follows, then, is a self-conscious dialogue between contemporary theology and Augustine. Because the topic under discussion is scriptural interpretation, interacting with his work *De doctrina christiana* is a logical choice. This text has acquired classical status, and thus one can assume it has something to say even today. Looking to the past may well provide important resources to move beyond problems of the present.[1] Augustine's problems were not our problems, but in *De doctrina* he discusses the reasons, and the tools necessary, for interpreting the words of the prophets and apostles. Because of his time and place, what he has to say will be different from what theologians in our own context have to say. And that is precisely where his example can be instructive. Moreover, by turning back to Augustine from the present in a self-consciously dialogical manner, I suggest that insights will also be gained with respect to *De doctrina*. Because theological hermeneutics is the topic, and because in this text Augustine speaks theoretically about scriptural interpretation, I confine myself in the pages that follow to discussion of *De doctrina*.

It has been argued on numerous occasions, however, that the work is not representative of Augustine's practice, and, for that reason, it will be helpful to dispel such a notion briefly here at the start.[2] If one wants Augustine's views on interpretation, so the argument goes, *De doctrina* alone does not suffice. Rather, one should view him in practice; there one finds the "true" Augustine. As Frederick Van Fleteren states, "Without study of Augustine's hermeneutic and exegetical practice, *De doctrina christiana* alone could be misleading."[3] While there is some truth to this statement—a hermeneutics would never be complete without some kind of practice to model it—one need not assume that an investigation of *De doctrina* alone will yield a distorted picture of Augustine's practice. As Karla Pollmann states, "Strictly speaking, the idea of a hermeneutics scattered throughout different works is a contradiction in itself, as it is precisely the task of a hermeneutics (in contrast to mere 'rules of exegesis') to display the issue in a coherent and systematic whole."[4] *De doctrina* is just such a work, written by Augustine to pass on "certain rules for interpreting scripture" (Prol. 1). Perhaps it does not touch on all the issues that arise in Augustine's practice, but it is an outline for what he envisions the interpretation of scripture to require. Indeed, that is perhaps how a hermeneutics should be. Were every aspect discussed, one might as well simply get on with the interpretive act itself. It is not as though *De doctrina* contrasts with Augustine's actual interpretive practice. Because he writes what I will term an "*a posteriori* hermeneutics"—one to aid an existing practice of interpretation—it would be surprising if there were such a conflict. In fact, it can be demonstrated even in his more exegetical works that he sticks to the rules he gives in *De doctrina*, while perhaps going beyond them.

For instance, one need only note that Augustine's major "commentaries" on John and the Psalms are sermons.[5] As the subsequent pages will argue, the sermon is paradigmatic for his interpretive program. One interprets the scriptural texts in order to share that understanding with others to elicit a certain response: progression in the love of God *and* the love of neighbor. Interpretation—a two-part process involving understanding the text and delivering that understanding to others—is one of the ways humans come together in love. Book i of *De doctrina* sets out two primary rules that govern scriptural reading: the *regula fidei* and the *regula dilectionis*. The *regula fidei* comprises those things of faith and hope, the *objects* to which one relates in love. As Augustine's *Enchiridion* stresses, faith, hope, and love are inseparable, but faith and hope are pointless without love: "For when there is a question as to whether a person is good, one does not ask what he believes, or what he hopes, but what he loves."[6] Likewise, in a late letter, Augustine insists that even *De civitate dei*, a book likely to be deemed simply "historical," follows the "paradigm" of a sermon:

> I see that in one of your other letters you make excuses about why you have put off accepting the sacrament of rebirth and thus, in effect, you are throwing away the fruits of all those books you love. What fruits? Not that someone may have some interesting reading nor that he may learn a lot of things he did not know before. But that the reader may be convinced of the City of God so that he enter it without delay or that he become even more determined to stay in it. The first of these two things is conferred by rebirth, the second by the love of justice. If those by whom these books are read and praised do not actually take action and do these things, what good are the books? As far as you yourself are concerned, when they have not been able to get you to take even the first step, however much you praise them, thus far they have failed completely. (*Ep.* 2*.3, *Ad Firmum*)[7]

Here, when responding to letters from Firmus, Augustine gently rebukes the intellectual for simply enjoying *De civitate dei*, for reading and discussing it with detachment without actually being moved to accept the cleansing waters of baptism. The work should convince the unbeliever to enter the baptismal waters, from which—as *De doctrina* tells us—"all ascend to bear twins, the two commandments of love, and not one of them lacks that holy fruit" (2.6.7). And it should persuade the believer to desire to remain in the church and to live in the appropriate manner. In other words, *De doctrina*'s emphasis on the sermon and its role in engendering the double love of God and neighbor remains consistent throughout Augustine's lifelong engagement with scripture.

In *Enarrationes in Psalmos*, Augustine deploys another of the principles enunciated in *De doctrina*, what I will call the "*caritas* criterion," the principle that states if something cannot be connected to the realm of love, then it must be interpreted figuratively:

Do not think that there are wicked people in the world for no reason and that God brings nothing good from them. Every wicked person lives so that he may be corrected or so that a good person may be exercised by him. If only the one who presently exercises us would be converted and so be exercised with us! Nevertheless, as long as they continue to exercise us, let us not hate them because we do not know which of them will persevere in wickedness to the end. In fact, often when it seems to you that you have hated an enemy, you have actually hated a brother and not known it. The devil and his angels alone have been revealed to us in holy scripture as destined for eternal fire. Of them only should we despair of amendment, against whom we have a hidden struggle for which the Apostle arms us, saying, "Our struggle is not against flesh and blood"—that is, against people you see—"but against the leaders, the powers, the rulers of the world, of this darkness.". . . Therefore, since this rule of love [*regula dilectionis*] is established for you, that imitating the Father you should love your enemy . . . how would you be exercised in the command if you endure no enemy?[8]

Such a move is crucial, as anyone who has attempted to pray the Psalms can testify.[9] In the one under discussion, the speaker is oppressed by his enemies and pleads with God to have mercy on him and to cast them down. Augustine preached this sermon in the midst of the Donatist controversy when it would have been easy to read such a psalm as directly applicable to his current situation, but the *caritas* criterion espoused in *De doctrina* comes into effect. To call down vengeance on one's opponents is not the duty of the Christian who lives after Christ. Rather, Christ commands his followers to love their enemies, and thus Augustine can posit the reason there are in fact enemies to love as well as the reason not to hate them. Furthermore, he insists that only the devil and his minions are assuredly damned. Thus, he implicitly suggests that such a psalm—when calling down wrath on enemies and insisting that they will not change—is figuratively speaking of the devil and his angels. Only God knows the humans who will persevere in their rebellion to the end.[10] The church must love even its enemies and pray that they too will one day be brothers and sisters who must persevere in loving their enemies.

The preceding—admittedly brief—discussion demonstrates that Augustine follows the principles laid out in *De doctrina* throughout his career. Perhaps there are other ideas that can be gleaned from his works, but this treatise presents at least a starting point for understanding why and how one interprets the Bible theologically. As will be discussed in the following chapter, Augustine actually completed *De doctrina* rather than let it be catalogued as unfinished in *Retractiones*. It is, therefore, entirely accurate to state that the dialogue that follows is between Augustine and contemporary theology precisely because *De doctrina* is Augustine's theological hermeneutics, that is, his theoretical reflection on the practice of interpretation.

I write what follows with two groups of people in mind. For scholars of Augustine, I offer a reading of *De doctrina* that takes the entirety of the work seriously and seeks to allow him to speak through the words he wrote at the beginning and end of his bishopric. My goal is to allow him to be a living voice, and that necessitates a close textual engagement with his ideas. Several works have been written about *De doctrina*, and I do not intend my study to replace them but to supplement them.[11] Still, it does appear that—in recent English-language scholarship anyway—a full textual engagement with this work is missing.[12] I intend here to follow one of Lewis Ayres's suggestions for reading texts of the tradition: when studying figures from the history of theology, theologians "need to develop the same sense of attention to the dead as they consider it appropriate to show towards the living."[13] I aim to push this idea further than Ayres himself likely intends: if such attention is demanded, then it seems reasonable to put the ancient theologian into *direct* conversation with contemporary ones. Of course, the use of "direct" can only really be metaphorical, since a good deal of historical work must be done to bring Augustine forward. But the dialogue is more than just "mediated," because the goal is actually to do the historical work so that Augustine can speak through his text into our contemporary context, in close proximity to modern interlocutors. This exercise, I propose, will allow new insights and new ways of describing the ancient text to come to the surface.

My argument seeks to provide a new and faithful way of talking about Augustine's text, but it also aims to offer an example in practice of how one engages theologically with the texts of the past. For theologians, therefore, I offer a model, and more than that, I offer the actual fruits of the engagement: suggestions for the discipline of theological hermeneutics and the practice of scriptural interpretation. One of the issues present in theological appeals to Augustine is that he often falls victim to a partial reading. One need look only at recent theological uses of *De doctrina* to see that the work is often fragmented and only a portion of it used to advance the theologian's viewpoint.[14]

Telford Work appeals both to Athanasius's *On the Incarnation of the Word* and *De doctrina* in order to develop an ontology of scripture.[15] He discusses Augustine's text in terms of its fundamental "analogy of the Word."[16] Work follows Mark Jordan and appeals to this analogy to argue that scripture's words are analogous to the divine *logos*. Just as the *logos* emptied himself and came in the form of a servant, so God "makes his words vulnerable, for a time, to abuse."[17] For Work, scripture is "God's *self*-involvement in the world, somehow analogous to his personal involvement in the incarnate Jesus."[18] Such a construal of scripture is at once compelling and provocative. By using Athanasius's text and Augustine's, Work develops a sophisticated trinitarian ontology of scripture that accounts both for the text's divine and human attributes without falling victim to some of the more polarizing versions of this construal.[19] By arguing for such an ontology, he perhaps attaches scripture much more firmly to God's presence than Augustine would do. Work states: "Our ecclesiology of Scripture focuses on the Bible as a means of God's presence to his earthly, eschatological community, and as an instrument of the worshiping community when it is present before God."[20] Augustine would agree that scripture is an instrument in the divine economy, but a close reading of *De doctrina* would put more emphasis on God's presence in the *interpretation* of scripture, thus moving the stress away from scripture's ontology—a particularly Protestant concern—and on to the biblical texts' instrumentality in the divine economy. This point touches on the discussion below in chapters 4 and 5. Work's theology of scripture remains thought provoking, and his use of Augustine in conjunction with Athanasius is commendable. The subsequent pages will differ, however, in their more precise engagement with Augustine's text.[21]

Matthew Levering provides another recent example when he utilizes *De doctrina* briefly on his way to analyzing Thomas Aquinas.[22] Levering pulls from the treatise a purpose for reading scripture: "Thus, understanding the texts of Scripture in themselves is not, in itself, the purpose of reading Scripture. Instead, understanding the texts has as its purpose the encounter with Love—none other than incarnate Wisdom, Jesus Christ—teaching through them, so that we might be caught up into Love's wise pattern for our lives. This proper reading and hearing involves us in Christ's communion, the church, in which we are configured to the heavenly image that Christ teaches us."[23] For Levering, Augustine is helpful because he points to the instrumentality of scriptural reading: it is not an end in itself but is instead an activity that brings about certain forms of participation with Christ and his church. God's teaching and humanity's are not in conflict, and Levering finds this stance helpful in Augustine's model. On the basis of Augustine and Aquinas, Levering combines the focus on history as currently understood with precritical exegesis, what he calls a "participatory-historical" mode.[24] His model focuses not only on the biblical texts but also on participation with the divine teacher speaking through them. Such a construal is undoubtedly nearer to Augustine's than speaking, as Work does, of scripture's ontology. But because Levering is interested in the theological reasons for scriptural interpretation, he stops short of examining the final three books of De doctrina, describing them as "filled with practical advice on how to acquire the canonical, linguistic, historical, grammatical, and rhetorical gifts useful for discerning and teaching persuasively the true meaning of Scripture."[25] He contends that Augustine's "most important contribution" is the first book, where he expands the hermeneutical task to include "existential participation."

While such a reading is helpful, and while Levering is correct to point out that Augustine does discuss the "why" of scriptural interpretation in Book 1 and the "how" in Books 2–4, too quickly dismissing the final three books leads to a truncated version of what Augustine develops in De doctrina. The "why" requires the "how" precisely because Book 4 emphasizes the communal nature of Augustine's program, and this communal location is integral to his hermeneutics. Levering does stress the communal location, and— as with Work—his construal is compelling. But because Levering utilizes two interpreters in order to develop his theology of biblical interpretation, he must skip some parts of De doctrina for pragmatic reasons.

In contrast to these two recent theological engagements with De doctrina, the discussion that follows will engage with the entirety of Augustine's work, allowing him to establish the parameters of the dialogue, precisely to avoid reading my own ideas back into De doctrina. If the goal is to hear Augustine's voice in order to help us move beyond current issues, a few things are necessary: a thorough engagement with the text, with its historical situation, and with contemporary scholarship on it.

Chapters 1 and 2 represent such an exercise. They will demonstrate that what I construe Augustine's version of hermeneutics to be is in fact his and not mine. In discussions about *De doctrina*, scholars often divide the work into two independent parts: Augustine's hermeneutics (Books 1–3) and his thoughts on rhetoric (Book 4). By dividing the work in such a way, Augustine's clear statements about its unity are ignored. In the first chapter, I will argue that its four books and prologue represent a unified treatise, and more than that: it is an eclectic hermeneutics originally written primarily for the clergy. For that reason, I will argue further that *De doctrina* represents an "expanded hermeneutics," that is, a hermeneutics that includes a turn to rhetoric. In contrast to Schleiermacher, Augustine's hermeneutics is not only the inverse of rhetoric, but it also includes a turn to rhetoric. Scriptural interpretation, the *tractatio scripturarum*, is not complete unless one understands scripture and then turns to deliver that understanding to the church. Understanding and delivery are two aspects of the one act of scriptural interpretation. In chapter 2, it will be concluded that Augustine utilizes philosophical and rhetorical concepts in what is at all times a theological hermeneutics. Such conclusions will set the parameters for the discussions that follow.

Because Augustine is writing a theological hermeneutics that engages with philosophical concepts, and because there are several modern proponents of theological hermeneutics who appeal to philosophical concepts in their construals, it will be useful to put *De doctrina* into dialogue with a representative advocate of this kind of hermeneutics. Chapter 3 will therefore analyze the nature of the discipline and will engage with those who discuss this topic in detail. As the chapter will demonstrate, discussion typically revolves around the relationship between general and local, theological, hermeneutics. Some argue that general hermeneutics must be privileged and that theological hermeneutics can only be developed on that basis; only after a detailed account of hermeneutics can the practice of interpretation go forward in a safeguarded manner. I will argue that such a dichotomy between general and local hermeneutics needs to be supplemented by a further delineation between *a priori* and *a posteriori* hermeneutics. Rather than simply addressing whether a theologian prefers general or local hermeneutics, this logical, or temporal, delineation will allow a more precise discussion concerning the relationship of theory to practice. On the basis of a reading of Augustine's text, I will argue that the point of contention between theologians is less about whether general or local hermeneutics should be privileged than about how hermeneutics and the practice of interpretation are related. In theological hermeneutics, the debate does not really concern the scope of hermeneutics—how many texts it accommodates—but it instead concerns the sequential order of the move from theory to practice.

Werner Jeanrond provides a concise, lucid, and forceful argument for why hermeneutics must in theory come before practice to guard both the text and the reader, that is, for an *a priori* hermeneutics. By placing Augustine in dialogue with Jeanrond, conclusions can be drawn about the nature of the relationship between philosophical and theological hermeneutics as well as between theological hermeneutics and the practice of theological interpretation. Briefly, the investigation will demonstrate that Augustine can utilize philosophical ideas without subordinating the ongoing ecclesial practice of biblical interpretation to theory. Such a view will highlight that he has a communal location in mind and that he therefore espouses an *a posteriori* hermeneutics. Because some argue that he does in fact develop a general semiotic theory that constrains a subsequent biblical interpretation, the third chapter primarily argues that Augustine actually locates both his semiotics and his hermeneutics in a theological web, mitigating the force of the argument that he develops a disinterested theory to discipline a subsequent practice.

Because the third chapter will not be able to demonstrate just what kind of community *De doctrina* presupposes, chapter 4 picks this up in order to fill out just how Augustine's hermeneutics is in fact *a posteriori*. This chapter engages at a close textual level with the work, making the case for the argument announced in chapter 1:

that *De doctrina* is an expanded hermeneutics that intends to be read in the first instance by the clergy. There are certainly theological reasons for widening the audience, and the work itself has generalizing tendencies. But such a construal is not only historically accurate and persuasive on internal and external grounds, it also will have tremendous theological pay off. The sermon, on Augustine's model, is paradigmatic for theological interpretation, "paradigmatic" because Book 4 of *De doctrina* actually allows for books and conversations to be the form of delivery, but always as an extension of a sermon, that is, as directed toward the ecclesial community to engender the double love of God and neighbor.

Because chapter 4 emphasizes the church's connection to biblical interpretation due to the *a posteriori* nature of Augustine's hermeneutics, chapter 5 places *De doctrina* into dialogue with Stephen Fowl, an interpreter who also stresses the ecclesial location of interpretation. Several interpreters highlight the necessity of locating scripture in its relationship to the church, and Fowl represents one of the more nuanced proponents of such a view. By putting him into dialogue with Augustine, both interpreters' programs will be thrown into sharp relief. In particular, Augustine's intense focus on scriptural interpretation as the activity that begets virtue stands in marked contrast to Fowl's dismissal of the term "meaning" in favor of the community whose (non)existing virtue affects interpretation. The differences between the two theologians, I will argue, concern how they construe the nature of grace and the human recipients of it and how they construe the way in which the Holy Spirit works through the community and through the text. Nonetheless, Fowl brings up important points for a theological hermeneutics to examine, and these points are taken up in connection with Augustine's text.

The goal in these chapters is never simply to criticize "bad" interpretive programs. The goal is to let the dialogue between the past and present highlight strengths and weaknesses of the contemporary projects, allowing the discussion to move beyond current proposals. But I have intentionally not selected interlocutors who are easy to dismiss simply because they are different from Augustine.

Both Jeanrond and Fowl appeal to him as a voice to be heeded. Both offer programs similar to his. To engage with them is to engage with some of the stronger examples of combining theology and inter-pretation. To allow Augustine to dialogue with them will inevitably reveal potential weaknesses and provide ideas for moving beyond them, but this occurs only on the basis that they offer compelling arguments for their programs, programs that—at the start—have much in common with *De doctrina*. Indeed, Augustine himself is open to questions from the contemporary practitioners.

In the pages that follow, I intend to provide an example of how one can appeal to the tradition, read it well, and also apply its insights to the contemporary context. By reading the ancient text through the questions of the present and by responding to current issues in Augustine's voice, this work will yield new ways of talking about the patristic text while providing helpful correctives for the ongoing practice of theological interpretation. Ancient and modern hermeneutics in dialogue, each mutually affecting the other, both given due attention: this is the method and the goal. By turning to the past in faith, we seek to hear a voice from outside, one not con-cerned with our immediate problems but one nonetheless describ-ing the same object: holy scripture and the triune God who speaks through it.

# Augustine's *De doctrina christiana*

## History and Context

If, as the introduction argued, the goal is to allow Augustine to be an active dialogue partner with contemporary theology, a good way to allow him a say—to allow him to be a voice from outside—is to allow him to set the parameters of the discussion. It has already been decided, on the basis of the topic under consideration—biblical interpretation—and on the basis of the classical status of *De doctrina christiana*, that this work will be the primary focus. Such a decision is pragmatic: it delimits the topic considerably. It is also necessary: *De doctrina* is unlike any other work by a church father in that it focuses explicitly on the act of biblical interpretation. Even more than Origen's *De principiis* and Tyconius's *Liber regularum*,[1] *De doctrina* represents a systematic, theoretical handbook on why and how one interprets scripture.[2] For a dialogue about scriptural interpretation, it is an ideal choice. Paying attention to the whole of Augustine's text will set the parameters for a dialogue with contemporary theologians while mitigating the worry that I am making Augustine say what I want him to say.

In addition to discovering insights for contemporary theological hermeneutics, I have suggested that engaging with Augustine in the manner I propose will also yield insights into the text of *De doctrina*. Putting it into close proximity with contemporary concerns will inevitably lead to new ways of construing its internal logic and its own concerns. The danger exists, however, that the contemporary concerns will override Augustine's voice. It would be easy simply to focus on the philosophical ideas of the work, or even upon its indebtedness to the classical education system. Indeed, such work has been done time and again. But to allow Augustine to be an out-side voice, it becomes necessary to follow him where he goes, and attention to only one of these areas would hinder the investigation. An interdisciplinary approach is therefore essential; Augustine—as all of us are—was a product of his culture. He was influenced by Plotinus and Cicero, among others. He is eclectic, unafraid to wander through the fields of philosophy or classical rhetoric, unafraid to pluck from them certain fruitful metaphors, certain ways of understanding the world. One reads him only partially if this point is forgotten. Nonetheless, attention to the whole of *De doctrina* reveals that, though he is eclectic in his sources, Augustine is in theological territory from the start. Such a point must be demonstrated, and allowing him to set the parameters for the subsequent dialogue will do so. *De doctrina*, in spite of being composed over the span of thirty years, and in spite of being partially released early on, is a unified theological treatise, intended principally for ministers of the gospel. Grasping its overall structure and its relationship to texts written around the same time will make this (contested) point persuasive.

## AUGUSTINE, BISHOP(S) OF HIPPO, ON INTERPRETATION

*De doctrina* represents a singular text in Augustine's corpus: not only is it one of the first works he began as a bishop, but it is also one of the last works he completed before his death in 430 C.E. As he says in *Retractiones* 2.4.1: "When I discovered that the books, *De doctrina christiana*, were unfinished, I preferred to finish them rather than leave them incomplete and pass on to the reconsideration of other works."[3] After beginning the work in 396 or 397, he ceased working on it sometime before 400. Theories abound as to why he stopped,[4] but they are less interesting than the fact that he picked it back up again.[5] He left several works incomplete,[6] even after reviewing them at the end of his life, but for some reason, the aging bishop found this text and decided that its four books were important enough to finish some thirty years later. He relates exactly where he stopped: "I had finished the third book, which had been written up to the place where the testimony of the Gospel is related concerning the woman who 'concealed yeast in three measures of flour, until the whole loaf was leavened.'"[7] R. P. H. Green is surely correct when he states: "If Augustine had not told us the exact place where he broke off, the join would probably have escaped detection."[8] The clear plan outlined in the first paragraphs of the work is followed. He finished Book 3 and wrote Book 4. One can argue about how well the ideas of Tyconius's fit at the end of Book 3,[9] but if we did not know of the break, it seems likely that a change in direction would not be noticed. After all, Book 3—as I will discuss below—treats ambiguities of scripture, and that is exactly what Augustine uses the handbook of Tyconius to do. Book 4 simply carries on with the project as outlined at its inception. The thirty intervening years aside, *De doctrina* has the feel of a unified treatise, which is a fascinating accomplishment, considering everything that occurred in those years. Arguments attempting to find differences in the theology of the work before and after the join are unpersuasive.[10] Augustine does mention the Pelagian controversy in 3.33.46, a controversy that had not occurred when he began *De doctrina*, but a survey of the texts composed at the start of his bishopric will highlight the fact that his theology need not have changed drastically in the intervening years. Even arguments that highlight the difference between Augustine's appeal to the classical tradition in the second and fourth books are unpersuasive.[11] The fact that some scholars think Augustine proposed a universal system of education in Book 2, while some argue exactly the opposite, suggests that any attempt to show how Book 4—argued by some to be entirely Ciceronian and by others to be a complete reworking of Ciceronian ideas—is different from Book 2 will continue unresolved, with no compelling argument either way. As it stands, Augustine himself thinks of the work as a single unit:

> Initially, I divided this work of ours, entitled *De doctrina christiana*, into two parts. After a preface, in which I responded to those who would have criticized the work, I said, "There are two things on which every interpretation of scripture [*tractatio scripturarum*] depends: the way of discovering [*modus inveniendi*] what should be understood and the way of presenting [*modus proferendi*] what has been understood. We will speak of discovery first, and then of presentation." Because we have said a good bit concerning discovery and have completed three volumes about this one part, we will now, with the Lord's help, say a few things about delivery. If possible, we will confine all we have to say to one book and finish this work in four volumes. (4.1.1, citing 1.1.1)[12]

At the end of his career, when he could have left *De doctrina* as it was, perhaps entitling it *De doctrina christiana libri duo imperfecti*, he goes on to complete it, apparently thinking his original idea important enough to continue. As the introduction to Book 4 demonstrates, the mature Augustine conceives of the work as a single unit. And as a unit, it encompasses his career in a way no other work of his does. Even *Enarrationes in Psalmos* (c. 392–c. 420) and *De trinitate* (c. 399–420/7) cover a shorter period of his life.[13] In *De doctrina*, Augustine, the young bishop of Hippo, and Augustine, the aged bishop, meet and pass on to posterity suggestions for interpreting scripture. Undoubtedly his views shifted on many topics, but his attention to scripture, from the beginning of his bishopric to the end, never wavered, and it is this with which *De doctrina* is concerned, and in this theological topic resides its unity.

## DE DOCTRINA AND THE LENINGRAD CODEX

In 391, Augustine found himself compelled into the priesthood in Hippo, and by 395 or 396, he was ordained to the bishopric.[14]

*Retractiones* specifies what works he was writing at the time and this gives some clues as to what issues concerned him then. The relevant works can be narrowed down even further due to a manuscript that dates back at least to the fifth century, Leningrad Q.v.I.3.[15] On the basis of manuscript evidence such as the amount of columns, the style of writing, and the rarity of abbreviations, E. A. Lowe declares: "The manuscript is certainly of the fifth century if not older, and it may be that it was actually written in Africa."[16] This manuscript concludes with the first two books of *De doctrina*—including the prologue as part of Book 1—bound with the three works that directly preceded it at the start of Augustine's bishopric: *De diversis quaestionibus ad Simplicianum, Contra epistulam Manichaei quam vocant Fundamenti*, and *De agone christiano. Epistula* 37 (to Simplician) precedes the first treatise in the manuscript.

Because the works are not united thematically and because the text of *De doctrina* ceases at the end of Book 2, William Green argues that the manuscript is a "collected works" (*Gesammelte Werke*) of Augustine up to that point.[17] There is no reason for *De doctrina* to have been included in its incomplete state after 426 or 427 when the work was finished.[18] The third book would not have been included because it was not completed. Augustine is clear that he did not like his works to be circulated before completion,[19] but he was not averse to releasing them in serial format, as *De civitate dei* demonstrates. In addition, he mentions *De doctrina* in *Contra Faustum* 22.91, which is dated between 397 and 400, suggesting that it must have then been in circulation. Green argues further in the *Praefatio* to his edition that the work was completed in Augustine's scriptorium. At the end of the Leningrad Codex, in uncial letters made by what appears to be a less-skilful hand (*manu minus perita, ut videtur*), is the following:

|   |   |   |   |   |   |   |   |   |   |   |   |
|---|---|---|---|---|---|---|---|---|---|---|---|
|   |   |   |   |   | P |   |   |   |   |   |   |
| L | E | G | E | E T | O R | A |   | P | E | C |   |
|   |   |   |   |   | O |   |   | C | A |   |   |
|   |   |   |   |   | M |   |   | T | O |   |   |
|   |   |   |   |   | E |   |   | R | E |   |   |
|   |   |   |   | A | G | * * * | I | N | U | S |   |

"Read and pray for me, a sinner, Augustine." Green argues that, unless further evidence comes along, this represents Augustine's own hand, and that, therefore, the manuscript was completed under his eyes, given his approval.[20] It has been argued, however, that the Leningrad Codex is probably not an autograph because of the frequency of errors in it.[21]

Rather than following Green, Kenneth Steinhauser suggests it was copied—still at Augustine's request—in Carthage. He argues further that the entire codex has a structure, and that, rather than being the *Gesammelte Werke* of Augustine, the Leningrad Codex is, in fact, a *Festschrift*, a gift from Augustine to Simplician.[22] *Epistula* 37 is therefore an introduction to the whole codex. Then, Augustine addresses questions that Simplician had himself asked, and he then responds to what appears to be a Manichean catechism. Simplician would have, after all, been familiar with Augustine's time as a Manichee.[23] The final two works—*De agone* and *De doctrina*—were handbooks, the former for the unlearned and the latter for the educated. While Steinhauser's argument is speculative, the point remains: the Leningrad Codex is early. The argument, as can be seen, is over *where in North Africa* the codex was copied, not *when*. The four works included in it are in the same order as in *Retractiones*. It is possible, therefore, to begin to understand the problems and controversies facing Augustine at the time he began *De doctrina*.

There are several ways to locate the work in Augustine's corpus. For instance, Tarmo Toom discusses it in the context of *Contra academicos* (c. 386) and *De magistro* (c. 389) to highlight Augustine's epistemological concerns, concerns that Toom finds throughout *De doctrina*.[24] B. D. Jackson, on the other hand, utilizes *De dialectica* (387) to highlight Augustine's logical concerns in *De doctrina* as well as *De magistro* to discuss his sign theory.[25] Karla Pollmann discusses *De doctrina* not only in connection with Augustine's and other pagan and Christian works, but also, and primarily, in comparison with Tyconius's *Liber regularum*, drawing out the differences between the two in order to highlight Augustine's distinctiveness: his is a hermeneutics built on *caritas*, while Tyconius's is built on ecclesiology.[26] In addition to these helpful studies, a good way to begin to understand

*De doctrina* is by grasping the issues surrounding Augustine at the time of composition. Therefore, it seems reasonable to highlight certain features of the three works included with it in the Leningrad Codex. The exercise will provide a point of departure for understanding *De doctrina*'s intended audience.

According to Augustine, *Ad Simplicianum* was the first work he began after becoming bishop, which places it sometime in 395. In it, he addresses several scriptural passages about which Simplician had written. Indeed, this detailed attention to scripture is the primary thing to highlight. Here at the start of his role as bishop of Hippo, Augustine struggles to understand scripture, especially the Pauline epistles, in his fight against the Manichees. In this text, he argues against them while also (inadvertently) preparing the way for his later anti-Pelagian views on grace.[27]

Upon turning to *Contra epistulam Manichaei*, one finds Augustine's concern with the church and its relationship to scripture: "I, however, would not believe the Gospel, unless the authority of the Catholic Church moved me" (*c. ep. Man.* 5.6). In the context of the argument, Augustine suggests that the Manichees want him to read the gospel to find testimony to Mani, but he asserts that he only believes the gospel because the church moves him to do so; the Catholic Church also tells him not to believe the Manichees. In other words, scripture and the Catholic Church are bound intricately together. Augustine's argument concerns the extent to which reason can arbitrate between Manichees and Catholic Christians. He thinks some presuppositions are necessary. Even the Manichees, who claim to use reason alone, end up asking for faith: "How, then, can you make me understand it? After so many promises to give knowledge, will you force me to take your word for it?" (*c. ep. Man.* 32.35). After his ordination, Augustine fights against the sect he has left behind by showing that scripture and the church are intertwined, indissolubly linked in a way echoed in *De doctrina*. Therefore, we have Augustine fighting the Manichees, while reading Paul, all at the start of his bishopric.

The next work Augustine mentions in *Retractiones*, and which is bound in the Leningrad Codex, is *De agone*, a work "written in a simple diction for the fellow Christians [*fratribus*] uneducated in Latin."[28] The reader is immediately struck not only by the simplicity of the language, but also by the accessibility of the ideas. Augustine's goal is to explain how Christians struggle against the devil whom they cannot see: "Many people, however, ask this question: 'How can we overcome the Devil, since we do not see him?'" (*agon.* 2.2).[29] He responds by showing that victory over the devil is victory over the sinner's evil desires: "We win an interior victory over the adversaries who assail us from without by conquering the evil desires by which those adversaries hold sway over us" (*agon.* 2.2). This, however, is not as easy as it might sound, so Augustine proceeds to discuss how to bring one's body under subjection. One begins by becoming a willing subject of God, for all creation is subject to God, some by servitude, and some by will (*agon.* 7.7). After faith, then, a Christian must follow the rules for correct living (*agon.* 13.14). By living correctly, the objects of faith grow clearer. Like scripture and the Catholic Church in *Contra epistulam Manichaei*, faith and virtue are united, tied together.[30] He discusses the articles of faith by moving through a credal structure, exhorting his readers and listeners: "Let us not heed those who say . . ." (*agon.* 14.16–32.34). The primary tenets of the Catholic Church's confession are considered: the Trinity, the equality of the Persons, the incarnation, the gift of the Holy Spirit, and the church that exists throughout the world. He concludes the credal exploration with a discussion of the resurrection of the body. The entire piece reads as a catechism, a simple guide for those who do not quite understand what they profess to believe.

Throughout *De agone*, Augustine speaks clearly, simply, and he stays away from overtly rhetorical structures. In it, we find him arguing against yet another important enemy: the Donatists. The Leningrad Codex shows Augustine at the start of his bishopric, already in full defense of what he views to be the Christian faith. The only thing missing is the Pelagian controversy that is prepared for in *Ad Simplicianum*. *De agone* stands out from the other works that surround it, however, because it is written for a different class of people. It is written for those to whom he preaches. In comparison to it, *De doctrina* appears to be something written for an entirely different audience. The work seems more theoretical, written no longer for the average person, but for the learned, for those who have some training in grammar and rhetoric.

As stated above, *De doctrina* was composed in two parts. These three works represent the period around the time of the first part's composition. The part completed in 426/7 was written at an entirely different period in Augustine's life. He was no longer the young, unseasoned bishop he was at the start. He had spent thirty years preaching and teaching, using the Bible to defend positions, to teach his fellow clergy and the laity, and to develop doctrine. The Augustine of the latter part of Book 3 and the entirety of Book 4 has written *De trinitate* and *De civitate dei*. He has spent the past fifteen or so years writing primarily against the Pelagians. But again, if we did not know this, it would be possible for the join to go unnoticed.[31] Augustine does mention the Pelagians when discussing Tyconius, and Book 4 spends a good deal of time speaking of divine grace and God speaking through humans, but nothing in this book contradicts the emphasis in the prologue and Book 1 on God raising humanity up, on God speaking to humans through humans. In short: when Augustine picks up *De doctrina* in 426/7, he finishes the book he began in 396/7. One might speculate how it would have been different, but the point still remains: we might not even notice the break had he not informed us of it.

One is left, then, with the original context. *De doctrina* was composed by the newly ordained Augustine who had recently written (or was in the process of writing) *Ad Simplicianum*, *Contra epistulam Manichaei*, and *De agone*.[32] At this point in time, the new bishop is experiencing one of the greatest periods of change in his life. He has engaged with Paul before and in *Ad Simplicianum*, starting him on the path to his mature thoughts on grace. He is combating what he perceives to be heresies, the refutation of which becomes a major aspect of his ministry. At the same time, the duties of a bishop require him to write and to preach simply, making himself clear to those who are not able to comprehend the intellectual refinement of a classically trained orator. Two aspects of these works are particularly important: the sense of overwhelming attention to scripture, whether it is in connection with the church or simply trying to understand its difficulties, and the sense that Augustine can write for the average person, who has difficulty with the Latin language. When one turns to *De doctrina*, then, we find the same attention to scripture, but we find Augustine sharing with others how to read and interpret it, an interpretation that includes a turn to delivery. Furthermore, one can note that *De doctrina* is more intellectually rigorous and stylistically demanding than *De agone*. He has not written *De doctrina* for the unlearned, for the average members of his congregation. It reads instead like a book telling people how to do what he himself does.[33] The summary and outline in the following chapter will make this abundantly clear. As I will argue, *De doctrina* is a hermeneutics written primarily for the clergy, albeit a well-educated, ideal clergy. It can have application beyond them, but they are its primary audience. By putting *De doctrina* in the context of Augustine's early career, especially near the time of the composition of *De agone*—where Augustine's simplicity emphasizes the intellectual rigor of *De doctrina* and where he spends time treating the basics of faith rather than emphasizing how to understand scripture and deliver that to others—this conclusion becomes more convincing, in spite of the arguments against it.

De doctrina sits comfortably in the company of the seemingly disparate works in the Leningrad Codex. Even if Steinhauser's argument that the codex represents a *Festschrift* remains speculative, it does draw attention to its location at the start of Augustine's bishopric, when he engages with what it means to read scripture, to connect scripture and the Catholic Church, to combat heresies, and to teach those who are uneducated. *De doctrina* sits at the pinnacle, as it were. In it, we have Augustine showing others how to read the Bible in order to move closer to God, which involves sharing with others what one understands. Book 4— though written later (but already announced in the prologue)—stresses speaking simply so that the uneducated can understand. Moreover, 2.13.19 and 3.3.7 stress the acceptability of barbarisms so that scripture can be understood by the less well educated. Both the earlier and the later parts of the work stand in continuity with the simplicity of *De agone*, but they speak theoretically while the simpler work represents the theory in practice. By keeping the differences between these two works in mind, one can begin to narrow down the target audience of *De doctrina*, preparing for a summary and outline of the work.

## *DE DOCTRINA*: HERMENEUTICS AND RHETORIC

Historically, there have been four main views concerning what *De doctrina* is and to whom it was written, and they range from the narrow to the increasingly comprehensive.[34] While Pollmann's *Doctrina Christiana* successfully undermines these distinctions, they can still be found in works utilizing *De doctrina*. Did Augustine write a biblical hermeneutics with a rhetorical appendix, a handbook for preachers, a rhetorical handbook, or an outline for a Christian culture?

### A Biblical Hermeneutics with a Rhetorical Appendix?

In the first and most narrow view, *De doctrina* is a biblical hermeneutics.[35] That is, the work is concerned specifically with biblical interpretation, and Book 4—the underlying thought seems to be—is about something entirely different.[36] Such a viewpoint is particularly prevalent in theological discussions, even if it is unstated. For instance, Toom only focuses on the first three books because they alone concern interpretation.[37] By intently focusing on Augustine's distinction between signs and things, he argues that Augustine's entire treatise sets out to affirm the usefulness of sensible signs after the Fall.[38] His argument, however, is not convincing for one primary reason: it divides the first three books from Book 4 in what seems to be an irrevocable way.[39] Toom contends that Augustine's christology is fundamental to *De doctrina*. Whether or not this is the case, to argue for a foundation of the first three books at the express exclusion of the fourth book is to miss out on the very structure Augustine establishes. The four books *together* represent his version of hermeneutics. When consideration of *De doctrina* focuses only on the first three books, one is left explaining the fourth as a change of subject, a rhetorical handbook in an appendix. Clearly, Augustine did not view his text in this manner, as he sees interpretation and communication as two parts of the same whole (1.1.1). Nonetheless, some division can be useful, as Augustine does, in fact, have two aspects to the one act of interpretation: a *modus inveniendi* and a *modus proferendi*. Yet, to divide the work strictly, focusing only on discovering the meaning or only on delivering what has been discovered, misses the entire purpose of *De doctrina*: it envisions one act of interpretation comprising two *modi operandi*.

Interpretation, that is, the subject of a hermeneutics, is not complete for Augustine without the requisite turn to delivery. It is not enough to understand what the biblical texts say; the interpreter he describes must also explain the truth discovered to someone else, and in the case of *De doctrina*, that someone else is a group of people, a congregation of the church. Likewise, the subject of Book 4 (how to deliver what has been discovered in scripture) is incomplete without the prerequisite determination of what exactly scripture says. The two parts stand and fall together. Division is useful for pragmatic reasons, but in the end, understanding and communication are part of the indivisible act of biblical interpretation. *De doctrina* is about the transmission of Christian truth, which is taught like anything else, though within the context of an ecclesial setting. Therefore, rather than describing the first three books as a biblical hermeneutics that is then supplemented by a turn to rhetoric in the fourth book (as proponents of this view seem to do), it seems more accurate to expand the definition of hermeneutics to include rhetoric.[40] By doing so, one holds the unified interpretive project together. Likewise, this redefinition helps take into account that the work presupposes a specific context. In order to espouse an Augustinian hermeneutics, one must hold together the duality inherent in his program as well as its communal location. In other words, the view that *De doctrina* is a biblical hermeneutics is, in essence, correct; its weakness is its failure to hold together the first three books with the last one. By redefining hermeneutics in Augustine's manner, that is, by suggesting it involves both the practice of discovering what a text says as well as the delivery of that to a group of people, one can begin to see just how the hermeneutics in *De doctrina* is in fact what I will call an *a posteriori* hermeneutics. There is an existing group of people to whom the biblical text must be explained, and this work exists to aid that ongoing process of explanation. Augustine's hermeneutics does not exist without this community in the background. It is important, then, to emphasize his explicit focus on *scriptural* exposition; he is not concerned with other texts in the first three books.[41] Likewise, Book 4 has a specific communal background, and it is here that the proponents of the other views begin to assert their positions.

### A Textbook for the Clergy?

The second view has come to be associated with Edmund Hill, who not only published an important (though short) article, "*De Doctrina Christiana*: A Suggestion,"[42] but also published a translation of *De doctrina* provocatively entitled *Teaching Christianity*. He argues that Augustine began *De doctrina* at the request of Aurelius, the bishop of Carthage.[43] The argument has three basic parts. First, he appeals to Augustine's *Epistula* 41, which states: "We entreat you through him who has granted that [blessing] to you, and who has poured this blessing through you on the people you serve, that you would order any of their [the priests'] sermons that you might desire to be sent to us after they have been emended. For I also have not neglected that which you have commanded, and concerning the seven rules or keys of Tyconius, as I have often written, I still wait to know what you think" (41.2). In this letter, Augustine praises Aurelius for accomplishing his *sancta cogitatio* (holy intention), which involved the "ordained brethren" (*fratres ordinati*) and the priests (*presbyteri*) who preached sermons to the congregation (*ep.* 41.1). The cited section comes near the end of the letter when he has finished praising Aurelius and entreats him to send edited sermons. But he wants more than the edited sermons; he wants Aurelius's opinion of Tyconius's seven rules or keys, which we now know form the end of Book 3 of *De doctrina*. Hill speculates that Aurelius wanted Augustine to write a manual to use in training clergy to teach and preach.[44] This follows, he suggests, because Augustine was clearly working on something Aurelius had assigned him, something concerning sermons and the rules or keys of Tyconius.[45] On the basis of the final form of *De doctrina*, Hill suggests that Augustine must have been midway through Book 3 when he sent the letter to Aurelius. He needed the sermons for Book 4 and wanted Aurelius's opinion about Tyconius for potential inclusion in Book 3.[46] One might suggest—going further than Hill—that Augustine wanted the sermons to help with Book 4 insofar as they would provide him with a sampling of the sermons and therefore the level of skill present in the target audience, preachers.

Hill's argument, however, is not based solely on conjecture from a letter between Augustine and Aurelius. He also points to a particular passage in *De doctrina*: "For even if they [the rules of rhetoric] could eventually be mastered by the slower spirits, we do not consider them of such importance that we would wish to impose the learning of them upon men of mature or even venerable age. It is enough that this subject [rhetoric] should be the concern of the young, and not even of all of those whom we desire to have educated for the service of the church, but only of those who are not yet busy with more urgent requirements, which undoubtedly take precedence over this one" (4.3.4).[47] According to Hill, this section stresses the fact that *De doctrina* concerns not Christian education, but the education of Christian teachers. In other words, Augustine intended the work to be a practical handbook for preachers and teachers of the church.[48] This citation shows that he envisions a group of people active in the church, one part of which comprises older men already dedicated to ministry, while the other comprises younger men able to take some time off and learn rhetorical rules.

Finally, Hill points to the overall structure, stressing that the work culminates in Book 4, where it finds its goal in the explanation of what has been discovered in scripture:

> [S]o the work leads up to the fourth book as to its goal. But Christian preaching is in terms of scripture; so the would-be preacher must first be taught how to interpret the Bible. And since some, if not most, of the clergy are always going to find interpreting

the Bible a fearfully bewildering business, however many guides to it they are provided with, it is as well to begin this text-book by telling them beforehand the substance, the *res*, that they are going to find in the Bible. And then if necessary, if they find scripture too hard for them altogether, they can preach about these *res*, God and Christ, and faith, hope, and charity, without opening their Bibles at all.[49]

The point of *De doctrina* is to teach priests how to preach. In opposition to Henri-Irénée Marrou, Hill sees *De doctrina* as specifically about helping teachers of Christianity, instead of about the formation of a Christian culture. To summarize: Hill builds his argument first on the historical evidence of *Epistula* 41, then on the explicit mention of ministers in 4.3.4, and finally on the trajectory of the whole work.

Though this argument seems convincing, several criticisms have been leveled against it. First, the objection has been made that Hill fails to take into account what Augustine himself states the work is about: how to read and understand the scriptures.[50] Hill's thesis provides a unified outline, but "the unity thus revealed is a very general one: the main parts are Books 1–3, on finding what to preach in the Bible, and Book 4, on preaching."[51] In other words, there must be a way to connect understanding and explanation without collapsing the former into the latter. This criticism suggests that Hill puts too much weight on the fourth book (explanation) at the expense of the first three (understanding). Nonetheless, it seems Hill has gotten the point of the work right; he has correctly highlighted that the reason to have the first three books is to move to the fourth. A bit more focus on the actual practice of interpretation might be helpful, and as I will suggest below, this supposed imbalance can be corrected by combining Hill's view with the one that *De doctrina* is a biblical hermeneutics, though in the qualified sense given above of an expanded hermeneutics.

Second, it has been argued that the work suggests an ideal situation—a minister conversant in Latin, Greek, and Hebrew, who is well-spoken and who is familiar with world history, philosophy, and several other subjects—one that makes it hard to believe Augustine could really imagine a priest fulfilling the demands imposed by the work.[52] Against this argument, however, one can point to his admission in 4.31.64: he himself does not fulfill the demands he makes. Augustine is aware that his work concerns an ideal situation, but that does not necessarily imply that he does not have in mind the preacher. In fact, after spending several paragraphs discussing the importance of knowing the languages that stand behind the Latin (i.e., Greek and Hebrew), he makes the following concession: "We should either aim to acquire knowledge of those languages from which the Latin scriptures come, or we should have before us those translations that stick [*obstringere*] closely to the words themselves" (2.13.19).

He goes on to state that word-for-word translations are not sufficient, but they do help the person unfamiliar with Greek or Hebrew uncover mistakes that might exist in Latin manuscripts. Augustine is well aware that not everyone (anyone?) will be able to do everything he sets out here. That does not mean, however, that he thinks it unnecessary to specify the high standard to which a teacher ought to strive. Furthermore, one might suggest that he could not conceive of the kind of division of labor seen today, when one person studies the manuscripts, another the history, until finally another delivers a sermon. The very people delivering the sermons were the ones who would need to read Greek and Hebrew before preaching eloquently. Raising the criticism that Augustine's expectations are too high does not in any way, therefore, disprove Hill's thesis. If everything the Christian teacher (*doctor ecclesiasticus*) teaches is weighty and important—*omnia sunt magna quae dicimus* (4.18.35)—because it refers to the eternal well-being of the listeners, then it seems reasonable to expect him to have high standards. To stress the point further: the person he has in mind here teaches "from a place above the people" (*de loco superiore populis dicimus*); in the context, it seems reasonable to suggest that this is not just a position of authority,[53] but is rather a *certain* position of authority: the pulpit.[54] More directly: Book 4 makes it clear that the person Augustine has in mind is a Christian teacher, who speaks from a pulpit about weighty, eternal matters. Why would he not have the highest standards, even if they are nearly unattainable?

A third objection to Hill's thesis focuses on the difficulty of imagining that Augustine, having been asked for such a work, fails to dedicate it.[55] Such an argument from silence, however, is not all that persuasive. There is no way of quantifying how many treatises were requested that Augustine did not dedicate. Just because he dedicates several does not mean the ones he failed to dedicate were not requested. Furthermore, the lack of a dedication does not imply that there was no original occasion for the work, and when taking into account that it took him thirty years to finish the treatise, is it any surprise that he did not say what the impetus for the work was? Of the unfinished works he catalogues in *Retractiones*, *De doctrina* sparked his interest enough to finish it; he must have seen some need for it even then. While it remains striking that Augustine does not explicitly state who the specific target audience is, to insist that he say at the beginning, "Aurelius wanted me to write this thirty years ago, but I could not manage until now," might be asking for a bit much.

One also has to address the fact that Hill's contention on the basis of *Epistula* 41 is, even by his own account, conjecture.[56] If there were nothing within the text to support his case, then it would need to be dismissed. However, as will be argued in chapter 4, the text itself calls for a background similar to the one he suggests. At the very least, his thesis—even if the originating historical scenario is wrong—gets to the heart of the community presupposed in the treatise: it is written primarily for preachers. This much will be argued below.

Pollmann argues that the above-mentioned reference in 4.18.35 to the "place above the people" as well as other references to the *vir ecclesiasticus* (4.15.32) and the *praedicator* (4.27.60) are too unspecific to narrow the addressees down to ministers only. In addition, she (rightfully) points out that Augustine widens the audience in 4.18.37 to include people speaking in public and private, talking with one person or many, and writing books.[57] Therefore, she contends, one cannot restrict the intended recipients exclusively to preachers.[58] But considering the overwhelmingly oral nature of Book 4's discussion, it seems likely that Augustine does in fact have primarily preachers in mind, for instance, those who were also trained at his monastic community in Hippo. As I will argue in subsequent chapters, Augustine appropriates pagan concepts of rhetorical communication and develops a specifically Christian concept of the sermon: it is the result of discovering the truth spoken through the biblical texts and turning to the gathered community to deliver that truth to them orally and persuasively so that they act appropriately. After recognizing this model, one can extend it to other rhetorical acts—books, debates, and so on—and see that these are only extensions of the sermon as Augustine conceives it.

Hill's evaluation of *De doctrina* helpfully emphasizes the continuity between the first three books and the last, while effectively highlighting the communal background, and Pollmann's recognition that the work has universalizing aspects helps remind the reader that the work as it now stands is potentially more than simply a preacher's handbook. Hill's intense focus on delivery at the near exclusion of discovery can be balanced by the first view, that *De doctrina* is a hermeneutics (see the discussion of Pollmann below). By putting these two together, the two-sided project of Augustine's hermeneutics comes into sharper focus. Before more is said, the final two views should be taken into account.

### A Rhetorical Handbook?

In direct contrast to Hill's narrower thesis, the third view shifts the focus from Augustine and his local community to the educational system that influenced him. On this model, *De doctrina* is indebted to rhetoric; indeed, he writes a rhetorical handbook. Though Press views himself as separate from those who describe *De doctrina* simply as a rhetoric,[59] he nonetheless describes it in those terms while emphasizing that the rhetorical aspects of *De doctrina* apply to the work as a whole. For that reason, he will serve as the model for this viewpoint.

In order to argue his case, Press highlights the clear and unambiguous statements Augustine makes concerning the purpose and structure of the work. In opposition to the suggestions of others who look to the title and try to establish the work's purpose by defining the term "*doctrina*,"[60] Press finds within these clear statements a more fundamental and more easily defined term, *tracto-tractatio*, one he constructs from the verb *tractare* and its noun cognate, *tractatio*: "And the term that recurs in these passages is, not *doctrina*, but *tracto-tractatio*, which, unlike *doctrina*, can be fairly clearly defined and which locates the DDC fairly clearly in relation to the ancient rhetorical tradition."[61] Press is right to point to Augustine's clear statements of intention to establish what exactly *De doctrina* is about. For instance, in the prologue, he states: "There are certain rules [*praecepta*] for interpreting (treating) the scriptures [*tractandarum Scripturarum*]. . . . I intend to relate these to those who desire to learn and have the ability" (Prol. 1).[62]

After highlighting the important location of *tracto-tractatio*, Press traces the term through the rhetorical tradition in order to determine what it means.[63] He concludes this section by stressing that, in the rhetorical tradition, *tracto-tractatio* means treating or investigating anything, whether written or spoken or simply considered mentally. The term implies, though it does not specify, some kind of analysis or exposition. He continues: "Thus it [*tracto-tractatio*] overlaps to some extent, and so cannot be said to supplement, invention, which in any case, unlike treatment, is often very carefully defined."[64] In other words—and Press makes this point explicitly later—the two parts of *De doctrina* that Augustine establishes (*modus inveniendi* and *modus proferendi*) are actually two parts of the same rhetorical activity of *tracto-tractatio*.[65] Press manages to grasp the work's unity, a thing that scholars focusing explicitly on the hermeneutical aspects (the *inventio* side) fail to do. The entire work fits neatly into the rhetorical tradition, though, Press stresses, Augustine espouses an older rhetoric, more in line with Cicero than that taught in his time, which was less focused on correct interpretation than on persuasive speaking.[66] This finds support in certain sections of Book 4, where

Augustine refers back to Cicero (e.g., 4.12.27, 17.34), while disparaging rhetors who focus on style at the expense of substance.[67] For instance, he states: "For since rhetoric is used to persuade people of both truths and falsehood, who would dare say that truth should stand in its defense unarmed against untruth, when clearly those who try to convince their hearers of what is untrue know how to make their hearers either good willed or attentive or docile in the opening words? Should those trying to persuade them of truth not be familiar with the same strategies?" (4.2.3).[68]

To illustrate that Augustine wants his form of rhetoric to be different from the prevailing tendencies, the passage just cited need only be compared to one in Book 2: "Now there are certain rules of a more copious kind of argument, which is now called 'eloquence,' which are nevertheless proper, although by them falsehoods can be put forth convincingly [*persuaderi*]" (2.36.54). Rhetoric, or *eloquentia*, can be utilized either positively or negatively; it is in itself a neutral entity.[69] Nonetheless, in Book 4, he does not simply repeat the rules of this neutral practice because he does not want to teach people simply how to speak persuasively; he teaches how to deliver the truth. Therefore, with Press, it can be concluded that Augustine does, at the very least, have a different view of rhetoric from his contemporaries. His rhetoric is not concerned simply with style, but with providing tools so truth can combat falsehood. The rhetorical devices in Book 4 are not for delivering any message irrespective of its legitimacy; they are for delivering truth.

Press argues further that Augustine goes beyond even Cicero in his express focus on texts, and more particularly, on the biblical texts. For Cicero, documents were treated because of controversy that arose from them.[70] Texts were simply one set of things that could be interpreted among many.[71] In other words, *De doctrina* returns to a form of rhetoric that involves both speaking and discovering what to say, while he moves beyond the old rhetoric to a focus on a certain text: "Thus rhetoric is reborn as an important social force."[72] Press draws this conclusion because Augustine in *De doctrina* aims to elucidate the truth of the biblical texts, a truth that is already known, and to teach it to other people. On this basis, Press argues that Christianity—a self-consciously new society—makes rhetoric an important social force because it is a religion based on a book, and thus rhetoric is required to carry that religion along.

He then makes the following move: Augustine was not only influenced by the rhetorical tradition but he also returns rhetoric to "a social importance that dates back to the beginnings of the ancient cultural world."[73] Press argues that *De doctrina* retains the "old ideal" of rhetoric while Augustine simultaneously transforms it by making rhetoric "book-centered" in opposition to the forensic rhetoric that previously existed. And because Augustine has made rhetoric so important, Press suggests a way of reconciling the positions concerning what *De doctrina* is actually about: it creates a new culture by being both a textbook on exegesis and on rhetoric because in order for the new culture to be promulgated, the truth upon which it is based must be taught, and this can only be done when the leaders (the priests) are taught how to get the truth out of the book and to present it to the people.

Press, then, appears to solve all of the issues concerning *De doctrina*'s aim. Initially, this appears persuasive. After all, if there are four competing ideas over what *De doctrina* actually is—a biblical hermeneutics, a handbook for preachers, a rhetorical handbook, a formulation of a new culture—and if there are good arguments for all of these, then surely a view that accounts for them all must be closer to the truth than the others. Press's argument then begins to blend into the subsequent one, that finds in *De doctrina* a rehabilitation of the ancient culture's focus on *paideia*, and thus the creation of a new, Christian culture. Before moving on to discuss that view, however, it will be helpful to highlight a few problems with Press's case.

First, by emphasizing Augustine's continuity with the earlier rhetorical tradition, he compresses the categories too far. To say that Augustine must be in line with earlier Ciceronian rhetoric because he stresses *inventio* certainly emphasizes the continuity, but only at the expense of the discontinuity, which is more fundamental. As Press states, Ciceronian rhetoric was not concerned explicitly with text-based exposition. Yet Augustine's concern is *precisely* this. Attempting to show that he returns to an earlier form of rhetoric concerned

with *inventio* overlooks the fact that, for Augustine, biblical interpretation was exactly that: interpretation of the biblical texts.[74] Further, Press himself notes that Cicero is not concerned with arriving
at a correct or true interpretation,[75] but again, Augustine's focus is
*precisely* this: figuring out the truth and delivering it to a congregation. Such discontinuities are weightier than the continuities. Press
fails to account for the Christian communal location of *De doctrina*.[76]
This is the primary issue: Augustine's *modus inveniendi* is not simply
research to get one's ideas together before presentation. Instead, it is
the active engagement with biblical texts to get to the truth that God
reveals through them. Augustine makes a theological move. This is
*fundamentally* different from a concern with discovering something
to say in order to argue a point. The interpreter, according to *De
doctrina*, interprets scripture *specifically* to present to others the truth
found in the Bible. Scripture has a *telos* that is intimately bound up
with its location in the divine economy of salvation. This specific
text has a specific function in God's relationship with his creation—
and a person's relationship with others—and that function comes
to expression in the act of interpretation, that is, in *tractatio*, which
involves understanding and proclamation. This theological location of the text is decisive. Too much focus on continuity with the
rhetorical tradition fails to account for Augustine's indebtedness to
the scriptural interpretation that has gone before him.[77] Focusing
on the rhetorical background of *De doctrina* fails to address a more
local background, that of the Christian community that has been
engaging with these texts for the past four hundred or so years, not
to mention the Jewish interpreters that had gone before. Likewise,
though he discusses ancient rhetoric's location within the law courts
and politics,[78] Press does not give enough weight to how different
the two types of rhetoric would be *due to* their social location.[79] One
is for the secular law courts, where good argument can be more
important to the rhetor than the truth. The other is for the prom-
ulgation of the truth of the gospel, where people come to learn of
God's will, where their souls are bound together in love. It is precisely the differing communal location that makes Augustine's work
and the ancient rhetoric different.

The second problem with Press's case is related to the first: by making the rhetorical background primary, he can then conclude that Augustine's program establishes a new culture. Yet it could be argued that the rhetorical background is incidental. He speaks the language of a rhetor because he was a rhetor. His goal need not be so grand as establishing a culture (see below). That could simply be a result of what he does. In fact he clearly states he is *not* writing a rhetoric (4.1.2).[80] That he is influenced by the rhetorical tradition, indeed, that he uses technical rhetorical terms, does not necessarily imply that he wanted to write a rhetorical handbook, much less establish a new culture through it. He discusses the act of interpretation in terms of understanding and delivery of what is understood. If he did not use language from rhetoric, what could he even say? Press's viewpoint fails to account for the fact that other contexts may well have had their influence on Augustine. Explicit focus on the rhetorical tradition—even as defined by Press—fails to account for the more local context, the more local and theological concerns that Augustine has: God has revealed his will to his church through scripture and the interpreter-preacher must find out what that will is and explain it to its members. It is therefore impossible to agree fully with the view that locates *De doctrina*'s meaning and goal in the aims and practices of the rhetorical tradition. Nonetheless, the rhetorical approach to *De doctrina* cannot be hastily written off. There are certainly rhetorical aspects in the treatise.[81] I am not disputing that point. Rather, I am suggesting it would be more precise to discuss *De doctrina* as a hermeneutical treatise rather than as a rhetorical handbook. By classifying the work as an expanded hermeneutics—that is, by utilizing insights from the first and second views presented above—the unity of *De doctrina* can still be maintained, as Press does effectively. At the same time, however, the specific ecclesial community presupposed is not missed out. Press points out that the person Augustine envisions is labeled *studiosus divinarum scripturarum*.[82] Can *studiosus* refer only to priests? This objection might draw the ecclesial background into question, if taken as a technical rhetorical term. If, however, one reads through the treatise and notes the ecclesial background, it becomes evident that *studiosus* has lost its apparent connection with the rhetorical tradition and the young men to whom it would have been applied. The *studiosi* are now preachers who deliver what they find to a congregation.

## The Formation of a Christian Culture?

Whereas the previous view focuses too narrowly on the background and influences on *De doctrina*, this fourth one mistakes the subsequent effects of the text with its purpose. At least as far back as Marrou's *Saint Augustin et la fin de la culture antique*, it has been argued that *De doctrina* is much more than a simple handbook concerning the education of the clergy ("un simple manuel *de Institutione clericorum*"); indeed, there is nothing specifically ecclesiastical, Marrou claims, in Augustine's program.[83] *De doctrina* is, by his account, a treatise devoted to Christian culture, a well-thought-out and mature view in which Augustine expresses the place that intellectual culture should have in the life of a person.[84] Kevane is a more recent proponent of this view, arguing on the basis of the title of the work that *De doctrina* is a treatise concerning education, but not in the narrow sense that Hill proposes. Kevane, instead, sees himself in line with Marrou: "[I]t seems beyond question that Marrou has established the correct perspective."[85] In order to establish his position, which he sees as a reconciliation of the views regarding *De doctrina*'s purpose, he traces the meaning of *doctrina* to determine Augustine's aim.

It should be noted that Kevane and Press have the same concern. Both see several differing views on what the treatise discusses, but both have different methods of reconciliation. Both follow similar modes of argument: tracing the definition of a word throughout classical culture and into *De doctrina*. For Kevane, the answer is not in discussing *tracto-tractatio*; rather, he pursues his argument by looking at the definition of the term *doctrina*.[86] This is, after all, the title Augustine himself gives the work.[87] *Doctrina*, Kevane determines, means the same thing for Augustine and the Latin tradition that *paideia* meant for the Greek culture: it is a comprehensive ideal for education.[88] Therefore, with Marrou, Kevane sees *De doctrina* as

Augustine's attempt to establish a Christian culture, one influenced by, but not fully continuous with, classical culture: "It is indeed 'the charter of Christian culture,' as Marrou sees it but not merely because it reflects Augustine's view of culture, or his personal acquisition of culture as a Christian convert and intellectual: it is this charter primarily because it programs the social process of Christian education which alone is the adequate cause of Christian culture, whether for persons on any general scale, or for society in the sense of the Christendom yet to be formed."[89] In other words, *De doctrina* concerns educating people in the broad sense of forming them in their culture. The work can therefore be seen as a hermeneutics, a handbook for preachers, and a textbook of exegesis "because it launched all of these upon their development in the Western and Christian civilization to come."[90] He also allows for it to be a treatise concerning rhetoric, if by rhetoric one means "the classical education system as a whole."[91] Similarly to Press, then, Kevane sees his solution as comprehensive, *the* answer among a range of suggestions.

Augustine addresses the various arts and sciences of the classical education system in Book 2 and gives directions for using them in the context of the work.[92] One can see how it is possible to make an argument that he takes over certain aspects of the ancient educational system in order to make a decidedly Christian educational system (*paideia* in Kevane's terminology). By taking into account the technical vocabulary Augustine uses in the prologue, Kevane argues that he responds to critics who are against education.[93] Then, coupling this insight with the aforementioned section in Book 2, one can argue that Augustine utilizes the ancient educational system by molding it into a Christian framework, a Christian culture or *paideia*.

Though Kevane's focus on Augustine's reinvention of classical culture is helpful, in the end, it is unpersuasive. The assumption is that, because the classical culture is transmitted through this work into the Middle Ages and beyond,[94] Augustine must have advocated it. Yet the program espoused in *De doctrina* is far narrower, far more pragmatic than passing on the tools of classical culture. The treatise is about how certain tools *already in existence* are useful for getting to the truth and sharing it with a congregation. The tools are means to an end: the interpretation and communication of God's will to a congregation. While Kevane, like Press, maintains the unity of the treatise, he also, like Press, fails to grasp fully the presupposed social location—the Christian community that has a specific set of texts that need to be interpreted to understand what God says to the community. The study of history, for instance, is not a separate study; it is a tool to discover what God says to his church through scripture.

Nonetheless, Kevane's view has its strengths. It focuses on Augustine's given title of the work: *De doctrina christiana* (4.1.1; *retr.* 2.4.1).[95] By focusing on the usage of *doctrina* in both the Latin tradition and in *De doctrina*, Kevane mounts a sophisticated argument that, when read closely, seems to address many of the worries that Press presents. For instance, Kevane quickly points to the Ciceronian rhetorical background of the work.[96] He also addresses the concept of *tracto-tractatio*, stressing that the core of the Christian culture is the *tractatio scripturarum*.[97] It can be argued, then, that Press's view—that the work is a rhetoric which then creates a culture—and Kevane's—that the work intends the formation of a culture through rhetoric—are not that far apart. Both build on the usage of words and ideas from the classical world, and both focus on the structure of Augustine's argument.[98] Clearly, they do not say the same thing, but functionally at least, their arguments are similar and reach the same conclusions.

Though *De doctrina* did in fact help restructure the educational system of antiquity as it moved into the Middle Ages, it seems unlikely that Augustine saw his work in that light. Moreover, the work itself does not seem to intend such a program.[99] Accepting Kevane's statement that it is one thing "to draw up a philosophical plan for the Christian education of youth and a program for a Christianized order of studies" and another thing entirely to organize and operate these institutions,[100] one is still left wondering if *De doctrina* is, in fact, such a philosophical plan. For one thing, the text does not appear to be written for youths, the very target of the ancient *paideia*. Instead, it is for those who interpret the biblical texts, who need to explain the will of God to those in the community, a target audience comprising both young and old people. Both Kevane and

Press fail to account for this more local community because they focus too much on either the background—whether classical education or rhetorical tradition—or the subsequent effects that they in the process miss out on the more specific social underpinnings of the work: the interpretation and communication of scripture *in the context of the church.*

## FOR PREACHERS (AT LEAST AT FIRST)

Each of these viewpoints offers something constructive to an understanding of *De doctrina*, but Hill's piece offers the best starting point because he helpfully emphasizes what a close examination of the work will demonstrate: *De doctrina* has the clergy as its primary target audience. Still, Press is perhaps correct to suggest that such a description fails adequately to address the importance the work places on *inventio*. For that reason, it would be helpful to describe *De doctrina* as an *expanded hermeneutics* because it concerns the interpretation of a text, but an interpretation that involves more than understanding. It involves a turn to rhetoric. For Augustine, as I will argue in chapter 4, this turn to rhetoric presupposes a particular community. For now, it is necessary only to stress the fact that *De doctrina* purports to be a biblical hermeneutics. That is, it concerns the interpretation of scripture, which Augustine insists comprises no less than two parts: understanding scripture and delivering that understanding to others.

Hill's view must then be combined with Pollmann's, who, unlike the four views discussed above, follows Augustine as he moves between different disciplines. *De doctrina* is, she says, Augustine's "*Universalhermeneutik.*" It utilizes every discipline that will aid the interpretation of scripture, and it is a hermeneutics for all Christians. While she points to numerous rhetorical influences in the work—from its sign theory to Book 4—she does not fall into the same trap as Press and compress all of *De doctrina* into a rhetorical handbook. In fact, she directly negates such a view by demonstrating that Augustine only covers two of the rhetorical topics in any kind of detail (*inventio* and *elocutio*, not *dispositio*, *memoria*, or *actio*).[101] While rhetoric is an "underlying theory" (*theoriebildende Grösse*), *De doctrina* is actually a hermeneutics that *uses* rhetoric, as Church Fathers before Augustine were already doing.[102] For Pollmann, *De doctrina* arose out of the tradition of the *Ars* or *Techné*; it is a textbook.[103] But it is more than this because it is more than the sum of its parts. Drawing from rhetoric, grammar, and philosophy, Augustine integrates Christian theology into their "soft spots" (*Weichstellen*) and surpasses them, forging the new discipline of hermeneutics.[104]

Such a description of *De doctrina* is helpful because it highlights Augustine's eclecticism while pointing out that what he creates has its own internal cohesion. Pollmann is correct to emphasize that *De doctrina* is not intended as a dogmatic textbook, something the title might easily suggest to modern readers: "*De doctrina*," she states, "is not primarily theological or dogmatic in its aims, though dogmatic reflections are included in the establishment of the hermeneutical normative-horizon in Book 1."[105] But she suggests that *De doctrina* is deeply theological in another sense when she emphasizes that a Christian hermeneutics has to define biblical exegesis as the deepest and truest Christian act of communication. Such a hermeneutics will insist that exegesis should result in the double love of God and neighbor, while at the same time being aware that all exegetical effort will become unnecessary in the eschaton.[106]

Building on these insights, the following discussion will demonstrate further that *De doctrina* is, from start to finish, theological because of the broad network of connections it presupposes, and because it intends to be read at the start primarily by ministers of the gospel who are in charge of interpreting and proclaiming the message of scripture to the gathered ecclesial community. Pollmann addresses this topic specifically, arguing that, while the sermon is the first and most obvious place to see Augustine's hermeneutics in practice, it would be too narrow to confine the targeted readership of *De doctrina* exclusively to a certain professional group, even if Augustine's high intellectual demands could only have been fulfilled in practice by the social elite of his time.[107] Again, Pollmann points to 4.18.37, where Augustine widens the subject of Book 4 from speeches to books and conversations, demonstrating that he has every Christian in mind.[108] While she is correct to insist that Augustine widens the potential addressees here, I will argue in chapter 4 that it is better to start first with the oral delivery of a preaching minister before widening the circle. This move allows one to describe interpretation as utilizing the sermon as its paradigm, a description that is faithful to the primarily oral nature of the delivery taught in Book 4. The theological payoff of this terminology will be seen in the final chapters. The discussion below will begin to prove this point, but it will not be until chapter 4 that it receives a thorough treatment.

So in the pages that follow, I will build on Pollmann's foundational insight that the whole of *De doctrina* is an eclectic hermeneutics, even one that is universal in scope, while attempting to maintain Hill's insight that the work begs to be read, at least initially, by practicing preachers, who, at the time of composition, would have consisted primarily of ordained clergy. Hill's thesis might be historical conjecture, but it makes sense of the text on internal grounds, even if the external ones prove to be incorrect. Thus, on the basis of previous research, it can be concluded that *De doctrina* should be read as a unity. The discussion that follows will corroborate this conclusion, while its primary point will be to emphasize by a close analysis of the text that *De doctrina* should be categorized as an expanded (theological) hermeneutics. And it must be borne in mind: the purpose of this historical exercise is to set the parameters for a dialogue with contemporary theology, making certain that I am not simply using Augustine as a mask for my own ideas, but rather allowing him to speak as a voice from outside the current discussions.

# De doctrina christiana

## Eclecticism in Action

*De doctrina* was important for the young Augustine: he seems to have released the first two books before he finished the work. The older Augustine, moreover, felt compelled to complete it. This demonstrates that the work is an entirety and that he did not mean for it to be split into two. If the first half could really stand on its own, he might not have bothered to finish the work. The fact that he did so shows that he thought its two parts are actually constituent parts of a single process of interpretation. A survey of *De doctrina* will demonstrate its unity, while also setting the boundaries for the discussion with contemporary theological hermeneutics.

Following the prologue, he establishes the program for *De doctrina*: "There are two things on which every interpretation of scripture [*tractatio scripturarum*] depends: the way of discovering [*modus inveniendi*] what should be understood and the way of presenting [*modus proferendi*] what has been understood" (1.1.1; 4.1.1). In other words, scriptural interpretation involves both understanding the text and sharing that understanding with others, and *De doctrina* follows this outline precisely: Books 1–3 treat the *modus inveniendi*, while Book 4 the *modus proferendi*. Already at the start, one can note

43

that Augustine speaks of interpretation—the subject of a hermeneutics—and includes within it not only textual understanding but
also rhetorical delivery. For that reason, categorizing *De doctrina*
as an expanded hermeneutics is particularly apt. Scripture has not
been interpreted unless one shares what one has understood with
another. By framing the issue in this manner, it becomes impossible to separate Books 1–3 from Book 4. They stand or fall together.
Furthermore, by stressing that Books 1–3 belong with Book 4, the
conclusion that the work is aimed primarily at the clergy proves
persuasive.

## SUMMARY

### The Prologue, Navigating Extremes

*De doctrina* begins with a prologue in which Augustine defends the
work against three potential criticisms.[1] The three groups of critics
can be classified into two categories: those who need to focus more
on the vertical relationship between humans and God and those
who need to focus more on the horizontal relationship between
humans and their fellow humans. Indeed, Augustine's more forceful words are aimed at those who would forgo human assistance
and appeal directly to God. His emphasis, in other words, is on
the relationship between humans, a point that prepares for his discussion of the biblical texts as texts composed by humans, as well
as his insistence in Book 4 on delivering to others what one has
understood from scripture. *De doctrina* is, through and through, a
book about humans being bound together in love. The prologue will
be discussed in depth in chapter 3. What should be emphasized at
this point is that Augustine prepares for the text of *De doctrina* by
navigating a middle path between a purely immanent and a purely
transcendent approach to biblical interpretation. That is, interpretation involves prayer to God as well as listening to and speaking with
humans. Both aspects are fundamental. Neither exists without the
other. So as the reader makes his or her way through *De doctrina*, it

must be kept in mind that while these rules are guidelines shared by another human, they are shared in connection to God's interaction with his creatures. The reader should pay attention to what Augustine says, while nevertheless praying for God to open his or her eyes to both Augustine's text and the text of the Bible.

## Book 1, The *res* of Scripture and How to Relate to Them

After the initial division between the *modus inveniendi* and the *modus proferendi*, Augustine begins the discussion of the *modus inveniendi* (Books 1–3) by further dividing the topic into signs and things (*signa et res*): "All teaching (*omnis doctrina*) is either of things or signs, but things are learned through signs" (1.2.2).[2] This semiotic division represents one of the most discussed aspects of *De doctrina*. In fact, it has been argued that Augustine invented what has become the discipline of semiotics.[3] His signification theory will be discussed below when treating Book 2; here in Book 1, Augustine simply states that signs "are those things which are clearly used to signify something" before he moves on to spend the rest of the book handling the *res* of scripture (1.2.2). At this point, his purpose is merely to set out the structure within which he will discuss biblical interpretation, hence, the simplified definition of a sign. In spite of pointing out that things are learned through signs, Augustine discusses things first. Only later, in Books 2 and 3, does he speak about signs. This mitigates the force of any attempt to make Augustine's sign theory foundational for his hermeneutics.[4] The semiotic discussion does not norm his hermeneutics; it is instrumental in it.

Nevertheless, scholars argue that his semiotics is the basis for the hermeneutics of *De doctrina*.[5] In a frequently cited article, Rowan Williams states: "Augustine's account of interpretation in the *de doctrina* . . . is a set of variations on a single theme, the relation of *res* and *signum*, thing and sign, reality and representation: I want simply to outline his account of this, and to look at one or two aspects of this scheme which may perhaps have some contemporary interest and pertinence."[6] Williams slightly overstates the point when he notes the pervasiveness of the sign theory throughout the work; the distinction exists only in Books 1–3. This fact demonstrates that the distinction between sign and thing is actually given with a specific purpose. *De doctrina*, as Jackson points out, is about handling difficulties in scriptural exegesis; the theory of signs is proposed "for a definite use and not for its own sake."[7] While Augustine does utilize his sign theory throughout *De doctrina* 1–3, a reading that pays attention to the entirety of the text and that follows Augustine as he moves fluidly between disciplines will notice that his sign theory does not serve as the basis of his hermeneutics. The subsequent chapter argues this point. His sign theory is more of a terminological distinction deployed with the aim of getting to a specific point: how to understand the words of scripture.[8] He is not writing a disinterested, comprehensive semiotics that will guard his interpretation. As I will argue in chapter 3, Augustine is more concerned with practice than with theory.

Book 1, then, discusses the *res* of scripture, and because scripture dictates a certain way of relating to things, he utilizes the language of *uti* and *frui*: to use and to enjoy. It must be stressed at this point that *uti* and *frui* are two divisions beneath the topic *res*, that is, a further subdivision within the previous distinction between *signa* and *res*. *Uti* and *frui* have nothing to do with signs, only with things: "We must be careful to remember that what is under consideration at this stage is the fact that things exist, not that they signify something besides themselves" (1.2.2).[9] He initially defines the pair thus: "To enjoy (*frui*) something is to hold fast to it with love for its own sake. To use (*uti*) something, however, is to refer what is in use to that which you love so that it might be attained, if indeed it should be loved" (1.4.4).[10] This pair structures Book 1, the goal of which is to reach the point where Augustine can say: "Of everything, then, that has been said in our discussion about things, this is the chief point: that it is to be understood that the fulfillment and end of the law, and of all the divine scriptures, is love of the thing which ought to be enjoyed and of the thing which is able to enjoy that thing with us" (1.35.39).[11] In other words, the entire purpose of Book 1 is to establish the importance of the double love of God and neighbor for Augustine's hermeneutics. A certain set of biblical passages, all discussing the relationship between the love of God and the love of neighbor drives Augustine's argument: Matthew 22:37–40 (the double-love command proper, *doctr. chr.* 1.22.21, 26.27), 1 Timothy 1:5 ("the end of the command is love from a pure heart, a good conscience, and true faith," *doctr. chr.* 1.26.27, 40.44), and Romans 13:9–10 ("The love of neighbor does no wrong," *doctr. chr.* 1.30.32).[12]

In the following chapters, I will analyze Book 1 more closely. For the purposes of this discussion, one should note two aspects implicit in Augustine's description: there are *res* and there are appropriate ways of relating to them. A further way to discuss this distinction is to speak of the *regula fidei*, which Augustine himself says is under discussion in Book 1 (3.2.2), and the *regula dilectionis*, the double-love command. The rule of faith explains the things to which one relates either by using or enjoying them. Generally speaking, after the delineations of *signa-res* and *res quibus fruendum est-res quibus utendum est*, Book 1 breaks into two sections, labeled appropriately by Jackson as "faith concerning things" (1.5.5–21.19) and "ordered love of things" (1.22.20–34.38).[13] The first section lays out the *res* behind scripture, those things to which it points, following a credal pattern. It begins with God the Father and moves through the Son to the Spirit and finally to the church and the resurrection. After the things of faith are summarized, Augustine moves on to the section, "the ordered love of things": "Among all these things, then, it is only the eternal and unchangeable things which I mentioned that are to be enjoyed; other things are to be used so that we may attain the full enjoyment of those things. We ourselves who enjoy and use other things are things" (1.22.20).[14] The *regula fidei* serves as a general hermeneutical criterion for slightly ambiguous signs, while the *regula dilectionis* becomes hermeneutically important in Book 3 when Augustine develops what can helpfully be termed "the *caritas* criterion," a rule that determines whether a passage should be taken literally or figuratively. He prepares the way for this understanding by placing the entirety of scripture within a certain framework, which itself derives from scripture: the end of the law and, for Augustine, all of scripture, is the creation of the double love of God and neighbor. The language of *signa* and *res* is important because he wants to speak in Books 2 and 3 of a certain kind of *signa*: *verba*, and more precisely, the words of scripture. *Uti* and *frui* helps him discuss things because he needs to speak of two types of things: those we love with all our heart, soul, mind, and strength, and those we love as we do ourselves. By structuring the discussion in this manner, he paves the way for the two hermeneutical rules of faith and love.[15]

As chapter 5 will argue, scripture, for Augustine, exists to engender the properly ordered love of God and humans; that is its *telos*.[16] In 1.34.38, Augustine speaks of the divine economy being established with the goal of teaching and enabling humanity. Within this economy, scripture can be described as having an intrinsic *telos*, something established with regard to the text, and this *telos* corresponds to a theological anthropology of the reader, who has his or her own *telos*. In Book 1, then, Augustine places scripture itself in a certain theological location, showing it to be a tool used by God to bring about a certain end: knowledge of the objects of faith so that one can respond appropriately with the double love of God and neighbor. Scripture has this *telos*, which establishes the need for certain, specific hermeneutical rules to read it. Hence, Book 1 has to establish the *what* of scripture before Augustine can move on to discuss the *how* of interpretation.

## Book 2, Understanding the *signa ignota* of Scripture

### Setting the Stage, Getting to the *verba* of Scripture

After discussing the *res* to which scripture points, Augustine then moves on to talk about the *signa* that point the student of scripture to these *res*. Books 2 and 3 both discuss signs.[17] In 2.1.1, he states: "A sign is a thing which from itself makes something else come to mind besides the appearance which it impresses on the senses." This definition narrows the one touched upon in Book 1 by stating the mechanism by which a sign signifies: it somehow brings something else to mind. He then—in good rhetorical fashion—further subdivides the category of signs into natural and given signs (*signa naturalia et data*).[18] He leaves *signa naturalia* quickly behind, demonstrating that he is not writing a disinterested, universal semiotic theory. His interest in *De doctrina* is only with a certain kind of sign: the words of scripture. For that reason, he moves on to words as a specific form of given signs, which, he says, exist for one person to communicate to another, and he discusses them for a pragmatic reason: "Because even the divinely given signs which are contained in the holy scriptures were transmitted to us by the humans who wrote them" (2.2.3). In other words, Augustine narrows his topic to the very point of interest: the human words of scripture, through which God communicates. The reader knows from the prologue that no hard-and-fast division exists between the human and the divine; the two work together. Augustine's divisions have been made in an effort to get to this point.

He now makes the following move: "The ones who read [scripture] desire to find nothing other than the thoughts and desires of those by whom it was written and through them the will of God, according to which we believe such men were speaking. But careless readers [*qui temere legunt*] are led astray by the many countless [*multis et multiplicibus*] obscurities and ambiguities, mistaking one thing for another" (2.5.6). As he states at the outset, *De doctrina* concerns the interpretation of scripture, and he has been narrowing his topic further and further until he finally reaches this point. One reads scripture to understand what its authors were communicating and, thereby, what God's will is. Nonetheless, there are instances where the reader cannot begin to grasp the meaning of the text. For the canonical books to move the reader from fear of the Lord to wisdom (2.7.9–11), a reader must understand them, which involves understanding human *verba* because God speaks to humans through humans (*per homines hominibus*) (Prol. 6).

Augustine then continues with his semiotic discussion by making a further division between unknown and ambiguous signs (*signa ignota aut ambigua*) (2.10.15). Signs can be unknown or ambiguous in either their literal sense (*signa propria*) or their metaphorical sense (*signa translata*). Literal signs "are employed to signify the things for which they were instituted." This is in contrast to metaphorical signs: "when those things we signify with particular words are themselves used to signify something else." The difference, he suggests, is between saying "ox" and meaning the four-legged animal grazing in a field, and saying "ox" in order that the four-legged animal represents something else—in his example from 1 Corinthians 9, a person working in the service of the gospel. That is, the sign represents a thing that becomes itself a sign for another thing (*signum → res = signum → res*).[19] Book 2 concerns unknown signs (*signa ignota*) (2.14.21), while Book 3 focuses on ambiguous signs (*signa ambigua*).

Unknown literal signs are dealt with fairly succinctly: one needs to learn the biblical languages, Greek and Hebrew, and ideally have a few translations at hand. By mastering such practical skills, the student can move past a concern with the signs only and to a concern for what is really important: the things to which the signs point (2.11.16–15.22). The best way to remedy difficulties of this sort is to gain a better understanding of the signs themselves. Nonetheless, there is another issue, which has to do with metaphorical signs. The person at this point might understand just what the signs on the page mean but nonetheless fail to grasp what they *really* mean. The remedy to this is a knowledge of things, the concern of the rest of the book (2.16.23–42.63). In other words, a reader might understand just how a dove bringing an olive branch back to a boat looks, but without a knowledge of what an olive branch signifies, he or she will not grasp that the passage is about the perpetual peace that the olive branch indicates (2.16.25, alluding to Gen. 8:11). To gain a better understanding of things, however, involves an entire discussion of the disciplines.

Plundering the Egyptians to Understand Scripture

As stated above, some find in *De doctrina*, especially in Book 2, the outline of an educational program built on the Bible.[20] Even L. Verheijen, who argues that the whole of *De doctrina* is not such an outline, still thinks that the "digression" in 2.19.29–42.63 is.[21] Within

Augustine's framework, however, the disciplines are all put to a specific use: interpreting scripture in the service of the church.[22] The "digression" actually fits perfectly well in the finely tuned structure of the work.[23]

After a brief introductory section discussing the beneficial knowledge of certain characteristics of natural things (like stones, olive branches, etc.), of numbers, and of music (2.16.24–18.28), he announces his final topic, which will help with understanding unknown signs, especially in their metaphorical usage: "But so that we might explain carefully that whole topic [*totum istum locum*][24]— for it is of utmost importance—there are two kinds of learning [*genera doctrinarum*] that also occur in pagan society: one of them concerns those things that humans have instituted [*quas instituerunt homines*], and the other those things which they observed [*quas animadverterunt*], which were either already developed, or divinely instituted. Concerning the former, which are according to the institutions of humans, some are superstitious; some are not" (2.19.29). The rest of Book 2 fills out these categories: *res quas instituerunt homines* and *res quas animadverterunt*. He further divides the things humans establish into things that are superstitious and things created simply to preserve the social order. He dismisses the superstitious institutions in 2.20.30–24.37, discussing them to show their futility: they are in fact created in conjunction with demons. After this dismissal, he moves on to those human institutions that are not superstitious but are created by humans for humans. Some of these are superfluous—like fictional stories—and they should be avoided. Some contribute to society and its order—like weights and measures—and should be learned and memorized. He ends the section by stressing the importance of the "usefulness" of the institutions: "They are useful, and it is not wrong to learn them, nor do they involve one in superstition, nor do they weaken one with self-indulgence, if they only occupy one so far that they do not become an impediment to the more important things, which they should serve to attain" (2.26.40) He has just been speaking of learning languages and shorthand, and here sums up the section: they are to help the Christian attain what he or she should attain, which the reader knows—both from Book 1 and the ascent to Wisdom described at the start of Book 2—is a properly ordered love of God and neighbor, a progression that ends in wisdom. Augustine helps the reader learn the proper tools to understand things correctly, all so he can demonstrate how to understand metaphorical and literal signs. This must be kept in mind, especially as he moves on to those things humans discover, that is, those things instituted not by humans but by God.

Beneath this category, he places two subdivisions: things that concern the physical senses (*ad sensum corporis*) and things that concern the mind (*ad rationem animi*). Regarding the things concerning the physical senses, Augustine stresses the focus on scripture.[25] A few relevant sentences will suffice:[26]

> Whatever the subject called history indicates concerning the succession of years past [*de ordine temporum transactorum*], it helps us a great deal to understand the holy books, even if it is learned by youth in an education outside the church. (2.28.42)

> Concerning which category [zoology], we dealt earlier and taught that a knowledge of it is useful when solving puzzles of scripture. (2.29.45)

> The knowledge of these things [craftwork, medicine, etc.] should be used rarely and in passing, not in a devoted manner [*non ad operandum*]—unless some duty makes it a necessity, but that is not our concern right now—but to help us decide, lest we are completely ignorant of what scripture wants to convey when it includes any figurative expressions concerning these skills [*artes*]. (2.30.47)

The final quotation makes the point succinctly: the disciplines Augustine discusses do have uses, but he is not concerned with their practical outworking. Instead, he stresses their utility when applied to the interpretation of scripture's figurative statements.

The second category—things concerning the mind—becomes the concern of the rest of the book. First and foremost for Augustine is the discipline of logic, which is "exceptionally helpful for penetrating and dissolving all kinds of problems that are in the sacred texts" (2.31.48). He punctuates the discussion with several comments stressing the need for humility when dealing with these disciplines; they are not for being puffed up with knowledge but for humbly approaching the scriptures. In addition, such things as logic and rhetoric can be applied to false things (2.25.53). That is, simple knowledge of them does not suffice for proper living. One must know the things to which scripture points, particularly the double love of God and neighbor.

Though it at times feels like a general meditation on what kinds of educational system Augustine might set up were he establishing a school, he nevertheless constantly reminds the reader that he is in fact discussing the kinds of tools already present within the pagan society that can be used for understanding scripture: logic "helps readers more when it comes to solving and explaining ambiguities—about which we will speak later—than when understanding unknown signs, which is the present topic" (2.39.59). The strict rhetorical structure of the work allows this flexibility. On the one hand, he has long, sometimes meandering discussions, which have application beyond his scope, but on the other hand, he continually reins the discussion back in to the topic at hand: the interpretation of scripture. Because he seems to presuppose the ancient educational system and offer advice as to what to take from it, rather than setting up his own disciplines,[27] it can be stressed that Augustine does not intend to establish a rival educational system but instead establishes what plunder the Christian can take from the Egypt of the Latin educational system: "Pagan superstition would never have loaned the disciplines it considered useful to all those people [the martyrs and early church fathers] if it had suspected they would be converted to the use of worshiping the one God" (2.40.61).[28]

After yet again stressing the need for humility (2.41.62), Augustine ends the section on the richness of scripture, the wonderful wealth available to its students, and he reiterates the point of the preceding: "The reader—provided with this instruction [*instructione*], when unknown signs will not hinder him, mild and humble in heart, being yoked lightly to Christ and burdened with a light load, founded and rooted and built up in the love that knowledge is not able to puff up—can now go on to consider and dissipate the ambiguous signs in scripture" (2.42.63). In other words, with the tools in place from Book 2, one should have no problem reading the clear sections of scripture, which are misunderstood for practical reasons—an ignorance of a word's meaning, or an ignorance of the metaphorical registers of certain flowers, or even the lack of an understanding of the way logic works. The Bible, however, is full of ambiguities and obscure places, things unclear even when one has as much knowledge about signs and things as possible.

### Book 3, Understanding the *signa ambigua* of Scripture

Determining If a Passage Is Literal or Figurative

In Book 3, Augustine tackles the *signa ambigua*, which occur either in literal or metaphorical usages. When he speaks of ambiguities in relation to literal usage, he has in mind the text's relationship to the *regula fidei*. Since texts were not punctuated and were more often than not read aloud, sometimes it would be difficult to determine where the punctuation should be placed.[29] For Augustine, one either consults the *regula fidei* or the context to determine where the punctuation goes. Some might frown at his usage of the *regula* to determine a text-critical issue,[30] but one must remember that the rule of faith represents the whole of scripture, as seen in its clear portions (3.2.2). So when a passage is difficult to understand, Augustine turns to the whole of which that passage is a part (scripture) and uses its entire canonical context to narrow down the proper punctuation. If this fails to limit the options, then the person addresses the preceding and following passages to determine which of the several meanings fits the context the best. Sometimes there is just no right answer, and he is fine with that (3.2.5). He then moves on to treat ambiguities that arise from the metaphorical use of words in 3.5.9: "they require no ordinary care and diligence" because it is dangerous to confuse literal and figurative, to think a sign is a thing and fail to raise one's eye from the letter to the spirit beyond it (3.5.9).

The main issue treated in Book 3, however, is how to distinguish a literal passage from a figurative one: "One should recognize as figurative anything in the divine discourse that cannot be referred in its literal sense [*proprie*] either to good morals or to the true faith" (3.10.14). The two foci of Book 1 should be recalled: the *regula fidei*, comprising the things of faith, and the way one relates to them, the *regula dilectionis*. Augustine puts it like this: "Good morals pertain to loving [*diligere*] God and neighbor, the truth of faith [*fides*] to recognizing [*cognoscere*] God and neighbor. But hope [*spes*] is in each person's conscience, insofar as he thinks he is progressing to the love [*dilectio*] and recognition [*cognitio*] of God and neighbor. All of this was said in the first book" (3.10.14). Here, he has the triad working again, with hope now related to the progress one makes in regard to the two aspects of faith and love that he discussed in the first book. Still, Augustine is not naïve. He is aware that people will judge good and bad morals on the basis of their time and culture, and he provides some guidelines: if scripture condones something that is not conducive to love, it speaks figuratively, and if it condemns something that is conducive to love, it also speaks figuratively. If, however, it encourages an action conducive to love, it is literal, and if it commands an act in keeping with the destruction of lust, it is literal. Chapters 2 and 4 pick up on this discussion, but it should be noted that Augustine operates with an active notion of the reader: one's time and situation play an active role in determining how one relates to the text and how its signs relate to that person (3.17.25).

Once the reader determines that a passage is figurative, he or she then uses the rules of Book 1 to reach the true meaning (3.24.34). The reader will realize that the figurative meaning is somehow connected to the things the words express (3.25.24). Here, after an example, the original composition ceases. Thirty years later, he picks up right in the middle of his thought: the connection between the things and what they mean figuratively can sometimes be elusive, and there is no hard-and-fast rule to determine how it works. After a few examples demonstrating this point, he stresses that multiple meanings are not necessarily a bad thing, presuming one can demonstrate a clear passage in scripture that backs up one's interpretation (3.25.37). He has a short discussion on grammar and tropes, where he states: "But here it is not fitting to teach them to the ignorant, or we might appear to be teaching the discipline of grammar. I recommend that they be learned sensibly outside the church, although I already recommended that above in the second book, where I discussed the necessary knowledge of languages" (3.29.40). Again, it can be stressed that Augustine has a specific interest: understanding scripture. All the discussions concern this, no matter how general (or how expansive) they might appear at first. In Book 3, he develops what has been called the "absurdity criterion."[31] That is, if the text says something that cannot be true, then it must mean something else. Rather than calling it an "absurdity criterion," however, it would be more accurate to describe it as a "*caritas* criterion."[32] That is, what makes something absurd is not simply its being absurd; something is absurd because it stands in fundamental contradiction either to God's nature as expounded in the clear portions of scripture, or in contradiction to the double-love command. If a passage forbids lust, it must be literal. If it commands lust, however, it must be figurative, because lust is condemned in scripture, while its opposite, love, is praised. And at this point, Augustine turns to an older hermeneutics to provide some help to his reader, a hermeneutics written by "a certain Tyconius."

## Tyconius's *Liber regularum*, Passing on a Helpful Text (with Some Caveats)

In order to further his discussion about interpreting figurative statements, Augustine utilizes the hermeneutical handbook of Tyconius, a Donatist.[33] Much has been written on the relationship between the *Liber regularum* and *De doctrina*.[34] In fact, it is one of the most discussed aspects of Augustine's hermeneutics. Arguments often revolve around whether Augustine understood Tyconius or not, but for my purposes, such a discussion is less important than grasping how Augustine uses Tyconius's work.[35]

Augustine thinks the rules of Tyconius will provide a useful guide for understanding ambiguous passages in scripture.[36] He recommended the *Liber regularum* on at least one occasion for its ecclesiology,[37] and it seems that Augustine also thinks Tyconius's rules are helpful and that they highlight well what he has already said:

> All of these rules except the one called "Concerning the promises and the law" cause one thing to be understood from another, which is a characteristic of figurative speech. . . . For whenever one thing is said so that another is understood, there is a figure of speech, even if the name of that trope is not found in the discipline of rhetoric [*ars loquendi*]. When it occurs as it normally does, understanding follows without effort, but when it does not, one must work to understand it. . . . Hence, just as with literal words [*verba propria*], concerning which we spoke about above, where the things that are spoken are understood, so in metaphorical words [*verba translata*], which occur in tropes, where one thing is understood from another—concerning which we have dealt here sufficiently—students of the venerable books should be admonished so that they might understand the styles of speech in holy scripture, and they should pay diligent attention and commit to memory in what way things are customarily said in scripture. (3.37.56)

He states earlier that: "Once that is clear [whether a passage should be taken literally or metaphorically], the words in which it is expressed are found either to come from some similarity of the things, or from some connection between them" (3.25.34). In other words, he has already discussed how to interpret figuratively because one must be certain that the metaphorical reading relates to the literal meaning of the words. Augustine passes on what he considers to be a helpful set of rules for untangling the ambiguous statements of scripture; at the same time, he makes certain that Tyconius's helpful rules are not taken on board without due care. He puts them into an appropriate context so they can be used correctly; as Augustine makes clear, he does not intend his summary to be read at the expense of *Liber regularum*, but he does want it to be read with appropriate caution (3.30.43).

## Summary of Book 3

In Book 3, Augustine treats the *signa ambigua* by discussing how to know when a passage is literal or figurative. He here develops the *caritas* criterion, which states that if a passage does not build up the double love of God and neighbor when read literally, then it must be interpreted figuratively. Book 3 follows directly from Books 1 and 2. In the first book, the *regula fidei* treats the things to which the signs point and the *regula dilectionis* how one should relate to them. Once he has established these two rules, he can then move on to the clear passages, where confusion arises from a lack of understanding regarding signs used in their literal sense, their metaphorical sense, or the things to which those signs point. Finally, he has helped the student get to the point where he or she is ready to tackle the obscure portions of scripture, where a good knowledge of signs and things makes little difference. One must, at this point, have a grasp of the whole (the *regula fidei*) and a grasp of how one relates to God and neighbor (the *regula dilectionis*). Then, and only then, will the obscure passages begin to make sense. But the initial definition of scriptural interpretation insists that understanding scripture for oneself is not its own end, or, to put it more radically: for Augustine, one has not understood scripture fully if one has not communicated its meaning to others. Books 1–3 lead purposely to Book 4, where Augustine covers how the understanding gained should be explained to others.

## Book 4, Communicating What One Has Understood (with Some Help from Cicero)

In Book 4, Augustine finally arrives at the end of his two-part hermeneutics, the *modus proferendi*. A good bit has been written on this book alone. In fact, Book 4 is the first of Augustine's works ever printed.[38] Recently, a reprint of Book 4 has been published, with essays discussing its influence and relationship to Cicero and the rhetorical tradition.[39] But as this chapter has attempted to make clear, Book 4 should not be treated in abstraction from the first three books; it is the essential second half of the two-part process of interpretation. It is the culmination of Augustine's hermeneutics. There is no Book 4 without the preceding three, even if a division naturally occurs. In Book 4, the ecclesial location of *De doctrina* comes to the fore. That is not to say it has been absent. The prologue alone has reference to the necessity of the church for interpretation, but in Book 4, the focus on ministers, on preachers, is foregrounded. Books 1 to 3 have prepared the way for this one. Without delivering what one understands to the pilgrim church, one has not fully interpreted scripture. Still, one cannot downplay understanding, and the fourth book is therefore tied directly to what has gone before. To separate the *modus inveniendi* from the *modus proferendi* puts asunder two things that together comprise the *tractatio scripturarum*.

Augustine's program is a remarkable theoretical achievement. When one thinks of ministers as the potential, original target audience of *De doctrina*, it is perhaps not surprising that he speaks of oral delivery here, but he goes further and stresses that all preaching should be firmly grounded on a careful and responsible interpretation of scripture. The meaning of scripture—and not the opinion of the preacher independent from it—should be the sermon's topic. If one then follows the universalizing tendencies of *De doctrina* and looks to a more general readership, Augustine's project implies that the task of scriptural explanation is not simply confined to those whose profession involves preaching. *Every* interpretation of scripture (*omnis tractatio scripturarum*) involves two parts, he says, and thus Augustine extends the sermon as a paradigm beyond narrower institutional confinements.

Much discussion centers around Book 4's relationship to the rhetorical tradition. Augustine utilizes rhetorical ideas then in circulation, ideas that can be traced back especially to Cicero's *Orator*, written in 46 B.C.E. Like Cicero, Augustine discusses the three styles of speaking, the *genera dicendi*—the subdued (*summissus*), the grand (*grandis*), and the moderate (*temperatus*) styles—and like Cicero, he connects these to the effects that a rhetor should have on his listeners: the rhetor should either teach (*docere*), delight (*delectare*), or appeal emotionally to (*flectere*) them (4.12.27). A primary issue in the discussions is whether Augustine is original or simply derivative.[40] Primmer argues compellingly that Augustine's use of Ciceronian rhetoric "represents a step forward."[41] As Primmer points out, Augustine cites Cicero in 4.12.27: "A certain eloquent man has said, and rightly, that the eloquent should speak so that he teaches, delights, and appeals emotionally. He then added: 'to teach [*docere*] is a matter of necessity; to delight [*delectare*] is a matter of attractiveness; to appeal emotionally [*flectere*] is a matter of victory.'"[42] Though he quotes from Cicero, Augustine nonetheless changes his emphases:

> Thus our orator, when he speaks of the just, the holy, and the good—for he should not speak of anything else—aims to be heard with understanding, pleasure, and obedience (insofar as he can when he speaks about these things). And he should not doubt that he can do these things—if in fact he can and insofar as he can—more from the piety of his prayers than from the skill of his oratory [*pietate magis orationum quam oratorum facultate*], so that when praying [*orando*] for himself and for those whom he will address, he is a person who prays [*orator*] before he is a person who speaks [*dictor*]. (4.15.32)[43]

Augustine has shifted the focus away from the law courts, where "speaking in a clear, probable manner is no more than a prerequisite, speaking pleasantly entertains the listener, but appealing emotionally to the audience insures the speaker's victory."[44] For Augustine, the focus is shifted from the speaker to God; the goal is obedient listeners, who are persuaded to live according to the double-love command. Likewise, his use of the *genera dicendi* represents a move away from Cicero, while nonetheless utilizing his terminology:

> It is the universal office of eloquence [*eloquentia*]—in whichever of these three styles—to speak suitably in order to persuade [*dicere apte ad persuasionem*]; the aim, however, that which you

intend to persuade when speaking, in whichever of these three styles, the eloquent speaker indeed speaks in order to persuade, but if he does not persuade, then he has not arrived at the end of eloquence. In the subdued style [*genus summissus*], he persuades people that what he says is true; in the grand style [*grandis*], he persuades them in such a way that they are driven to do what they know they should do even though they have not done it yet; in the moderate style [*temperatum*], he persuades them that he speaks beautifully and elaborately. But what is the point of that for us? . . . We should refer this style to another end, namely, that what we aim to do in the moderate style is the same as when we speak in the grand style (that is, that good morals might be loved and bad ones avoided) if they are not so distant from that action that they might seem to need urging to it with the grand style of speaking, or if they already do it, so that they are made more eager and persevere steadfastly in it. (4.25.55)

Here, Augustine takes Cicero's three styles and insists that the moderate style, in which the orator is recognized as speaking beautifully, has no place for the Christian preacher. Instead, it should be related to the same end as the grand style, to persuade listeners to live correctly. The three styles are united to the three effects, and the Christian preacher really only has two goals: to teach, which predominately utilizes the subdued style, and to persuade his or her listeners to live correctly, which is accomplished through all three styles. Augustine points out that the three aims are not exactly correlated to each style (4.26.56) but that the aims to teach and to persuade (but never simply to delight) must always be kept in mind. As Carol Harrison puts it: "It is in this sense . . . that we can speak of a Christian aesthetic, a new Christian literary culture; one which rhetoric holds as central a place as it did in classical culture, but where it is transformed from a practice that primarily aims to please and persuade, to one which aims to inspire love of, and the practice of truth."[45] It is this focus on truth that sets Augustine apart from his classical forebears. Cicero's concern is persuasion of the audience and admiration of the orator.[46] Augustine, on the other hand, puts the focus beyond the preacher and on to the truth, which in his case is Christ. Hence, even if a speaker lives inappropriately, he or she can still teach and persuade the congregation (4.27.59). Augustine is still concerned with persuasion—like Cicero—but persuasion to the truth, which means that the Christian orator (preacher) does not seek to delight except to hold his or her audience's attention (4.26.57), which means Augustine has turned the classical order "on its head": teaching first, persuasion (and delight) second.[47] The preacher, in reality, is not the one speaking: "But because good, faithful people listen obediently not to just any person, but to the Lord himself, who says, 'Do what they say, but do not do what they do, for they say one thing and do another,' it is appropriate to listen even to those who act inappropriately" (4.27.59, alluding to Matt. 23:3).

The arguments for Augustine's originality over his indebtedness are therefore compelling. He uses Cicero but only when Cicero says what Augustine himself wants to say.[48] The precise structure of Augustine's work allows him the flexibility to use this pagan author's ideas without having to surrender to his exact emphases.[49] Augustine wants the Christian preacher to come to scripture to find what God says to his church, which sits continually in the background as interpretation goes on. In fact, interpretation is not complete until this community hears what the minister has understood. Book 4 demonstrates that Augustine envisions applications beyond the sermon (4.9.23), but these discussions and books are extensions of the primary act of interpreting scripture, which includes preaching. Why else would Augustine spend so much time discussing speaking aloud? Thus, as I will argue in chapters 4 and 5, the paradigm for Augustine's model of biblical interpretation is the sermon.

## Summary and Translation of the Title

In sum, *De doctrina* represents a finely structured work that lays out a bipartite interpretive practice: one reads scripture to understand what God says through the prophets and apostles, and then one turns back to the church and delivers that understanding. It is an inherently theological exercise, but a kind of theology unafraid to make excursions into other disciplines to utilize anything they have to offer. Because Augustine operates with such a structure, he can roam freely in the midst of it, allowing his thoughts to range over a wide variety of topics. In the first book, he divides interpretation into two parts: understanding and communication. Understanding is then broken down into the difference between understanding signs and things. Because he has a clear focus—Books 1 to 3 are under the heading of the *modus inveniendi*—he can discuss different disciplines that may or may not be useful for biblical interpretation, that is, for understanding the signs of scripture. This section may seem to be a general discussion on a general educational system, but Augustine continually states how these different topics are useful for the interpretation of scripture. By noting the overarching structure, this fact stands out sharply. Book 3 finds him once again on theological grounds with a discussion of the *caritas* criterion. Nonetheless, because his structure is so precise, he can yet again roam into territories normally out-of-bounds: he can go to the quasi-heretic Tyconius and plunder what is of most help in his treatise and, in so doing, provide directions for how his readers can benefit from the entirety of the *Liber regularum*. Finally, in Book 4, Augustine moves to the *modus proferendi* and, as he has done throughout, utilizes tools found outside the church to demonstrate how one should deliver the results of understanding the biblical text. He bends Cicero even more than he adjusts Tyconius, not utilizing either of them fully, but pulling from them what he thinks is of use in the quest to understand God's will in the words of the human authors of scripture. It is an eclectic work, one that feels at one moment as though it is a general discussion on signs and things, and at another, a meditation on the ineffability of the Godhead.

One question remains: How should one translate its title? *De doctrina christiana* can have several resonances. In English, it has been translated as "On Christian Doctrine," "Teaching Christianity," "On Christian Instruction," "On Christian Education," and "On Christian Teaching." Pollmann translates it as "*Die christliche Bildung*," which has resonances with "On Christian Education."[50] The editors of the *Bibliothèque Augustinienne* translate the title as "*La*

*Doctrine Chrétienne,*" "Christian Doctrine."[51] As this summary has shown, however, any title that suggests the book concerns Christian doctrine—in the sense of the dogmatic teaching of the Christian faith—can be ruled out; only the first book has to do with this topic. Likewise, "Teaching Christianity" can be ruled out because it suggests that the work concerns teaching *about* Christianity, rather than about how to go about teaching the Christian church. "On Christian Education" suggests that the book is concerned with education in general, a position that does not bear scrutiny. Book 2 might be construed as the establishment of a Christian *paideia,* but the structure I have demonstrated mitigates the force of this argument. The section on the pagan education system might feel like a general discussion, but it is in fact very narrow in its focus: what exists in the pagan world that is of use in the understanding of scripture. As with "On Christian Education," "On Christian Instruction" may give the impression that the treatise concerns something akin to teaching in a more formal environment, perhaps like a catechism. "On Christian Teaching," therefore, seems to be the best option for translating the title. "Teaching" can have both the active and the passive meanings in English that *doctrina* has in Latin.[52] Thus, "Christian" modifies the content as well as the manner of teaching. Books 1–3 are about Christian teaching in the passive form: they concern the subject matter, while Book 4 is about Christian teaching in the active form: it concerns the moment the preacher stands up and teaches the congregation the teaching discovered in the divine books.

## OUTLINE OF *DE DOCTRINA*

Though there are several outlines of the work available, it seems fitting to provide another to orient the reader:[53]

1) Prologue
   A. There are certain rules for interpreting scripture (*praecepta quaedam tractandarum scripturarum*) that can be helpfully passed on to those who want to learn to understand it [1].

B. Three groups might disapprove of this work [2].
　　I. Those who fail to understand my rules should pray for understanding [3].
　　2. Those who understand my rules but still fail to understand scripture should also pray [3].
　　3. Those who think there is no need for such rules in principle are being prideful because they fail to recognize that God works through humble, human means [4–9].
2) The Interpretation of Scripture (*tractatio scripturarum*) [Books 1–4]
　　A. The way of discovering (*modus inveniendi*) what should be understood [Books 1–3]: all teaching (*doctrina*) is about either things (*res*) or signs (*signa*) [1.2.2].[54]
　　　　I. Things (*res*) [Book 1]
　　　　　　a. There are two ways to relate to things [1.3.3–4.4].
　　　　　　　　I) Some things should be enjoyed (*res quibus fruendum est*): the Trinity.
　　　　　　　　2) Some things should be used (*res quibus utendum est*): the whole created order.
　　　　　　b. The things of scripture that are believed represent the *regula fidei* [1.5.5–21.19].
　　　　　　c. How to relate to the things of scripture represents the *regula dilectionis* [1.22.20–34.38].
　　　　　　d. All scripture teaches the double love of God and neighbor [1.35.39–40.44].
　　　　2. Signs (*signa*) [Books 2–3]
　　　　　　a. Natural signs (*signa naturalia*) [Briefly: 2.1.2]
　　　　　　b. Given signs (*signa data*), particularly those of scripture [Books 2–3]
　　　　　　　　I) Signs in general are not the concern; the words of scripture are [2.2.3–9.14].
　　　　　　　　　　a) There are written words because spoken words do not last [2.2.3–5.6].
　　　　　　　　　　b) Scriptural words are often misunderstood because God organized scripture that way [2.6.7–8].
　　　　　　　　　　c) One must progress from the fear of God to wisdom [2.7.9–9.14].

      1. The interpretation of scripture is the third of seven stages [2.8.12].

      2. There are certain canonical books on which the interpreter should focus in order to progress in holiness [2.8.12–9.14].

2) Unknown signs (*signa ignota*) [2.10.15–42.63]

    a) There are a few aids to understanding signs unknown in their literal (*propria*) sense [2.11.16].

      1. One should gain an understanding of Greek and Hebrew [2.11.16].

      2. One should consult translations [2.12.17–15.22].

    b) There are a few aids to understanding signs unknown in their metaphorical (*translata*) sense [2.16.23].

      1. Some can be resolved simply by learning languages [2.16.23].

      2. The rest can be resolved by learning about things, with which some disciplines taught by the pagans are helpful [2.16.24–42.63].

        a. There are disciplines instituted by humans (*instituerunt homines*) [2.19.29–26.40].

          1) Some are superstitious (*superstitiosum*) [2.20.30–24.37].

          2) Some are not superstitious [2.25.38–26.40].

            a) Some are superfluous (*superflua*) [2.25.38–39].

            b) Some are good and necessary (*commoda et necessaria*) [2.25.38–26.40].

        b. There are disciplines discovered by humans (*quae investigando homines prodiderunt*), whether occurring in the passage of time (*transacta temporibus*) or divinely instituted (*divinitus institutas*) [2.27.41–42.63].

          1) Some pertain to the outward senses (*ad sensum corporis*) [2.28.42–30.47].

          2) Some pertain to the mind (*ad rationem animi*) [2.31.48–42.63].

3) Ambiguous signs (*signa ambigua*) [Book 3]
    a) There are a few aids to understanding signs that are ambiguous due to literal (*propria*) usage [3.2.2–4.8].
        1. One should check punctuation and articulation [3.2.2].
        2. One should consult the *regula fidei* discussed in Book 1 [3.2.2–4.8].
        3. One should consult the context [3.2.2–4.8].
    b) There are a few aids to understanding signs that are ambiguous due to metaphorical words (*verba translata*) [3.5.9–37.56].
        1. Be careful not to interpret a figurative statement literally and vice versa [3.5.9–10.14].
        2. A passage is figurative when it cannot be related either to good morals (the *regula dilectionis*) or to the true faith (the *regula fidei*) [3.10.14–28.39].
            a. Scripture condemns nothing but lust and commands nothing but love [3.10.14–16.24].
            b. Be aware of the reader's situation because this affects how the passage applies, either literally or figuratively [3.17.25–21.31].
            c. Nearly all Old Testament passages are both literal and figurative [3.22.32–23.33].
        3. A knowledge of tropes is useful, but also rather commonsensical [3.29.40–41].
        4. The Rules of Tyconius are helpful for handling ambiguities [3.30.42–37.56].
B. The way of presenting (*modus proferendi*) what has been understood [Book 4][55]
    1. These are the goals and responsibilities of the preacher (*officia*) [4.4.6–14.31].
        a. Biblical wisdom (*sapientia*) is more important than human eloquence (*eloquentia*) [4.4.6–7.21].
        b. Clarity (*evidentia*), that is, an emphasis on the listener's capacity, is a necessity [4.8.22–11.26].
        c. There are three duties (*officia*) of rhetoric [4.12.27–14.31].

    1) To teach (*docere*)

    2) To delight (*delectare*)

    3) To appeal emotionally (*flectere*)

2. The preacher must pray because God speaks through him or her [4.15.32–16.33].

3. Cicero's three styles (*genera dicendi*) are useful guides for preaching [4.17.34–29.61].

    a. The subdued style (*genus summissum*) convinces of the truth of what is said.

    b. The grand style (*genus grande*) persuades one to perform an action.

    c. The moderate style (*genus temperatum*) urges one to continue and persevere.

4. God's grace and prayer are imperative for the speaker [4.29.62–31.64].

## *DE DOCTRINA* AS A VOICE FROM OUTSIDE

The preceding outline should provide some orientation to the work, while at the same time demonstrate just how intricate Augustine's text is. The finely structured outline allows him to have general discussions while never losing sight of the work's topic: the interpretation of scripture. It is a unified project in spite of its breadth. When reading *De doctrina*, it can be easy to forget that Augustine has such a narrow concern because many pages feel like excurses on a wide range of topics. Nonetheless, as this summary and outline demonstrate—and as the following pages will bear out—*De doctrina*'s seemingly general discussions are put to a specific use, demonstrating an eclecticism at once expansive and focused.

By keeping an eye on the text as a whole, it becomes possible for Augustine to set some parameters for the dialogue that will follow. I have emphasized the overt, theological nature of *De doctrina*. While classical and philosophical ideas are present and must be reckoned with, they are subsidiary to the theological and scriptural interests. Because our concern is biblical interpretation, and because

hermeneutics is the theoretical reflection on the practice of interpretation, it makes sense to allow Augustine's version of theological
hermeneutics to engage with contemporary construals. He couples
philosophical ideas with theological ones, and so it will make sense
to seek out theologians who do the same. By allowing them to enter
into dialogue with Augustine, insights into the contemporary context will come from Augustine's text, and the dialogue should also
provide helpful language with which to analyze *De doctrina*. The discussion will lead us to specific sections of the work, which will in
turn lead us to the examination of other theologians.

The entire process is dialogical. The goal is to allow Augustine
to be a voice from outside in the sense that he not only speaks from
outside our historical context, but that precisely by doing so, he can
open our eyes to different ways of framing issues and analyzing our
situation. He began *De doctrina* as a newly ordained bishop and
he finished it at the end of his career. Within its pages we have his
thoughts on how the Bible should be read, thoughts that span the
entirety of his tenure as bishop of Hippo. To read Augustine is to
embark on a journey. One enters into a flow of thought unlike contemporary patterns. One looks for something to latch hold of, only
to find it swept along the current of another way of expressing the
problem or solution to it. One reads Augustine as a contemporary at
one's peril. He is refreshing because his concerns and emphases are
different. He can appeal to philosophy because he thinks God reveals
truth everywhere, and he can make statements like this because he
has not been affected by later arguments about natural theology.[56] He
can interweave biblical interpretation with theoretical thought about
the place of logic and history. Reading Augustine requires effort. On
the one hand, the reader cannot expect him to write about exactly
what one wants to ask, and on the other, one cannot doubt that his
concerns will mesh in some way with the concerns of the present.
In *De doctrina*, we come upon an Augustine who wants to share his
insights into biblical interpretation. As contemporary discussions
revolve around this very question, it seems reasonable to turn back
to this text with fresh eyes and an inquiring mind to discover what
Augustine might say were he speaking to theologians today.

# Theological Hermeneutics

*A priori* or *a posteriori?*

An initial problem confronts the contemporary theologian who wants to make use of *De doctrina christiana* as a hermeneutical text: on one hand, it looks similar to hermeneutical treatises written today—it contains philosophical concepts, discussions about the text and the reader, and so on—while on the other, it is unlike such contemporary texts—it does not shy away from talking about God, human sin, and the like. Moreover, the contemporary theologian begins with a set of presuppositions about the nature of hermeneutics that propels the investigation in certain directions from the moment he or she begins to read the text. For instance, what exactly is the purpose of hermeneutics? Does the discipline exist to describe human understanding in general, or does it help the reader grapple with how to read a text? Do theological categories like sin and grace have a place in discussions about how to read, or should one speak more about texts and readers than about divine and human agency? For that reason, it will be helpful to discuss *De doctrina* as a hermeneutical treatise in general before moving on to what it has to say about its particular version of hermeneutics. In other words, this chapter discusses what the text says about the nature of theological hermeneutics as a discipline. Such a discussion runs the risk of anachronism, but by bringing contemporary concerns to a close reading of an ancient text, the theological payoff should outweigh the potential risk.

When Schleiermacher pronounced that "misunderstanding results as a matter of course," he ushered in a new era for hermeneutics.[1] No longer could a reader assume that the act of reading was for the most part unproblematic; it now required a degree of attention that had not, until that moment, been thought necessary. Along with the assumption of misunderstanding, a general hermeneutics could be formed that would be unlike what had gone before.[2] The discipline could finally, with Gadamer, move to declare itself foundational not only for understanding texts, but for the process of understanding itself: "[hermeneutics] denotes the basic being-in-motion of Dasein that constitutes its finitude and historicity, and hence embraces the whole of its experience of the world."[3] Hermeneutics no longer concerns only interpreting texts because one's existence itself is hermeneutical.[4]

Gadamer's description of hermeneutics is distant from the modest "hermeneutics" Augustine espouses in *De doctrina*, where he describes his treatise as a rulebook to help a reader unravel the obscurities found in the biblical text: "Likewise the person who accepts the rules that we are attempting to teach, when he finds an obscurity in the text, will not require another to reveal to him what is hidden because he has comprehended certain rules" (Prol. 9). He is concerned not with understanding per se, but with understanding texts, and even more narrowly, with understanding the obscurities present in one particular text. After Schleiermacher, on the other hand, the discipline of hermeneutics becomes foundational, as it were, an *a priori* exercise; only after comprehending how texts and understanding fit together in general should a person move to a special or local hermeneutics. On the basis of Schleiermacher's ideas, the discipline continued to develop until Gadamer could finally declare it the basis of all understanding. Such a conception derives from the acknowledgment of the linguistic nature of all human understanding.[5] In contrast, Augustine's suggestions for interpretation have the appearance of ad hoc rules, given in order to help the reader of scripture understand how, in fact, scripture says what it should. Interestingly, his influence can be felt in philosophical hermeneutics, although without the theological matrix present in *De doctrina*.[6] For this reason, when surveying contemporary theological hermeneutics, one might expect to find Augustine's example exerting its influence.

In contrast, however, discussions often seem to focus on philosophical ideas to the near exclusion of explicitly theological concepts, while at the same time they appeal to Gadamer and Ricoeur at the expense of an appeal to Augustine or, say, Luther.[7] For instance, David Tracy and Werner Jeanrond—both theologians—describe the discipline of hermeneutics in philosophical terms; they ask how texts and understanding are related, rather than, say, how God uses scripture to speak to the church.[8] Hermeneutics is for them a foundational exercise meant to evaluate the understanding of self and of texts; only after grasping the general process of understanding can the theologian turn to the Bible. Such appeals to philosophical hermeneutics in theological discussions lead one theologian to ask: "Why, for example, is Augustine's untroubled appeal to the grammatical and rhetorical tools of ancient interpretative practice so different from modern theology's heavily theorized—and often anxious—investment in a philosophical view of 'interpretation' or 'understanding'?"[9] This chapter aims to answer the question by putting Augustine in dialogue with a contemporary theologian, drawing his use of the philosophical ideas of his day and contemporary theology's respective use into sharp contrast. In the course of discussion, I hope to show that Augustine's hermeneutics as espoused in *De doctrina* represents a significant alternative to the hermeneutics espoused by, for example, Tracy and Jeanrond. Because he locates scriptural reading—and therefore hermeneutics—within the divine economy in a specific way, Augustine can utilize philosophical as well as theological ideas. In fact, he would see no rigid disjuncture between theology and philosophy, and that explains to some extent his attractiveness both to philosophers and theologians. By determining what he says about his hermeneutics in general, the chapter will go some way in preparing for the subsequent discussions about what he says concerning the interpretation of scripture.[10]

## CATEGORIZING HERMENEUTICAL THEORIES: SPATIAL AND TEMPORAL MODELS

In order to discuss Augustine's hermeneutical treatise and its relationship to contemporary theological hermeneutics, it will be helpful to make a terminological distinction between what I will call the spatial model for categorizing hermeneutical theories—general and local—and the temporal or logical model—*a priori* and *a posteriori*. The spatial model depicts hermeneutical theories in terms of what the theory is envisioned to describe: general hermeneutics pertains to a broad range of texts and perhaps to understanding itself, while local hermeneutics exists within general hermeneutics and pertains to a specific text or a limited group of texts. The temporal model, on the other hand, describes the moment appeal is made to hermeneutical theory, whether before practice to guard it or in the context of practice to aid it; at issue is not how broad the theory is but how the theory is envisioned to stand in relation to the ongoing interpretive practice. Both models are useful, but in discussions about theological hermeneutics, often a sharp polarization develops between general and local hermeneutics, where one is privileged and the other subordinated (or excluded altogether). Such an opposition does not exist in practice, however, because even the most local of hermeneutics appeals to general concepts. Rather, the spatial model actually operates more as a continuum than as a sharp opposition. For this reason, the temporal model will supplement and describe the situation in different, though complementary terms. This conceptual delineation will help clarify just what makes Augustine's model of hermeneutics a considerable alternative to the theological hermeneutics present in many contemporary discussions.

Again, debate in theological hermeneutics often concerns whether one should prefer a general (or universal) hermeneutics, within which local, theological, hermeneutics exists, or a special, local, hermeneutics only. First, there are those who argue that theology should begin with a general hermeneutics (whether on the basis of philosophy or literary theory) in order to guard interpretation of the biblical texts. For instance, a driving force behind Anthony Thiselton's appeal to general hermeneutics is the attempt to protect them from misreading. In *New Horizons in Hermeneutics*, he seeks to provide tools to avoid the misuse and ideological reading of the biblical texts: "[A]dequate use of suspicion and self-criticism in hermeneutics is essential if we are not to worship idols, projecting our own wishes and images onto revelation"; here, Thiselton explicitly references Paul Ricoeur.[11] Thiselton develops a general hermeneutics in order to prevent theological concerns from overriding the concerns of the text. Elsewhere, he explicitly states that hermeneutics must be separate from theology in order to resist "reduction and domestication";[12] without an external critique, it seems, theology will subvert the Bible and make it say what the reader wants to hear.[13] Theology can be described as practice, while hermeneutics is the theory that undergirds it. If practice comes first, Thiselton seems to suggest, interpretation is suspect.[14] In response, he formulates a theory that comes logically before practice in order to ensure that the practice can be corrected. Because his main concern is safeguarding interpretation from theological imposition, Thiselton is not as concerned as other theologians with finding alternatives to so-called historical-critical methodology.[15]

Especially driven to move interpretation away from biblical criticism,[16] a second trend in contemporary theology comprises scholars who emphasize the importance of localized, or special, hermeneutics.[17] Underlying this appeal to local hermeneutics seems to be the affirmation that general hermeneutics is just that, a generalization, and useful only to a limited degree. For instance, Charles Wood states: "[T]here is no understanding in general, of which every achieved understanding is an instance. Several fields of inquiry may of course have some common criteria for 'understanding,' so that a shared paradigm might be abstracted from their accounts. But it is well to remember that this is an abstraction, not a foundation.

'Understanding' is context-dependent not merely in its more remote outworkings but at its center."[18]

Crucial to the argument for special hermeneutics is this notion that understanding cannot be abstracted from its locale: "What constitutes understanding depends a great deal on the use one wants to make of the text, as well as on the character of the text itself."[19] Wood's argument locates biblical interpretation within the context of Christian understanding, returning the church to the discussion of hermeneutics, putting the focus on local hermeneutical issues. Crucial to such a theological position is the definition of "hermeneutics" used: "[H]ermeneutics is critical reflection upon the practice of interpretation—its aims, conditions, and criteria."[20] It is not defined as an all-encompassing philosophical program but as a practical aid to an ongoing act of interpretation, a local practice.[21] Such definitions can remind one of the typical descriptions of hermeneutics before Schleiermacher.[22] In fact, they sound similar to the hermeneutics found in *De doctrina*, where Augustine formulates rules to aid the interpretation of obscure passages in scripture. Those arguing for local hermeneutics at the (near) exclusion of general hermeneutics have to appeal to an ongoing practice that needs to be corrected.[23] The issue is less about the applicability of the theory to a certain number of texts than it is about how the theory relates to the tradition of interpretation within a certain community.

With these two positions outlined, it is helpful to note that both have their strengths. For instance, focusing on general hermeneutics might help prevent an ideological reading, while focusing on local hermeneutics could guard a certain interpretation from collapse if the general hermeneutics underlying it is dismantled.[24] More importantly, it should be noted that the focus on local hermeneutics has some overlap with the focus on general and vice versa. Those theologians interested in local hermeneutics concede that much can be learned from the realm of general hermeneutics, and those interested in general hermeneutics do have theological concerns.[25] "General" and "local," then, operate more as ends of a continuum than as firm polarities; the focus can shift in a discussion from local to general concerns and back again.[26] As the foregoing discussion

demonstrates, the debate has less to do with these two spatial categories than with how the theologian wants his or her theory to relate
logically to interpretive practice: Does the envisioned theory come
before the practice to safeguard it, or does the theologian think it
actually supplements and aids a certain group's existing tradition of
interpretation?

While the discussion typically utilizes this terminology of "general" and "local" hermeneutics, different terms could be employed
in light of the overlap just expressed. The new terminology would
supplement the distinction between general and local hermeneutics.
Rather than viewing the two as a binary opposition, the new terms
would self-consciously allow the spatial terminology to function as
a continuum. Framing the issue in terms of "general" and "local" is
essentially to use a spatial model, suggesting that "local" hermeneutics exists within the realm of "general" or universal hermeneutics.
One covers a broad range of texts, while the other is more specific,
covering only a select group. And though this spatial imagery is
helpful, a temporal model is more accurate for describing the situation in theological hermeneutics because the argument actually
concerns how theory relates to practice; both groups want to interpret the Bible. That is, both want a local hermeneutics in the end;
the debate really concerns just how the theologians envision their
theory to relate to the act of interpretation. Therefore, rather than
referring to a preference for "general (philosophical) hermeneutics"
or "local (special) hermeneutics," it would be more precise to refer
to "*a priori* theological hermeneutics" and "*a posteriori* theological
hermeneutics."[27] This temporal model suggests that the criterion for
distinguishing between the two trends is *when* the hermeneutical
theory is employed: Is it more important to develop a theory before
moving to practice, or does theory serve a subsidiary role to interpretive practice? Such temporality is perhaps artificial, but it nonetheless expresses particularly well the differences between the two
camps. Undoubtedly, it is impossible to put theory before practice in
any strict fashion. Some practice always goes before theory. "Temporal" is a metaphor for a logical move made by the proponents of this
kind of theological hermeneutics.

Briefly, to demonstrate why this logical move should be high-lighted, one can compare Gadamer's self-description to the discussions I have just outlined. In his "Autobiographical Reflections," he states: "In fact, my development of a 'hermeneutical philosophy' can be traced back to nothing more pretentious than my effort to be theoretically accountable for the style of my studies and my teaching. Practice came first. For as long as I can remember, I have been concerned not to say too much and not to lose myself in theoretical constructions which were not fully supported by experience."[28] For Gadamer, then, hermeneutics is descriptive of what actually occurs in practice. It is not a safeguard for a future practice, though it is the essential aspect of our Being. Though later philosophical hermeneutics might be concerned with avoiding ideological distortion, Gadamer's example is illustrative because it demonstrates that the move in philosophical hermeneutics is from local examples of practice to a conceptual *description* of general similarities over a broad range of instances. As demonstrated above with the example of Thiselton, however, a theological hermeneutics that would typically be described as "general" makes exactly the opposite move: the theologian wants to guard a local practice from distortion, so he or she steps back from the practice of reading and envisions a logically primary step, the development of an appropriate general interpretive theory that can then be applied to the local practice. "General" does not therefore accurately describe the distinction in theological hermeneutics. Gadamer writes a "general hermeneutics"; he investigates legal and theological hermeneutics before he discusses how human existence comprises what he has extrapolated from them.[29] His *conclusion* is called "general" philosophical hermeneutics. Theologians like Thiselton, however, want to read a specific set of texts. Their concern is not with the general hermeneutics of Gadamer or Ricoeur, except insofar as it protects the specific hermeneutics they want to develop at the end. The move is temporal, or logical. It concerns not the range of texts but the way the theory relates to the specific theological texts at hand. By highlighting this difference between Thiselton and Gadamer, the metaphor of *a priori* and *a posteriori* temporality becomes helpful: the differences between theologians really concern the logical progression from theory to practice and which one is privileged.

The terminology "*a priori* hermeneutics" accurately summarizes Thiselton's program. For instance, it would step back from the text to be interpreted and develop in abstraction, as it were, a general theory of understanding that disciplines the subsequent interpretation.[30] On this basis, the practice of interpretation could go forward in a more safeguarded way than would have been the case without such an underlying theory. An *a priori* hermeneutics can be identified by the way a theologian appeals to theory: Is it described in such a way that it is primary or foundational, a constraint to practice? The theory, in other words, would be fundamental, grounding and making the practice of interpretation more secure.

The general trend of an *a priori* theological hermeneutics would then be: (1) A suspicion exists that misreading is common and that any existing tradition of interpretation is therefore potentially untrustworthy. (2) The interpreter therefore makes a self-conscious step back from the text(s) to be interpreted, in this case, scripture. (3) This step back is followed by a development of criteria for understanding in general to guard against ideological misreadings; this would probably come from insights found in the realm of philosophical hermeneutics (or perhaps in literary theory). (4) After developing criteria for understanding, the theologian would move back into the realm of theology, perhaps adding some distinctly local attributes to his or her theory. (5) Finally, the theologian would be able to interpret the text. The primary emphasis of an *a priori* hermeneutics would be the crucial importance placed on theory, followed by a subsequent move to practice, which is subordinate to (and constrained by) the developed theory.[31] It should be emphasized that the temporal move I am describing is a metaphor for how the theologian intends his or her theory to stand in relation to the interpretation. As the steps above show, theory can never come temporally before practice in a literal sense, but such a temporal, or perhaps logical, metaphor demonstrates the difference between theological debates better than the spatial metaphor because theologians like Thiselton do consider their developed theory vitally important to any appropriate subsequent act of interpretation. "*A priori*" differs from "general" because it describes when the theory comes into play, as opposed to whether or not the theory is generally true for all texts.

An *a posteriori* hermeneutics, in contrast, would find its starting point not in abstract issues, but in an actual tradition of interpretation. The suggestions of an *a posteriori* hermeneutics would be similar to ad hoc rules, given in order to solve specific problems.[32] The theologian would, as with a local hermeneutics, have a concern for the location of the reading, that is, in and with the church, but this is not the crucial point of difference between the two groups. Rather, the distinctiveness of an *a posteriori* hermeneutics in comparison to an *a priori* hermeneutics is its move from concrete practice to ad hoc rule and back to practice. In a sense, this is pragmatic. An *a posteriori* hermeneutics is less concerned with abstract theories than with helping an ongoing interpretive practice, though abstract theories may prove helpful. It must be kept in mind, then, that an *a posteriori* hermeneutics need not reject all appeal to general hermeneutical principles. This is one of the strong points of distinguishing between *a priori* and *a posteriori*: an *a posteriori* hermeneutics can still make use of general principles, as the discussion about Augustine will demonstrate. The general principles would be more like analogies, resources for particular purposes. The primary point of the distinction is to emphasize the way in which one envisions the relationship between philosophical and theoretical categories and the practice of interpretation.

Therefore, an *a posteriori* theological hermeneutics would be described as follows: (1) There is a tradition of biblical interpretation within the context of the church. (2) A problem arises within the process that cannot be explained. (3) After deliberation, the theologian suggests a rule that makes sense of the problem. (4) Interpretation continues. Crucial to this particular model are the focus on practice prior to theory and the comparably less suspicious approach to interpretation than an *a priori* hermeneutics.[33] An *a posteriori* hermeneutics concerns itself with an ongoing act of interpretation. It may step back from the situation at hand in order to develop a general notion, but it is important to note that the general notion is developed within the context of an ongoing tradition of interpretation. The theory is secondary. "*A posteriori*," therefore, differs from "local" because it is open to general discussions and indeed is unafraid to appeal to general criteria, albeit only in the light of local practice.

The primary difference between *a priori* and *a posteriori* hermeneutics, then, is how (when) appeal is made to theory—from the beginning or only in light of practice? Said differently: Is the hermeneutical theory a constraint upon a logically subsequent practice, or is it an aid to an ongoing practice? Clearly, any hermeneutical rule affects subsequent practice, and equally clearly, any hermeneutics can—strictly speaking—only be written in the context of a practice of interpretation. Nonetheless, this temporal distinction helps highlight what is actually at issue in theological discussions. Theologians are not arguing over whether they want to use general hermeneutics or whether general hermeneutics is inappropriate for local, biblical interpretation. They are actually arguing over how theory and practice fit together. Is it necessary to develop a preliminary general theory in order to safeguard biblical interpretation before it can go forward? An *a priori* hermeneutics answers affirmatively, while an *a posteriori* hermeneutics answers negatively.

The terminology of "general" and "local" hermeneutics remains a useful delineation, especially when discussing the difference between, say, Gadamer and Wood, but the distinction between *a priori* and *a posteriori* more precisely describes what occurs in the realm of theology than the spatial model can do alone. Indeed, one can still say that Thiselton privileges general hermeneutics above local, but the term *a priori* more accurately describes his actual program. He does want a theological hermeneutics (i.e., one concerning biblical interpretation), but only on the basis of a general hermeneutical theory does he think the practice of biblical interpretation can and should go forward in a safeguarded manner.

Such terminology helps one discuss the difference between Augustine and contemporary theological hermeneutics. As the driving question of the chapter suggests, Augustine—like contemporary theology—appeals to philosophical and theoretical categories within *De doctrina*. The developed terminology will help conceptualize just how his appeal is different from similar appeals in contemporary theology. Jeanrond represents an ideal candidate for comparison, as his two works on hermeneutics lucidly and succinctly address the problems of interpretation and the benefits of what I have described as an *a priori* hermeneutics. By putting Augustine and Jeanrond in dialogue, it should become clear, first, that the distinction between *a priori* and *a posteriori* describes the situation of theological hermeneutics with greater clarity than the local and general distinction can do alone, and second, that Augustine's *a posteriori* hermeneutics in fact represents a significant alternative to Jeanrond's *a priori* hermeneutics.

## WERNER JEANROND:
## AN EXAMPLE OF *A PRIORI* HERMENEUTICS

In his two books and several articles on the subject, Jeanrond insists on the necessity of what I have termed *a priori* hermeneutics.[34] More than Thiselton or Tracy, he explicitly and cogently argues for the importance of such a hermeneutics and thus represents a good way into the problem at hand. He wants "to give a further development of the theory of understanding of texts in order to ground theological text interpretation in an appropriate foundational theory."[35] Theological interpretation thus occurs on the basis of an explicitly general hermeneutics. Though he frames the issue in terms of general and theological hermeneutics, it should be noted that he is concerned with both. He wants to make certain that a general hermeneutical theory disciplines a subsequent theological reading: "[A]n all too quick understanding of a text from an exclusively theological perspective raises the question of ideological reading."[36] First and foremost, Jeanrond wants to protect the biblical texts from theological distortion. The text is the weaker partner in a conversation, as it were, where the reader may impose his or her understanding too quickly.[37] Likewise, he wants to guard the reader from "text-slavery";[38] in other words, the text might impose an improper or dangerous viewpoint upon the reader who, if not vigilant from the beginning, might succumb to the text's ideology.[39] His theory provides a safeguard for both the text and the reader, and it does so by establishing a logically primary set of principles that will constrain and guard later practice. In addition to this "double critique" of self and of text, Jeanrond seeks to return theology to the discussion of biblical interpretation—a viewpoint he considers endangered and attacked by such critics as Räisänen[40]—while providing a public justification for such a return.[41] These emphases are fundamental to his methodology.

He begins with the textual basis of theology: "Theology . . . has no choice but to involve itself with texts."[42] For this reason, he suggests that one must develop "a total outline of text interpretation" because this alone can adequately handle the textual character of theological statements.[43] This textual nature of theology serves as an entrance into and foundation for the discussion of interpretation.[44] "To refuse to consider the primacy of textual understanding would mean to expose oneself right from the beginning to the possibility of denying the importance of that which constitutes the sustaining sources of Christian theological thought, namely the texts."[45] Jeanrond not only wants to protect the texts from theological distortions, but he also wants to ward off purely historical or literary readings; this balancing act is the "old dilemma in biblical interpretation."[46] By starting with textuality, he aims to safeguard the texts from misreading, and this move highlights well the usefulness of the temporal term "*a priori* hermeneutics." Jeanrond wants a theological, local, hermeneutics but only on the basis of a prior general theory. He appeals to general hermeneutics to protect his theological hermeneutics, which in turn will protect the actual act of interpretation. He confronts what he considers the two negative aspects of biblical interpretation: theological misreadings and monistic historical-critical readings. In essence, he wants a modified form of objectivity, a way for a theologian to approach the biblical text as text and not to read in his or her own views. In order to accomplish this, he begins in abstraction from the biblical texts, establishing a general theory of "text" and only later moving to formulate an explicitly theological hermeneutics on the basis of his foundational, philosophically derived hermeneutical theory. The term "general" does not do justice to Jeanrond's method because, in the end, he wants a localized hermeneutics. The crucial difference between Jeanrond and those arguing for an expressly "local" hermeneutics is, in reality, not the appeal to general hermeneutics but how exactly he intends his hermeneutics to sit in relation to the practice of interpretation. He envisions a logically primary hermeneutical theory that disciplines subsequent practice (an *a priori* hermeneutics), while they envision a tradition of interpretation aided by a logically secondary theory. In other words, the primary issue is how one envisions the logical, theoretical relationship between the philosophical and theological categories.

He derives his methodology primarily from Gadamer, Ricoeur, and Tracy.[47] There are three dimensions of interpretation: understanding, explanation, and assessment.[48] Understanding occurs when the reader grasps the sense of the text; explanation concerns the methodological aspect of interpretation, where the results of understanding are corrected or validated; finally, assessment involves critiquing the self and the text.[49] This third dimension, according to Jeanrond, is his contribution to general hermeneutics. He finds in Gadamer and Ricoeur a dangerous "idealism." One should not speak directly of understanding, explanation, and comprehension because this leaves out the necessary double critique of text and reader. In his focus on "assessment," Jeanrond develops the notion of "text-" and "reading-genres": each text calls for a complementary genre of reading.[50] These concepts allow him to insist that the biblical texts require a theological reading: "Thus, whichever way one turns this thematic phenomenon [of the biblical texts describing certain theological relationships], no reading perspective seems adequate which does not include some sort of a theological dimension. But this discovery of the theological dimension of the biblical texts must not be confused with the ongoing projects of a Christian reading of the biblical texts through a confessional, though ecumenically informed, theological perspective."[51] It is crucial to catch the significance of his move. Instead of beginning with the presuppositions of theology and moving directly to the biblical texts, he abstracts from the ongoing, ecclesial interpretation to develop a theory of texts, which he only subsequently applies to the practice of interpreting the biblical texts. Then he can argue that the text-genre of the Bible itself requires a theological reading. This theologically motivated reading can then be, and indeed is from the beginning, disconnected from ecclesiology.[52] Jeanrond, therefore, seems effectively to prevent theology from illegitimately reading into scripture because the texts themselves call for a theological reading.[53] Thus, his reading does not appear presuppositional, as an ecclesiologically motivated reading does.

Again, it can be stressed that he does, in fact, have local interests. This highlights once more the usefulness of the temporal model because he moves between general and local concerns; the important point is his theory's relationship to his practice. As with his earlier formulation of a general notion of hermeneutics, he seeks to provide safeguards against impositions on the text by the reader and on the reader by the text. His theological hermeneutics finds its model in Tracy's notion of "the classic,"[54] but: "Classics are not to be excluded from criticism, their normative claim . . . must also be responsibly assessed by the community of interpreters. Otherwise ideology slips stealthily in . . . and we are back with Gadamer's notion of entering into tradition without knowing what repercussions are there to come upon us."[55] Jeanrond's primary focus can here be seen: the text must be protected from ideological readings, while at the same time the reader must be protected from the text's inappropriate ideologies. As a preliminary concern, his focus is helpful. It allows him to make the biblical texts "publicly justifiable," interpretation "transparent, public and responsible,"[56] and he can return biblical interpretation to the realm of theology. Furthermore, by beginning with the human aspect of the texts, he has avoided a kind of docetism: "The very different focus of theological thinking, i.e., God's revelation in this universe, from that of other disciplines of human knowledge does not only not justify a different interpretation theory, rather it demands the application of a general hermeneutics both in order to point out this different focus and precisely because of the fact that we have been able to proclaim in our human language God's presence in our human world and history."[57] His hermeneutics, then, seems to address a multiplicity of issues that, in our contemporary climate, are particularly pertinent.

To summarize: Jeanrond, on the basis of the Bible's textual nature, steps back from the texts and develops a theory of text- and reading-genres with the aid of philosophical hermeneutics, upon which he builds a theological hermeneutics, which he subsequently applies to the texts. Such an exercise helps prevent ideological impositions on both the biblical texts and on the reader. The strength of describing his method in temporal terms as "*a priori*" can now be seen: for him, the theory is not only important to, but also fundamental for, the practice of interpretation. It is less important to note that he wants a general or universal hermeneutics within which local hermeneutics exists (obviously he does). Rather, the crucial distinction between Jeanrond and, as shall be seen, Augustine is better described temporally: Is the theory envisioned as coming before the practice or after? Is the theory intended as a constraint to a logically subsequent practice or simply as an aid to an existing one? In the case of Jeanrond, the answer is clear: ideological distortions constantly threaten the text and the reader, and a logically primary theory must therefore be developed to discipline the subsequent practice of interpretation.

Jeanrond does raise important issues that an *a posteriori* hermeneutics must be able to address. First, ideological distortion of scripture and its ideological imposition on a reader must both be avoided. Is there a theological way to solve these issues? Second, Jeanrond's notion of text-genres is helpful because he can connect biblical studies and theology without appeal to presuppositions alone. Can an *a posteriori* hermeneutics address this issue? Finally, Jeanrond discusses the importance of a critical eye on tradition. In an *a posteriori* hermeneutics, the location within a particular tradition is taken for granted. Is it possible, then, for an *a posteriori* hermeneutics to address his fear of solidified, rigid, and distorted tradition? As I noted earlier, one might expect to find Augustine as a helpful resource in the discipline of theological hermeneutics, yet explicit use of him is peculiarly minimal. In fact, *De doctrina* is a perfect example of an *a posteriori* hermeneutics, and it offers several responses and queries to the *a priori* hermeneutics so cogently defended by Jeanrond.

## AUGUSTINE:
## AN EXAMPLE OF *A POSTERIORI* HERMENEUTICS

Expressing the problem of theological interpretation in terms of *a priori* and *a posteriori* hermeneutics makes it necessary first to consider the claim that Augustine has an aprioristic hermeneutical theory. For instance, in *Theological Hermeneutics*, Jeanrond portrays him as an ally, as a watershed in the development of theological hermeneutics, bringing the schools of Antioch and Alexandria together in a new synthesis: "[H]e advocated a thorough linguistic analysis of a text in order to control the accompanying spiritual reading of it."[58] According to Jeanrond, this semiotic dimension of Augustine's theory proves foundational: "In sum, Augustine's biblical hermeneutics is based on a well-defined general semiotic theory."[59] Augustine, it would seem, offers the precise kind of *a priori* hermeneutics I am suggesting he challenges. He appears to build the practice of biblical interpretation upon his theory of signs, a prior theory intended to discipline a subsequent practice. Jeanrond only takes issue with his use of the faith praxis of the church, which is itself an interpretive construction.[60] But Augustine, Jeanrond maintains, is less of a problem than those who followed him. In fact, he even becomes a tool for Jeanrond's critique of Barth: "[U]nlike Augustine, Barth did not engage in a thorough reflection on the linguistic conditions of the communication of God's Word in the Bible."[61] Jeanrond considers Augustine's methodology only flawed insofar as he fails to recognize the presupposition of ecclesiology. For all intents and purposes, Augustine represents an *a priori* hermeneutics that controls the act of interpretation by positing a general theory of signs to safeguard the ensuing practice of interpretation. If Jeanrond is correct, and Augustine does in fact promote such a hermeneutics, one based on semiotics, my argument fails.

Though Jeanrond's depiction of Augustine is in the end unpersuasive, his position is not without evidence, and he is certainly not alone in thinking that the discussion of signs in *De doctrina* represents the theoretical underpinnings of the entire work. As the second chapter demonstrated, after the prologue, Augustine begins his interpretive discussion by highlighting the distinction between *signa* and *res*. Signs are "those things which are clearly used to signify something" (1.2.2), and, later, he defines a sign as "a thing which from itself makes something else come to mind besides the appearance which it impresses on the senses" (2.1.1). As R. A. Markus points out, there are three components to Augustine's version of a sign—sign thing, signified thing, and sign user/receiver—and the third term varies.[62] In the first definition, Augustine discusses signs from the perspective of the sign user, the one who utilizes a sign to communicate a message;[63] in the second, he has moved to discuss signs as things to be interpreted. Things, on the other hand, "are not employed for signifying something" (1.2.2). In other words, a thing does not refer beyond itself. His examples are logs and stones. The moment they are employed to signify something else—such as Moses throwing a log into the waters at Marah, making them sweet—they become signs and are no longer strictly things (1.2.2).

The entire work at first appears to be constructed upon this distinction between sign and signified. Augustine begins with a semiotic discussion; surely, then, he uses it as the basis for what comes later. When Markus states, "The triadic relation of signification is the key to Augustine's entire hermeneutic theory,"[64] his statement seems to require no defense. Williams agrees: in Book 1, Augustine develops his theory of signs and things, and of using and delighting in things, while in Book 2 he moves to apply the theory to scripture. By Williams's account, Book 1 is the theory on which Books 2 and 3 are built: "Book 2 of DDC turns to apply all this [the fact that we are trapped in a world of signs, "the shifting, mobile realm of representation"] to Scripture."[65] Williams does not remove Augustine from local hermeneutical concerns; he stresses that God is the ultimate thing in Book 1 that relativizes all love to use.[66] But Williams's prioritizing of Augustine's theoretical framework at the expense of his overall focus is problematic. Augustine explicitly states that the goal of his work is to help readers understand the ambiguities of scripture for themselves (Prol. 9). Williams, in contrast, seems to give Augustine concerns that would probably have been outside of his purview, as the following remark suggests.[67] Here, Williams has been discussing Augustine's concern that *signa* not be privileged over *res*: "[T]he importance of the application of all this to Scripture is that Augustine has in effect defined Scripture as the paradigm of self-conscious symbolic awareness: it is a pattern of signs organized around—and by—the incarnate Word in such a way that all the signs *remain* signs, all are kept open to the horizon of God, in virtue of their relation to the central acting out in cross and resurrection of God's otherness from the realm of representation."[68] By Williams's account, Augustine's concern is signs as ever-open signifiers, meant to break down pride, to convince the reader that he or she cannot control the text, that learning from scripture is "an extended play of invitation and exploration."[69] Augustine's notion that signs always remain open derives from the incarnation, Williams suggests, and this idea is then applied to scripture. Yet this reading of *De doctrina* is ultimately unpersuasive. Perhaps Augustine's ideas can be used to encourage a more open reading of scripture, or at the least a reading that allows for polysemy, but not on the basis of such a reading of his sign theory. Augustine employs the delineation of *res* and *signa* not as a purely theoretical notion but as a specific way of getting into the problem he wants to address: the interpretation of scripture as one aspect of the divine dispensation employed for our salvation (1.35.39). To imply that his primary concern is signs endlessly referring, as Williams does here, misses the point of Augustine's sign theory.[70] As the previous chapter demonstrated, such rhetorical divisions are made in *De doctrina* with explicitly theological intentions. Though his sign theory may be usefully employed in philosophical discussions, to insist that Augustine thought signs were problematic in all communication obscures the fact that he thought only one thing was incommunicable: God, who has nevertheless sanctioned the human voice's praise (1.6.6).

The difficulty in describing Augustine's treatise seems to arise from the confusing use of the distinction between general and local hermeneutics in theological hermeneutics, where general hermeneutical ideas become foundational for local hermeneutics. In our contemporary context—where "philosophy" and "theology" are often thought of as two spheres—one works to see how to relate them, but in Augustine's context, such a conceptual distinction did not exist in exactly the same way. Because he offers a general hermeneutical discussion on the nature of signs and things (one that even reminds the reader of certain branches of current philosophical discussion), it becomes difficult to decide whether to classify *De doctrina* as a theological hermeneutics built on the basis of a general, philosophical hermeneutics—as Jeanrond does—or as a theological hermeneutics that simply offers theologically informed rules for interpretation. Neither of these categories sufficiently describes what exactly Augustine does. Rather, the temporal model of *a priori* and *a posteriori* describes the phenomenon better than the spatial model can do alone. In fact, the temporal model relaxes the tension between "general" and "local," allowing them to serve as ends of a continuum, ends between which Augustine can move freely. It can be noted once more that "temporal" refers less to methodology and more to how the theologian views his or her theory; it is a logical distinction. Clearly, Augustine starts with a general discussion of signs and things, but this "sign theory" in no way constrains an ensuing practice. Instead, it serves more as conceptual clarification, a way into the problem he seeks to address.

As chapter 1 demonstrated, he continually appeals to his general hermeneutical distinction between *res* and *signa* (in Books 1–3), yet it also established that this distinction is primarily a structural way of discussing a theological topic. He begins with things, even after expressly stating that "things are learned through signs" (1.2.2). This reversal suggests that he is not as concerned with signification as it initially appears. Indeed, the fact that he begins with things suggests, as William Babcock states, that Augustine "is acutely aware, from the beginning, that signs can be construed wrongly," and that: "His procedure provides the corrective. It stipulates in advance what the *terminus* of the scriptural signs is and thus establishes the control in light of which we are to interpret those signs. Augustine's is not, then, a neutral or disinterested concern with signs and with signification."[71] Instead, the discussion is instrumental to the construction of *De doctrina*, which, as I argued above, is a tightly structured work, whose topic is the interpretation of scripture (*tractatio scripturarum*). Furthermore, when he first posits the distinction between *uti* and *frui*, Augustine has in sight the end goal of loving a thing in and of itself, hinting toward the double-love command that is so crucial to the whole of his interpretive scheme. Within the initial delineation, he states almost presuppositionally that the Trinity is the one thing that should be enjoyed (1.5.5).

As the outline and discussion of the work demonstrated, the distinctions Augustine makes have a very precise goal: to highlight the theological objects to which scripture testifies and how we are to relate to them. His theory of signs, then, is in no way foundational. Instead, his concern is the interpretation of scripture, and more specifically, teaching others how to understand the obscurities of scripture on their own (Prol. 1). The general hermeneutical comments he makes are not his primary concern, and they are certainly not the foundational theory that Jeanrond suggests they are. Once again, it can be noted how helpful it is to distinguish between general hermeneutics and *a priori* hermeneutics. Upon a close reading, Augustine's semiotic analysis seems to be given for preliminary conceptual clarification in order to express the terminology about to be used in the discussion concerning the interpretation of the specific text at hand. In other words, his semiotic theory is structural, not foundational. His general, or, one might say, philosophical, comments on the nature of language are embedded in a complex theological web, one that stresses the fallenness of humanity and the incommunicability of the triune God. Now it remains to detail this theological web and the theological presuppositions that inform his discussion of signs and things and indeed the whole of the work. Augustine's delineation of *signa* and *res* in Book 1 fits precisely into the overall structure, and it occurs within a theological web, illustrated by Augustine's appeal to credal language. In Book 2, he also locates his hermeneutics, that is, the theoretical concepts he offers for interpretation, within a theological matrix.

## The Credal Structure of *De doctrina* 1

Once Augustine distinguishes between *signa* and *res* and *res quibus fruendum est* and *res quibus utendum est*—each, as has been illustrated, an instrumental part in his overall argument—he begins to expound upon theological themes in the order of a creed.[72] After he establishes that the only thing to be enjoyed is the triune Father, Son, and Holy Spirit, he traces the basic outline of the Christian faith. It will be helpful to summarize this section in order to highlight the credal features. At the end, it will become clear that these affirmations are not an excursus, or even one of Augustine's sometimes maligned (sometimes appreciated) ramblings, but instead are crucial to his overall argument.

First, he announces the ineffability of God and begins to describe the Trinity:

> The Father is neither the Son nor the Holy Spirit; the Son is neither the Father nor the Holy Spirit; the Holy Spirit is neither the Father nor the Son, but the Father is purely the Father, and the Son purely the Son, and the Holy Spirit purely the Holy Spirit. These three have the same eternity, the same unchangeableness, the same majesty, the same power. In the Father there is unity, in the Son equality, in the Holy Spirit a concord of unity and equality. And these three are all one on account of the Father, all equal on account of the Son, and all joined on account of the Holy Spirit. (1.5.6)[73]

He has expressed, to the best of his ability, what the *res* to be enjoyed is. Yet he recognizes in the following section that his language cannot adequately express the thing he wants to describe. He instead admits the inexpressibility of God while affirming the fact that God has sanctioned the human voice's praise (1.6.6). Subsequent discussions of the incarnation and Wisdom's descent to humanity

(1.7.7–13.13) flow from this affirmation. When Augustine offers his analogy between human words and the divine Word, he is making just that—an analogy—in order to discuss the ineffable:

> How did he come except that "the word [*verbum*] was made flesh and dwelled among us"? It is like when we speak, when what we have in our minds sinks through the listener's fleshly ears into his mind: the word [*verbum*] which we have in our heart becomes a sound, and an act of speech occurs. Nonetheless our thought is not converted into the sound itself, but it remains untouched in its proper place, not taking on any defect from its change into the form of a voice which pushes into the ears. Thus, the word of God was not changed even when he became flesh so that he might dwell among us. (1.13.12, citing John 1:14)[74]

He has to discuss how the word became flesh, and he uses an analogy to do so. He does not stop to meditate on how Christ as the Word fits together with words in general. Perhaps he dwells theoretically on how the Word and words fit together in *De trinitate* (though this itself is questionable), but here in *De doctrina*, Augustine simply offers a metaphor to describe the ineffable.

By assuming that his general remarks on language are foundational, one can be misled into thinking that this section on the incarnation is a further elaboration of the underlying sign theory. But such a reading fails because the metaphor of Word and words operates in one direction: the way words work helps understand the incarnation of the Word.[75] He says nothing here about what the incarnation reveals about the way words operate in everyday communication.[76] His semiotic language at this point is clarificatory, a way to talk about God and his relationship with humanity (and humanity's with him). This discussion is not part of the earlier, more general discussion of *signa* and *res*, which itself has a definite theological point: to move to the *verba* of scripture. Augustine's general comments there are subsidiary to the theological rationale for reading scripture within a relationship with a gracious God. The distinction between local and *a posteriori* hermeneutics is helpful here:

Augustine uses general concepts, but never apart from the specific, local context of a worshiping community in relationship with God. His sign theory fits into a theological web. It is a component of it, but he does not seem to envision it as some sort of guard to a later act of reading scripture. In fact, he interprets scripture, elaborates the theory, moves through a credal outline, and utilizes theoretical notions of language to help define the incarnation, all the while continuing to interpret scripture, only to come back to the sign theory in Book 2.

Because the ineffable, unchangeable God is the one thing to enjoy, because the quest for God requires purity of mind, and because humanity is fundamentally unable to make any progress on this journey, wisdom humbled itself and came in human form. In the process, the very place to which humanity travels (God) became the very way to get there (1.11.11). Augustine moves immediately from his discussion concerning words and the Word to the incarnation itself, mitigating the force of any argument for his serious investment in the Word/words analogy. Throughout this passage, he alludes to verse after verse of scripture, illustrating the way God condescended to humanity in order to redeem us (1.11.11–14.13). He next asks why God had to humble himself, and the answer is because humanity fell by pride (1.14.13). Humanity is fallen, sinful, and God condescended to save us, becoming the way to himself. Augustine here stresses the fact that Christ was born to a woman, and that he lived a virtuous life, and finally that he died in order to free the dead. It begins to become clear that some form of a creed, perhaps an early form of the Apostles Creed, structures his discussion, especially considering that he immediately moves to the resurrection and ascension, both of which reinforce faith with hope: "By how much confidence is the hope of believers cheered," says Augustine, "when they consider the great price he suffered for those who did not yet believe" (1.15.14).

Continuing to expound on an underlying creed, he discusses Christ's imminent return when he will judge the living and the dead. This return should encourage believers and instill fear into the uncommitted. Augustine then moves to highlight the role of the Spirit, whom Christ has given to support those who believe on their journey and who also enables believers to perform the necessary acts in the church, which is Christ's body: "For with what words can we describe, or with what thoughts grasp the reward he will give in the end, when he has given so much of his Spirit as consolation during this journey, so that in the adversities of this life, we might have such a great confidence in, and love for, him whom we have not yet seen; and when he has given each person particular gifts for the instruction of his church, so that we might do what he shows we ought to do not only without murmuring, but indeed with pleasure?" (1.15.14). To recollect: the discussion has moved from the Trinity, to the Father, to the Son, to the Holy Spirit. Indeed, as with the Apostles Creed, he links the Holy Spirit explicitly to the church. The Spirit gives consolation during life while providing particular gifts for the instruction of the church, which is where a person can know that his or her sins are forgiven (1.18.17). After this description of the church, he moves to consider the resurrection of the dead, stressing the resurrection of both body and soul (1.19.18). Finally, he returns to his primary argument: "Among all these things, therefore, only those things which we said are eternal and unchangeable are to be enjoyed; others, however, are to be used so that we may be able to arrive at the full enjoyment of those things" (1.22.20).

Augustine has come full circle, and in a treatise on interpretation, a discussion about theology might seem out of place. Precisely for this reason, the distinction between *signa* and *res* must be seen as a useful, preliminary clarification, not as a foundational theory meant to buttress the interpretation. As the previous chapter demonstrates, Book 1 establishes the *regula fidei* and the *regula dilectionis*: there are *res* and appropriate ways of relating to them. The distinction between *signa* and *res* is instrumental in getting to this point. It becomes difficult to agree with Jeanrond's claim that "Augustine's biblical hermeneutics is based on a well-defined general semiotic theory."[77] Instead, from the beginning, Augustine employs his divisions—between signs and things and between things to be enjoyed and things to be used—in order to help him get to the meaning of scripture, which has to do with the two *regulae*. In other words, while he freely deploys philosophical notions, they are embedded within his theology. The credal discussion—the *regula fidei*—has laid out the things of scripture; only the Trinity should be enjoyed, and therefore Augustine must move to the other things of scripture in order to determine how one ought to relate to them. It is useful to note that the distinction of *uti* and *frui* runs throughout the book. This expressly theological commitment comes to the surface in Augustine's next section, where he discusses the proper love of things (1.22.20–34.38).

In this section, he first moves to the question of the proper use of oneself. The body is not a natural enemy to be fought against and destroyed. Rather, it is in conflict with the spirit, to which it should be subservient. Again, this kind of practical theology seems out of place in a treatise on interpretation, but for Augustine, interpretation is intricately bound together with the creed, with life in the flesh, and with morals, that is, the love of neighbor, which he treats in the next discussion (1.22.20–1.30.33). He continues to explore the relationship one ought to have with the other things of scripture expressed in the credal affirmations. Finally, he wants to know if God loves us by using or by enjoying us (1.31.34–32.33). This distinction should put to rest any hesitancy over the polarity of *uti* and *frui* because both are ways of loving. God loves us in relation to himself; thus, he "uses" us, but this "use" is related solely to his goodness and is in no way reminiscent of the way fallen humanity uses other people or things, except insofar as Christians "use" others by loving them in the course of loving God:

> That use [*usus*] which is attributed to God, by which he uses [*utitur*] us, is not related to his advantage [*utilitatem*] but to ours; it is instead related only to his goodness. When we show mercy to and care for someone, we certainly do so for that person's advantage [*utilitatem*], and that is our goal, but in some curious way, some benefit occurs for us as well because God does not fail to reward the mercy we show to the needy. But this is the highest reward: that we might fully enjoy [*perfruamur*] him, and that all

of us who enjoy [*fruimur*] him may fully enjoy [*perfruamur*] one
another in him. (1.32.35)

It here finally becomes clear that the entire discussion, including
the credal affirmations, remains within Augustine's initial rubric of
*uti* and *frui*, which is his way of discussing the appropriate love of
things, the *regula dilectionis*. Love is the message of scripture, the
love of God and the love of neighbor, the way one relates to the *res* of
the biblical text. The distinction between *uti* and *frui* exists to help
him describe this message of scripture.

Before reaching the summary of Book 1, Augustine discusses
the difference between loving one another in ourselves or in God
(1.33.36–33.37), showing that ethics are integral to his program of
interpretation, that the double-love command informs the entire
argument of the book. By keeping in mind his distinction between
*uti* and *frui*, this section on ethics is crucial to the argument. Augustine once again discusses the incarnation, showing that the Word
made flesh did not allow us to love his flesh only; instead, he
returned to heaven, thus insisting that we continue to the supreme
and unchangeable good. He begins: "Look in what way, when the
same Truth and Word through whom all things were made [*per quod
facta sunt omnia*] was made flesh [*caro factum esset*] so that he might
dwell among us" (1.34.38),[78] and concludes: "From which it is understood that no thing should detain us on the way, because neither did
the Lord desire to keep us, in so much as he became our way, but for
us to cross over, not clinging weakly to temporal things—although
they were undertaken by him for our salvation—but rather let us
eagerly run through them, so that we might approach and draw
near to him [*provehi atque pervehi mereamur*] who has liberated our
nature from temporal things and placed it at the right hand of the
Father [*conlocavit ad dexteram Patris*]" (1.34.38). One might expect
the words/Word analogy to come back in at this point, were it as fundamental as some suggest. The fact that it does not demonstrates
the weakness of such a position. Instead, Augustine here focuses
on flesh and temporality, ideas arising from the biblical texts he
uses as well as from the credal structure. The sign theory stands

in the midst of a complex theological web, a web as comprehensive as a creed. Augustine does not say all signs endlessly refer; rather he takes for granted that signs do in fact refer. In the incarnation, God has sanctified our flesh (and hence our language) in order to communicate himself and to raise us up. For this reason, Augustine stresses that wisdom did not become in any way foolish when it condescended to us in the way that we grow wiser when we draw near to it (1.11.11). For him, the only thing language cannot communicate is God, yet God has nevertheless sanctioned its use to talk about and praise him. Augustine's theory of signs, then, is not a theory that serves as the basis for his hermeneutics.[79] Rather, his semiotic analysis in Book 1 is preliminary clarification to establish the terms he will use to discuss the treatment of scripture. God, who is the only thing to be loved, communicates to us through scripture, which he uses to engender in us the appropriate love for himself and others. The particular problem is not how language works but is far more specific: scripture has a meaning, and this meaning is communicated through signs that point to things; these signs can be obscure, and therefore Augustine wants to discuss how to interpret them correctly.[80]

As I hope is becoming clear, the general versus local hermeneutical model does not adequately describe just what Augustine does. He has what looks like a general semiotic theory in Books 1 and 2, and he gives general hermeneutical rules throughout Books 2 and 3. Yet he is writing a treatise intended solely for the process of biblical interpretation, in other words, a local hermeneutics. More fruitful, then, is the temporal distinction between *a priori* and *a posteriori* hermeneutics. The preceding discussion has shown that Augustine does not build his hermeneutics on a semiotic substructure. Rather, his careful structuring of *De doctrina* reveals that the general, philosophical (or rhetorical), *signa-res* distinction is part of a discussion concerning the *tractatio scripturarum*. Indeed, this distinction is located explicitly within the first partition, the *modus inveniendi*. Furthermore, the distinction is put to explicit theological use: the *res* to be enjoyed is the Trinity, and from this point, Augustine explores the biblical text through credal language, illustrating the things that are communicated by scripture. The fact that he further explores the questions of how to love neighbors, angels, and ourselves demonstrates that the overall distinction between sign and thing, and the subsequent distinction between use and enjoyment, are employed for expressly theological purposes: to get the reader to the conclusion that scripture teaches nothing but the double love of God and neighbor. Therefore, it can be concluded that Augustine's hermeneutical treatise is not built on his semiotic theory. Rather, the theory is subordinate to the ongoing theological practice of interpretation within a relationship with the triune God, in which love for God and neighbor are of supreme importance. The semiotic discussion is located in a theological web where he uses general hermeneutical principles for explicitly theological ends.

As the previous chapter demonstrated, Book 1 can be divided helpfully into the *regula fidei*, which concerns the *res* of scripture, and the *regula dilectionis*, which concerns how one relates to the *res*. The *regula dilectionis* represents Augustine employing the *uti-frui* distinction. Book 1 is intensely theological; even general points are made in the service of an ongoing practice of interpretation occurring in the context of the relationship between God and humanity. Furthermore, he appeals back to Book 1 throughout the treatise and, when he does so, appeals not to the distinctions between things and signs or using and enjoying, but to its theological conclusion: the scriptural signs are there to engender one thing, the double love of God and neighbor.

For instance, his first rule of biblical interpretation is to know the canonical books, and this means understanding the clear passages, all of which point to faith, hope, and love, and on the basis of them to interpret the obscure passages:

> The first observation in this laborious task [of seeking the will of God in scripture] is, as we have said, to know those books, if not yet with understanding, nevertheless by reading either to commit them to memory or at least not be completely unfamiliar with them. Then those things which are stated clearly in them—whether commands for living [*praecepta vivendi*] or

rules for believing [*regulae credendi*]—should be carefully and diligently investigated. . . . For in those passages that are stated clearly, all those things can be found that comprise faith and the morals of life [*fidem moresque vivendi*], certainly hope and love, about which we have spoken in the previous book. Then, after acquiring a certain familiarity with the language of the divine scriptures, one should proceed to open and unravel the obscure parts, by taking examples from the clear passages to illuminate the obscure ones, and by using the testimony of plain passages to remove the uncertainty of those in doubt. (2.9.14)

One can note the constant interchange between faith and ethics, which leads him to refer the reader to the first book, where he has already discussed them. For Augustine, the *regula fidei* alone does not express the mind of scripture; one also needs the *regula dilectionis* to understand how to relate to the things expressed therein. When he summarizes and points back to Book 1, he does not point to the discussion of signs and things but to faith, hope, and love, which he finds to be the summary of scripture. The sign theory and the *uti-frui* distinction are only structural signposts, helpful clarificatory terms to get to his theological point. Furthermore, he states later in Book 2 that his rules are not enough to aid understanding; rather, the interpreter must grasp the truth concerning the happy life, which we know from Book 1 is the love of God (2.37.55).[81]

In Book 3 as well, he makes reference back to Book 1 in order to clarify how to understand which passages in the Old Testament are meant to be figural and which ones are meant to be literal (3.6.10–24.34). Again, he stresses that a passage, if it cannot be connected to love, should be studied again and again until it becomes clear how it connects: "Now, after ascertaining that a passage is figurative, and after consulting the rules of things [*regulis rerum*] which we discussed in the first book, it is easy to turn it around in several different ways until we arrive at the correct meaning, especially when the use [of these rules] is aided by the exercise of piety. We discover whether a passage is literal or figurative by considering the criteria discussed above" (3.24.34). One should note that Augustine connects the discernment of figurative passages back to the first book while he also connects it to the exercise of piety. In other words, the manner of living is directly connected to interpretation. Or, in the terms I am utilizing, his theory is intimately bound up with an already existing practice; his are not the methods of one who puts hermeneutics before interpretation. Instead, Augustine establishes, in the context of Book I, what the *res* of scripture are and how to relate to them, and his general principles are used in order to solve difficulties. Once it has been determined that a passage cannot be taken literally, he refers the reader back to Book I, and again, not to the *res-signa* or *uti-frui* divisions but to the fact that all scripture points to the double love of God and neighbor (3.10.14). These examples of Augustine referring to Book I in the context of his discussion of hermeneutics illustrate that semiotics is not his foundation or a constraint on subsequent practice. Rather, within an explicitly theological web, he has determined what scripture means and the uses to which it ought to be put; the semiotic analysis in Book I serves as a component within this much larger web in order for Augustine to get to the meaning of scripture, which is the love of God and the love of neighbor.

Worded in this way, it might seem that Augustine is open to the charge of ideological distortion, that his practice allows no room for critique because it remains localized, or ecclesiological. One passage in particular, however, serves to illustrate that even Augustine knew that people tend to read what they want, especially in a time when allegorical interpretation was practiced widely. He stresses that, when unclear passages are confronted, the double-love command and the *regula fidei* serve as criteria by which to judge interpretations (3.2.2). Though this may sound like an appeal that will obscure what the biblical texts state, he is convinced that the two derive from the clearer passages—the overall communicative intent—of scripture (3.2.2).[82] Indeed, he spends a good portion of Book I illustrating these affirmations with scripture.[83] In contrast to the charge Jeanrond makes, a charge found at least implicitly in Thiselton—that the problem with precritical exegesis was its ecclesiology, which is founded on the *regula*—Augustine finds that love is the overall communication of scripture, and that the *regula fidei* is used in order to show the things to which scripture points, only one of which ought to be enjoyed, loved for its own sake. In Book 3, after Augustine has discussed how to tell if a passage ought to be taken metaphorically, he decides, quite simply, that if the passage does not promote good morals or the true faith, then it should be taken figuratively; in other words, he refers back to the double-love command espoused in Book 1 (3.10.14). Yet, he states, it is human nature to judge sin by the standard of our own practices, and thus, when a person comes across a command forbidding something that he or she does not consider a sin, then the passage will be interpreted figuratively. Likewise, people can be convinced of a particular thing, and when scripture says something against it, then they interpret it figuratively. Augustine comments:

> And so it happens that if scripture either commands something which is inconsistent with the customs of the hearers, or censures what is not inconsistent, and if the authority of the words has a grasp of their minds, they suppose the expression is figurative. Scripture, however, commands nothing except love, nor does it censure anything but lust, and in that way it informs the customs of humanity. Similarly, if belief of a certain error occupies their minds, whatever scripture asserts to the contrary, humans think it is figurative. But it does not assert anything but the catholic faith in things past, future, and present. It is a narrative of the past, a prophecy of the future, a demonstration of the present. But all these go into nurturing and strengthening love, and they overcome, conquering and extinguishing lust. (3.10.15)

He stresses that scripture stands above the subjectivity of the reader, whether moral or ideological. If a command encourages love, then a person must follow it, and if a command forbids an action, then the reader must submit. Likewise, if a person holds a doctrine that does not coincide with the catholic faith, and believes that he or she has found it within the text, Augustine asserts such a reading is faulty.[84]

The text only presents the catholic faith, the faith found in the *regula fidei*, which arises ultimately from scripture itself. In other words, Augustine, within his theological web, assigns the text the function of critique and judge, an aid to break down pride.[85] Scripture is God's chosen vessel for communicating to humanity; it is only part of the temporal dispensation, but it is nonetheless supremely important. It breaks down pride and does not allow the reader to superimpose his or her thoughts on the text. The text—because of its location in the divine dispensation—is an equal, if not a more powerful, discussion partner with the reader than either Jeanrond or Thiselton maintains. But as will be shown in the following section, it must be kept in mind that this is a reader who fears God and is pious. For that reason, the hermeneutical "tool" of utmost importance for Augustine is prayer (see 2.7.10; 3.37.56; 4.15.32).

Thus, he allows for a critique of the community in which the text is read.[86] The critique may begin with the presupposition that the *regula fidei* is an adequate—if limited—summary of scripture, but it is a presupposition that, at least for Augustine, arises out of the text itself. Further, the *regula fidei* requires a synchronic and not a diachronic reading, but he never stops to question if these texts should be read this way.[87] This is a presupposition on the basis that God has lowered himself to speak to humanity. The text is part of the temporal dispensation God has set up for the salvation of humanity. To construe the text otherwise is out of Augustine's thoughts. Though scripture can offer historical information (*civ.*), and though it certainly tells us things about God (*trin.*), it has an end, a use, and that is to get humanity to love God and neighbor and to aid them on their journeys to God. Yet even on the basis of this construal, Augustine does not let the reader override the text. He sets in place aids for interpretation. And, as we have seen throughout the discussion concerning Book 1, the criterion for interpretation is love, love either for a thing in and of itself, God, or love in the form of use, loving something in the course of loving God. The *regula fidei*, then, exists to describe the things of scripture and to identify the one whom we are to enjoy.[88]

The preceding discussion has demonstrated that Augustine's theoretical aspects of Book 1, though general in nature, are not actually foundational in the sense that they constrain the interpretations that follow. Rather, he employs his semiotic distinction between *signa* and *res* to allow him to move to his next distinction, *uti* and *frui*. Both sets of distinctions are general, even philosophical, in scope, but they find their location within his prior notion of God as the ultimate *res*. This is illustrated by the credal affirmations. That Augustine begins with a discussion of things, after explicitly stating that things are learned through signs, shows he considers the theory less foundational than it seems at first. Instead, he demonstrates how scripture says what he already knows it says: there are certain objects of faith that must be related to in love. This is his concern, not semiotics. The semiotic discussion exists to clarify the terms. It is structural; once he has established that God is the ultimate *res*, he can leave the distinction behind. There is no discussion of "thing-ness," nor a comparison of the "thinghood" of God with that of creation, something one might expect if his semiotic analysis served as a foundation that constrained the subsequent practice. Furthermore, when he begins to discuss *signa* in Book 2, he does not follow up every delineation he makes; for instance, he briefly discusses the *signa naturalia* before moving on because they are not his concern. And it can therefore be concluded that his hermeneutics serves as an ideal example of what I have termed *a posteriori* hermeneutics: his general semiotic theory fits with his local theological interests. The semiotic theory is not meant as a constraint to a practice not yet existing. Rather, it fits with the practice of interpreting scripture in order to love God for his own sake—to enjoy him—and to love one's neighbor in the context of loving God—"to use" him or her. The sign theory is a conceptual clarification to aid the argument and to elucidate the *telos* of scripture: to engender the double love of God and neighbor. Augustine can effortlessly move between the general and the local, without subordinating his interpretive practice to his analysis of signs and things. In the terms of this chapter, the theory stands in the midst of the practice rather than in a logically prior point as a safeguard.

## The Location of Hermeneutics in *De doctrina* 2

Having illustrated that Augustine's sign theory is not foundational to his hermeneutics, it still remains to demonstrate more fully that his hermeneutical theory is not a prior constraint on his practice. Instead, he locates scriptural interpretation directly in the midst of the spiritual life, showing that the hermeneutical principles espoused in Books 2 and 3 are not such an *a priori* theory. Instead, the tradition of interpretation exists within a broader network of practices, all meant to bring one closer to God, and the hermeneutical theory is an aid to this set of practices. In the context of Book 2, the reflection on scripture and the act of interpretation occurs within an ecclesial context exemplified by a certain ethos. This can be illustrated by a close reading of the seven stages that Augustine lays out in 2.7.9–10. Throughout the work, he continually refers back to the first two stages, demonstrating that his hermeneutics actually plays a subordinate role to the ongoing spiritual life in which biblical interpretation occurs. The seven stages are influenced by the Neoplatonic idea of purification and the ascent of the mind.[89] The structure of the seven stages, however, comes from an inversion of Isaiah 11:2–3:[90]

> And the Spirit of the Lord will rest upon him,
> the Spirit of wisdom (*sapientiae*) and understanding
> (*intellectus*),
> the Spirit of resolve (*consilii*) and fortitude (*fortitudinis*),
> the Spirit of knowledge (*scientiae*) and piety (*pietatis*).
> The Spirit of the fear of the Lord (*spiritus timoris Domini*) will
> fill him.[91]

He inverts the passage on the basis of Psalm 110:10 (LXX; Hebrew: 111:10): "For the beginning of wisdom is the fear of the Lord" (*Initium enim sapientiae timor domini*; 2.7.11; cf. Prov. 1:7). His seven stages progress as follows: first, the would-be reader or interpreter of scripture will be moved by the fear of the Lord (*timor domini*) "towards learning what God's will is, what he commands us to seek or to avoid." This step brings the person's mortality into sharp focus, which leads to sacrificing all prideful inclinations (*omnes superbiae motus*) (2.7.9). Second, piety (*pietas*) will lead the interpreter not to contradict scripture or to think that he or she is better able to offer instruction, even if scripture is obscure. The pious reader recognizes that "what is written there—even if it lies hidden—is truer than any thoughts that we ourselves can have" (2.7.9). One can note the preparatory nature of these steps: they do not concern scriptural interpretation itself but instead focus on the mind and heart being put into an appropriate state to receive the results of biblical interpretation.[92] The first two steps concern the reader's relationship to God; first, one wants to learn the will of God, and second, one finds it in scripture. A range of practices—indeed, even a communal location—lie at the back of these two steps.

Only after these two stages is the third one, knowledge (*scientia*), reached, at which point "every student of the divine scriptures" (*omnis divinarum scripturarum studiosus*) will be ready to interpret them, and the student will find nothing in them other than that he or she must love God for God's sake and his or her neighbor on account of God (2.7.9). Here, it can be noted that the double-love command still structures Augustine's approach to scripture. In fact, the presence of the double-love command here as well as in the first book demonstrates well that *De doctrina* itself is located in this third stage. That is, the hermeneutical treatise exists as an aid to an ongoing interpretation of scripture that occurs in the midst of a range of theological practices, all revolving around the person's movement to God in the midst of the ecclesial community. Within the discussion, Augustine asserts that the student must learn that the scriptures show that he or she is entangled in love of the present age—not the appropriate love—and this, combined with fear (the first stage) and piety (the second stage), leads the person to lament his or her own condition (2.7.10). To trace the steps to this point: because a person fears God and wants to seek his will, and because he or she recognizes that the divine books are where God expresses it, the person approaches the text with humility, recognizing that God speaks even in the obscure portions. After these two steps, the student turns to scripture and finds that God's will is to love him on his own account and to love the person's neighbor as him- or herself. Here in this third stage, though, the reader recognizes that he or she does not in fact love God or neighbor appropriately and is therefore driven to prayer: "Such knowledge of good hope makes the person not boastful but remorseful; in this disposition, he obtains by attentive prayer the consolation of divine assistance, so that he is not broken by desperation, and he arrives at the fourth stage" (2.7.10). In other words, the third stage—where Augustine explicitly locates his hermeneutics—concerns learning where one stands in relation to God's will, and this knowledge drives a person to desperation or to the practice of prayer, and on to the fourth stage, which is fortitude, or strength (*fortitudo*).

Here, the student turns from the love of transient things to the love of eternal things, which on the basis of Book 1, is the unchangeable unity of the Trinity. The student, however, cannot bear to gaze upon the light of the Trinity because of his or her weakness of vision,[93] a weakness connected to sin, and this brings the student to the fifth stage, which Augustine calls "the resolve of compassion" (*consilium misericordiae*), a strained expression tying back to Isaiah 11:2, which does not mention *misericordia*. Still, it is tied to his overall concern with the love of neighbor and God because the student continues to turn away from temporal things and to eternal things, and in the process, grows to love even his or her enemy: "Here, he diligently exercises himself in the love of his neighbor and becomes accomplished in it . . . coming even to the love of his enemy" (1.7.11). Thereby, the sixth stage is reached, which is unnamed, but which surely parallels Isaiah 11:2's "spirit of understanding" (*intellectus*).[94] The student continues to grow so that the divine light becomes not only bearable but even enjoyable, and the love for neighbor becomes wholly subordinate to the love for God. And, though still in enigma (*in aenigmate*) and as through a mirror (*per speculum*) (1 Cor. 13:12), this person (now called a "holy person") will progress to the seventh stage, which is wisdom (*sapientia*): "Therefore, this holy person [*sanctus*] will have such a single-minded and purified heart, that he will not be turned from the truth by either an eagerness to please people or a desire to avoid whatever disadvantages come against him in his life. Such a son ascends to wisdom [*sapientia*], which is the seventh and final stage, which those who are peaceful and tranquil enjoy [*perfruitur*]" (2.7.11). As the discussion of the third stage demonstrated, no stage is entirely separate from the others. So, one must pass through the first two steps to get to the third, but the person in the third step must continue to fear God and practice piety. In addition, the third stage serves as the driving force to the fourth stage, where one begins to thirst after righteousness; this desire for righteousness is a product of the third stage's conviction that a person does not love properly. The stages advance to wisdom, but one does not leave behind a previous stage in the move to another. Rather, each stage is taken up into the movement toward wisdom. Thus, a person must love his or her neighbor on the way to loving God, but this love must finally reach the point where it is subordinate to the love of God. This does not mean it is forgotten; rather, the love for neighbor continues, a component within the love of God, no longer its own end.

Augustine's focus is the third stage, *scientia*, where the discussion of scriptural interpretation takes place: "But let us move our consideration back to the third stage" (2.8.12). He thereby subordinates the interpretation of scripture to the fear of God and holiness, which hints at the ecclesial context in the background and the ethos informing his interpretive schema. Furthermore, as was illustrated in regard to the first book, he places scriptural interpretation in a theological web. Here, the focus is on sin and purification, pride and humility. A certain anthropology of the reader is presupposed: one reads scripture because one needs to move closer to God. Sin prevents the reader from knowing what God desires; indeed, sin may well prevent the reader from even *wanting* to know. For that reason, scriptural interpretation is just one part of the process of moving to God, and it is not even the first step. Even in Book 1 of *De doctrina*, Augustine makes this clear: "Therefore, this entire temporal dispensation was established for our salvation by divine providence so that we might know this truth and have the ability to act on it; and we must use (*debemus uti*) it, not with such permanent love and enjoyment, but rather as transitory means, as our vehicles or other such instruments (there may be a better way to say this), so that we love that by which we are born on account of that to which we are born" (1.35.39). When this passage is taken together with the seven stages Augustine describes—with scriptural interpretation located in step three—it becomes clear that even the interpretation of scripture is not a foundational enterprise, let alone the theoretical account of interpretation (i.e., hermeneutics). Instead, he relativizes his hermeneutics, and it becomes a set of rules that are meant to show how scripture aids us in our progress toward the eternal, unchanging God.

This location of interpretation within the progress toward God occurs throughout *De doctrina*. First, after establishing the canon to be interpreted, Augustine points back to stages one and two: "In all these books, those who fear (*timentes*) God and are gentle with piety (*pietate mansueti*) seek the will of God" (2.9.14). Only after establishing that the interpreter is a person who has come through the first two stages does Augustine offer his first practical hermeneutical rule: to know all of the canonical books. The entire hermeneutical discussion in Book 2 is intended for a person who fears the Lord and who seeks God's will in piety. In fact, Book 2 ends on a note of progression: "Therefore, provided with this instruction, a reader will not be hindered by unknown signs. Gentle and humble in heart, gently subject to Christ and laden with a light burden, founded and rooted and built up in love, which knowledge cannot puff up, he can approach the ambiguous signs of scripture in order to consider and to solve them, about which I will strive to teach in the third volume" (2.42.63).

Thus, even the progression from interpreting literal signs to interpreting ambiguous signs is connected to an advance in holiness. Scriptural reading is one practice among many, and it is intimately bound to holiness and one's relationship to God. If scriptural reading is tied to these practices, itself not foundational, how much more is the hermeneutics written to aid it relegated to a subsidiary role?

This progression in holiness and its connections to the different types of signs (literal and ambiguous) is also picked up in Book 3, which begins with a reference back to the first two stages described in Book 2: "The person who fears (*timens*) God diligently seeks his will in the holy scriptures, and he should not love controversy, being mild with piety (*pietate mansuetus*)" (3.1.1). Then such a person can use the practical discussion of Book 3 to approach scripture. After using those tools, the student will still find passages that are obscure because of metaphorical words (*verba translata*) (3.4.8), but he or she knows where to turn in this instance: back to Book 1 and the double-love command. Book 3, then, also rests within the explicit framework of the seven stages of ascent to wisdom. And since Book 4 rests on the basis of the preceding books, it is clear that Augustine locates his hermeneutics, and indeed all focus on signs and things and use and enjoyment, within the temporal dispensation, which is set up by God in order to bring humanity to knowledge and love of him. Augustine's hermeneutics, then, is in no way foundational in the sense that it serves as the theoretical basis for the actual act of interpretation. Instead, on the basis of Book 1, God is the ultimate thing that relativizes every other thing, and on the basis of Book 2, interpretation is one of the seven steps to use in order to reach him. Hermeneutics is located within the church, the congregation of those who take part in the interpretation of scripture, knowing they should fear the Lord and be pious, and yet Augustine makes several appeals to general hermeneutical tools (e.g., semiotics, grammatical rules, tropes, etc.).

Once again, it becomes evident that the general-versus-local model of hermeneutics fails on its own to describe aptly what actually occurs. It is more useful, and indeed more precise, to supplement this spatial model with the temporal model of *a priori* and *a posteriori* hermeneutics. And on the basis of this discussion, it seems fair to conclude that Augustine's hermeneutics is an example of an *a posteriori* hermeneutics. He writes to aid an already existing ecclesial tradition of interpretation of scripture in the pursuit of God, and he does not attempt to make his theory foundational. Rather, he does exactly the opposite; his semiotic discussion in Book 1, as useful as it may be for a general theory, is not foundational. It does not constrain his subsequent practice. It serves as prolegomena. Likewise, in Book 2 Augustine locates interpretation squarely within the context of the spiritual life. He wrote *De doctrina* to aid the communal reading practices that exist solely to help the Christian in his or her journey home, yet, in this very theological work, he did not refrain from self-consciously using the general, philosophical and theoretical ideas of his day.

## MELDING GENERAL AND LOCAL CONCERNS

By placing Augustine into dialogue with Jeanrond, the foregoing discussions demonstrate that the temporal model, *a priori* versus *a posteriori*, helpfully supplements the spatial model, general and local. The general-versus-local hermeneutical model accurately describes the difference between, say, Ricoeur's hermeneutical theory and Wood's. In the context of theological hermeneutics, however, viewing the two as a sharp antithesis is unhelpful. The issue is no longer as clear cut when describing the practices of theologians; instead, the distinction between theologians is more precisely described in terms of whether the theologian privileges theory to practice or vice versa. This helps diffuse the rigid polarity between "general" and "local," while effectively utilizing those very terms. In the case of the preceding discussions, it can be seen that the *a priori* and *a posteriori* model helps describe what occurs in both Jeanrond's and Augustine's hermeneutical discussions. Jeanrond self-consciously steps back from an ongoing interpretive act to begin with an abstract theory of texts, and on the foundation of that general theory, he moves to a more localized theory and only then does practice go forward in a safeguarded manner; his theory is meant to come into operation before—logically speaking—the subsequent interpretive act. Augustine, on the other hand, makes appeals to general hermeneutical rules and observations, while all the time focusing on explicitly theological issues, and this in turn highlights his communal location and the ethos of that community. His hermeneutical rules are not meant to be foundational to a practice that is not yet occurring; they are meant to aid an already existing interpretive practice.[95] It has also become clear that, unlike Jeanrond or Thiselton, Augustine subordinates his theory to practice.

The answer to this chapter's driving question—What makes Augustine's appeal to the philosophical resources of his day different from that of much of contemporary theological hermeneutics?—is: Augustine uses the general philosophical distinction of *res* and *signa* for explicitly theological purposes. He embeds philosophical ideas into his theology, making philosophy a field to be plucked, not a master to serve.[96] That is, theology has every right to correct philosophy, to *use* its ideas for theology's own ends; it need not assume philosophy has a grasp on some truth that theology does not. All truth is God's (2.42.63). Augustine thereby shows that "general" and "local" need not be hard-and-fast antinomies; rather, they can be ends of a continuum. He can give due attention both to the *res* about which the text speaks (God) and the text itself. He holds the two together in a way not often duplicated.

The previous discussions illustrate forcefully that Augustine does not, in fact, view his theorizing as foundational to practice. Instead, he locates his theory within a comprehensive theological web. The careful structuring of *De doctrina* illustrates this point and shows that the delineations he makes, though theoretical in tone, are actually put to very specific uses. Because the double-love command described in Book 1 and the first two of the seven stages described in Book 2 are continually referenced throughout *De doctrina*, the appropriateness of the web imagery can be seen. Scripture is a vehicle that brings us to God. For that reason, biblical interpretation works to understand what God says through scripture. Any other construal would seem to Augustine wrongheaded. The biblical text is construed as an instrument in the divine economy; it is—somehow—the place where God's will can be learned and it is thereby a vehicle to God. If, however, one construes the text as primarily a human text, a move which requires an *a priori* hermeneutics to guard it from misinterpretation, then this begs the question: How can an *a priori* hermeneutics answer questions posed to it by the church, which views this text as the *viva vox dei*?[97] Perhaps the construal of the text as an instrument in the divine economy is not as publicly justifiable as Jeanrond might want because of its explicitly presuppositional nature, but one could ask if Jeanrond's method is any less presuppositional, with its underlying anthropological assumptions.[98]

In addition, Augustine's hermeneutics does not simply perpetuate the tradition.[99] Instead, scriptural interpretation occurs within the schema of convicting the reader of his or her sin, and leading him or her to God. In fact, Augustine assumes that the reader will come to the text with all sorts of presuppositions and sinful proclivities. Scripture, because it is an instrument used by God in the economy of salvation, exists to break down prejudices that a sinful reader brings to it. Though the *regula fidei* is part of the tradition, Augustine is certain that the overall message of scripture is love of God and of one's neighbor. That is the "mind" of scripture. The *regula fidei* describes the things of scripture, and the double-love command—the *regula dilectionis*—tells how to relate to them. This can be seen in the extended credal discussion in Book 1. Augustine shows how these beliefs are scriptural by continually citing scripture. The beliefs, then, are not accepted as a rigid body of tradition, or as—in the words of Jeanrond about "petrified" interpretation— "reductionist, repetitive and formal";[100] instead, Augustine shows how they are in fact the things of which scripture speaks.[101] This suggests that an ecclesiological reading may not be as dangerous as Jeanrond suggests.[102] Furthermore, Augustine's construal of scripture puts the focus to some extent off of arriving at a "correct" interpretation and on to progression to God. Augustine's anthropology assumes that the interpreter is in need of more than knowledge. An instrument that corrects sin and moves the person closer in love to God and neighbor is more important than getting stuck at the level of understanding the things of which scripture speaks and failing ever to relate to them appropriately.[103] Reading the biblical texts is part of a larger exercise.[104] Admittedly, a focus on the text's agency and its correction of the reader's presuppositions only answers half of Jeanrond's criticism. What about the text's inappropriate ideologies? More will be said about this in subsequent discussions, but briefly, one can note Augustine's criterion of love does mean that certain portions cannot—for the contemporary reader—be taken at face value. Moreover, his attention to the community where interpretation occurs—one existing after the incarnation—mitigates to some extent the worries over the text's inappropriate ideology.

This chapter has primarily addressed the contention that Augustine develops what I have termed an *a priori* hermeneutics. On the contrary, it has become clear that he develops an *a posteriori* hermeneutics; his theoretical discussions are secondary to his driving practice, the ongoing interpretation of scripture within the community of the church.[105] Not much has been said about the communal aspect of his interpretive program; more will be said in the following chapter. In his discussion on logic, he describes the process of learning to walk in order to show that rules are often less important than practice (2.37.55). Someone could give rules about how to walk; for instance, do not pick up your back foot until your front foot is on the ground. Then the person could describe in detail how the different joints of the limbs and knees work. Though the person would be correct, it does not actually work that way: "People find it easier to walk by actually doing these things than by paying attention when they do them, or by understanding instruction about them." Augustine uses this kind of example a few times in *De doctrina* (e.g., 4.3.4, 4.5). The point in every case is the same: it is better to practice than to learn rules. This analogy could be extended: though learning to walk begins with practice, there comes a time when a child can be told certain things about how to walk that will help even more, such as not to walk when the crosswalk light is red, or not to walk in front of a person trying to go through a door. These ideas are helpful and at some points crucial, but they are not the basis for walking. In the same way, Augustine shows that an *a posteriori* hermeneutics has a place for the good aspects of general hermeneutical discussions. This can be seen in his semiotic treatment, a discussion that still reverberates in philosophy today. Indeed, to remove the general discussions would impoverish just what he does in *De doctrina*. Still, he does not lose out on the specific applicability of local hermeneutics. His hermeneutics effectively melds general and local concerns, without subordinating practice to theory.

I suggest that this fusion is just the sort of thing contemporary theological hermeneutics can learn from the dialogue in the preceding pages. It shows just one reason why an *a posteriori* hermeneutics—which emphasizes practice over, but not at the expense of, theory—offers a significant alternative to an *a priori* hermeneutics—which views theory as a constraint upon subsequent practice. Theological hermeneutics has the freedom and indeed every reason to utilize the insights of general, philosophical hermeneutics without ever having to surrender its local, theological concerns.

# Community, Hermeneutics, Rhetoric

While it has been established that Augustine's hermeneutics, as espoused in *De doctrina christiana*, is what I have labeled an *a posteriori* theological hermeneutics, it remains to be seen just what ongoing interpretive practices inform *De doctrina*, that is, what communal location he presupposes. Bearing in mind the first two chapters' analyses of *De doctrina*, it might seem unnecessary to discuss the presupposed community. After all, Augustine began it at the start of his bishopric and finished it at the end, making it a thoroughly ecclesiastical book. Furthermore, when compared to *De agone*, the language and structure of *De doctrina* reveal that it is written for a learned audience, not for the average person, for a person who needs to know how to understand the Bible and to deliver to others the results of that understanding. In the fourth and fifth centuries, it seems a bit of a stretch to expect even the priests to have the qualifications Augustine lays out here, much less the average lay person. He even states that the person he has in mind is an ideal, rather than an actuality: "I give thanks to our God because I have been able to discuss in these four books—with what little skill I have—not the kind of person I am, because I have many faults, but the kind of person he ought to be who desires to labor in sound teaching [*doctrina sana*], that is, Christian teaching [*christiana*], not only for himself but also for others" (4.31.64).[1]

Taking these things into account, one might think the presupposed community is self-explanatory. This quotation alone forces the reader to reckon with a specific target audience: a person who works to understand Christian teaching *in order to share it with others*. As I said in the first chapter, Hill's view that *De doctrina* was composed for a clerical audience makes good sense on internal and external grounds. I suggested that his view should be combined with Pollmann's suggestion that the work is a universal hermeneutics, that is, one that utilizes every available resource to explain how one should understand scripture. In contrast to Pollmann, it will prove helpful not to widen the target audience of the work until the original target audience of the clergy is addressed. The theological payoff of this move will be seen in due course. It will be helpful to keep in mind that the execution of *De doctrina* might be slightly different—more ambitious perhaps—than the treatise Aurelius (may have) requested, especially when Augustine set about writing the last sections in 426/7. Certainly, there are reasons to argue that the target audience includes more than simply ministers, but paying attention to the text's internal structure and argument will bring to the surface a set of presupposed interpretive practices that all highlight the initial focus on a certain community—the church—and a specific set of people within it—the clergy. Any universalizing tendencies present in the work begin from this point.

Textual analysis will best help to determine the specific community Augustine has in mind. By paying attention to his theological movements, the precise role of scripture in the divine economy can be seen. For instance, the prologue emphasizes the necessity of human teachers, demonstrating that an image of the community he envisions emerges even from the start of the work. The discussion of the canon in Book 2 provides a further clue to the importance of the Catholic Church for his interpretation. In addition, the continual importance of the *regula fidei* and its connection to the *regula dilectionis* demonstrate the precise nature of the community and the role of the biblical text within it. Finally, in Book 4, Augustine is clear about the goals and aims of the practice he sets forth in the entire work. It is not just for anyone (at first), and the investigation will demonstrate the precise nature of the community and the people within the community that Augustine has in mind. In the course of discussion, echoes of contemporary issues will ring forth, and these will continue into the following chapter. By analyzing the ongoing interpretive practice underlying *De doctrina*, this chapter will demonstrate just how the treatise is an example of an *a posteriori* hermeneutics, and the merits of such a hermeneutics will also become more apparent.

## THE PROLOGUE: DIVINE AND HUMAN IN HARMONY

Often, arguments against the view that *De doctrina* was composed for the clergy begin with the prologue. Here, it is suggested, Augustine shows he has the general reader in mind, not a priest.[2] Such a viewpoint might seem persuasive on the first reading of the prologue, but upon closer examination, the reader begins to notice that even here Augustine has in mind a group of people who read in order to proclaim. Individual interpreters are not the target audience at any point in *De doctrina*. More than that, a precise set of theological judgments informs his entire argument: God speaks to humans through humans (*per homines hominibus*), and this takes place when God uses the human words of scripture as well as when God speaks through those who interpret them.

As Press points out, Augustine begins his treatise by stating what he intends to do: "There are certain rules for interpreting the scriptures, which I think can be usefully related to the students [*studiosis*] of them" (Prol. 1). Here, at the start, is a statement of purpose: the treatise is a set of rules elaborated with the express goal of teaching people how to understand the scriptures on their own (Prol. 9). As Kevane points out, *studiosus* is a technical term from the Latin educational system, but this does not necessarily imply that Augustine here envisions such a system. More importantly, the treatise has one subject: the interpretation of *scripture*, not of literature in

general but of scripture, the divine books (*litterae divinae*). He specifies what he means in Book 2: "The most skilled investigator [*soler-
tissimus indagator*] of the divine scriptures [*divinarum scripturarum*],
then, will be the one who, first, has read all of them and is familiar
with them, and if not fully with understanding, nevertheless now
with reading, precisely [*dumtaxat*] those that are called canonical"
(2.8.12). In subsequent sentences, it becomes clear that, eventually,
one can read the noncanonical books. Nonetheless, the important
books are the canonical ones. These and these alone are the subject
of his work. More will be said on the canon below.

In the prologue, as the first chapter stated, Augustine registers
three potential objections to his treatise, each one helpfully drawing the communal location to the surface. Two groups of critics are
lumped together because they would have some difficulty with the
text of *De doctrina* itself. The first set of critics would fail to understand the rules Augustine imparts. They are like people who want to
see the moon, but when it is pointed out to them cannot even see the
finger guiding their eyes (Prol. 3).[3] The second group of objectors
understands what he says in the work, but when they turn to apply
his rules to scripture, they fail to understand what they could not
understand to begin with (Prol. 2). Again, he utilizes the metaphor
of the moon and the finger: these objectors can see his finger and
the way it points, but they still fail to see the moon. He responds to
both groups: "They should both stop blaming me and pray that God
would give them insight" (Prol. 3).[4] Augustine couples the first two
potential objections together, demonstrating that his rules are not
the end of the matter. They are his way of aiding those seeking to
understand the scriptures, but they are not infallible. Instead, prayer
is required in both cases. *De doctrina* is nothing more than a guide,
a practical aid to understanding the obscurities of scripture. These
rules must be utilized in the context of prayerful consideration,
calling out to God for insight. *De doctrina* is written to help these
people, but it cannot be utilized apart from God's divine help.[5] Without prayerful appeal to God, what Augustine says and what scripture
says might well remain a mystery. For these objectors, more focus
should be put on God, less on the human Augustine.[6] At the same

time, the appeal for them to pray is also a plea for them to continue reading his treatise. He seems to recognize that this text might
prove challenging for some to understand and still others to imple-
ment correctly. Augustine envisions actual people who have difficulty understanding scripture. He intends this work to help them,
but they must struggle through it prayerfully in order to understand
what exactly it says, and what scripture says, in order that they might
deliver it to others.[7]

The third group of objectors—the so-called "charismatics"—
receives exactly the opposite response:[8] they should place less weight
on divine illumination and more on human interaction. Whereas
the first two are lumped together and addressed in a matter of sentences, Augustine dedicates several paragraphs to the third potential
group, who would object in principle. They interpret the scriptures
well (or at least think they do) without recourse to the kinds of rules
he will be expounding: "Those, who see (or at least suppose) that
they themselves have the capacity of explaining [*exponendorum*] the
sacred books without having read observations of the kind which
I have now set out to relate, exclaim that these rules are not necessary for anyone, but instead everything that is correctly revealed
about the obscurities of the texts comes from a divine gift" (Prol. 2).
Briefly, one should note that this group's boast concerns not only
understanding for themselves but also the ability to explain scripture without human assistance, highlighting an ongoing practice of
understanding *and* explanation. One might have expected Augustine to have sympathy for this view after reading his response to
the first two objections, but that is not the case. It is one thing to
have difficulty understanding human instruction and thus to need
to pray for divine aid and quite another to reject human instruction
altogether and appeal directly to divine illumination. There is a necessary human component to scriptural interpretation. Focus purely
on the vertical relation to God at the exclusion of the horizontal
one to humans fails to take into account the double-love command,
which becomes the focal point of the work, as the first chapter illustrated. In other words—and Augustine labors this point throughout the prologue—failing to take into account the importance of

inter-human relationships is a symptom of something much deeper, pride, but he has a long way to go to make this charge stick. He is, after all, a well-educated rhetor telling a group of people intent on appealing to the Holy Spirit that they are, in fact, prideful. But his focus later on the double-love command makes this charge possible because humans exist in two types of relationships: a vertical one with God and a horizontal one with others.[9] His stress on prayer when handling the first two objections highlights the vertical relationship, while the stress against the third is on the horizontal relationship with teachers. To fail to account for either relationship is an error. Nonetheless, Augustine has to make the case that, when these people appeal to God and refuse to listen to him, they are prideful. Again, there are actual people who Augustine thinks will object that they do not need his work to help them understand scripture or to help them teach what they have understood.[10] He, however, thinks otherwise and tries to persuade them to read what he has to say.

At this point, it can be suggested that Hill's thesis makes considerable sense of the prologue. Augustine envisions two groups of ministers who will attempt to put what he writes into practice but for one reason or another fail. He here encourages them not to give up but instead to pray for help to understand both his treatise and the Bible itself. This plea suggests he is aware that the work might not be the simplest text for many to understand. He envisions a third group, however, which has an ideological problem with his treatise; they do not think they need any help from his treatise *at the start*. They think they need only appeal to God for understanding. Rather than seeing the prologue and the entire treatise as Augustine's "pro-*paideia*,"[11] a close reading reveals a more narrow concern — convincing actual people to read his book. These people seek both to understand scripture and to deliver that understanding to others. Such a suggestion becomes more plausible when Augustine claims to be doing what they themselves do by explaining what they understand:

> But if he reads and understands without any human explaining it to him, why does he desire to explain it to others, and not rather send them back to God, so that they likewise might

understand not through humans, but through God's inner teaching? Because, clearly, he fears that he will hear from the Lord: "Wicked servant, you should have placed my money on deposit." Just as they reveal to others what they understand, whether in speech or writing, so do I. Surely I should not be reproved by them if I offer not only what I understand, but also the rules observed in the act of understanding. (Prol. 8, citing Matt. 25:26–27)

These potential opponents are already reading scripture and sharing what they understand with others. Augustine's concern is not with defending education per se; instead, he, writing to ministers, knows they read scripture and explain it to others. Because he is in essence doing the same thing, why would they not listen to him? The only difference between him and his critics, he suggests, is that he wants to reflect on the *process* by which both he and they understand scripture.

In addition, he sees in this third viewpoint something more sinister and more theologically dangerous: pride. If these people do not want to read his book because they can hear from God, then why should anyone listen to anyone else? If God operates through divine illumination and there is no need for Augustine's work, then there would be no need for church attendance at all.[12] The logical conclusion of the third view, he suggests, is departure from the church's fellowship:

> Let us not tempt him in whom we have believed, so we are not deceived by the cunning and perversity of the enemy and actually refuse to go into the church to hear the Gospel and to learn, or to read the book, or to hear a person reading and preaching [*legentem praedicantemque hominem*], and instead expect to be snatched up "to the third heaven, whether in the body or out of the body," as the Apostle says, and there to hear "ineffable words which a person may not speak," or there to see the Lord Jesus Christ and to hear the Gospel from him rather than from humans [*hominibus*]. (Prol. 5, citing 2 Cor. 12:2–4)

This passage forces the ecclesial background of the prologue to the foreground. He wants especially the third group to read his text. To convince them, he demonstrates the logical conclusion of their objection: people stop going to church and risk falling prey to the devil. Such an argument would have no traction if the target audience were not ministers themselves.

In the third objection, there is a deeper, broader issue, and he goes about attacking it head-on in the following sections. Perhaps— he is willing to concede—some people can learn to understand and to interpret the divine books without human assistance, but before they get too excited about such a great gift from God, they should remember that they learned at least the alphabet from humans (Prol. 4). And—again, granting an argument—even if someone has learned the alphabet simply as an answer to prayer, one nonetheless only learns one's native language by hearing it spoken from childhood or through some other teacher. Here he applies his *reductio ad absurdum*: if these critics are correct, then they should cease teaching their children how to read and how to speak because the apostles, after all, were inspired at a single moment by the Holy Spirit (Prol. 5). His response is simple: stop being prideful. Again, this charge might strike the targets of his criticism as odd, especially coming from so highly trained a rhetor who dares think he can tell them what to do. His primary concern is highlighting the practical, underlying problem preventing them from reading his work, which he associates with pride. By insisting that humans can learn from the Holy Spirit on their own, these objectors are on their way to removing any reason for church attendance, any reason to read the biblical text or to hear it read and preached. Instead, they might wait for the Spirit to snatch them up to heaven. These are "very prideful and very dangerous temptations" (*temptationes superbissimas et periculosissimas*).[13] Augustine's primary concern with this third group is therefore not their reliance on the Holy Spirit, or even necessarily their distrust of education,[14] but what he sees as the result of their prideful state of mind: departure from the church. Such a point is corroborated by paying attention to the first two potential opponents, who are encouraged to rely more on the Spirit. The members of the third group think they have no need to be taught by humans and that they can appeal directly to divine illumination. This, to Augustine, is the epitome of pride. These criticisms only work if the people he wants to read his text themselves preach and teach.

After all, he says, even the apostle Paul, struck down and enlightened by a divine voice from heaven, had to go to Ananias to receive the sacrament of baptism and to join the church. Augustine phrases it emphatically: "Although he was struck down and instructed by a divine and heavenly voice, *to a human*, nevertheless, he was sent so that he could receive the sacrament and be connected to the church" (Prol. 6). Further, he continues, an angel actually appeared to Cornelius the centurion and told him that his prayers had been heard. But did the angel instruct him in what he should believe, hope, and love? No, he had to learn from Peter—from a human person—and be baptized by him. Here, Augustine pauses to emphasize: "The human condition would be debased if God appeared unwilling to minister his word to humans through humans [*per homines hominibus*]" (Prol. 6). God's temple, the human person, is holy. Yet how could this be the case if God simply bypassed humans and communicated straight from heaven? This observation cuts both ways: Augustine uses the necessity of human teachers to chastise his objectors into humility, while he shows that God insists on using human teachers to raise the status of all of humanity.[15] One who appeals solely to God is prideful precisely because he or she attempts to go beyond God's established order of revealing himself to humans through humans.

Again, the balanced focus on the vertical and the horizontal is crucial to Augustine's argument; there is a double-love command, not a single. It is not enough to be in relationship with God; this relationship remains incomplete when not connected to the one between neighbors: "Then, if humans learned nothing from one another, love itself, which binds people together in the knot of unity, would not have any means of pouring and, as it were, of mixing souls with one another" (Prol. 6; cf. 1.34.38). He seems here to allude to his warning that the third position leads to forsaking church attendance. His argument begins with the fact that, if this third group of objectors were consistent, then people would cease coming to church, where they are encouraged. At the end of the argument, he points out that the targets of his criticisms still preach and write, implying that they see some need for churchly attendance. The path between the two traces the examples in scripture of people hearing from other humans. These arguments would be ineffective unless the target audience were fellow ministers that Augustine wants to read *De doctrina*; in it, he does nothing other than what they do every time they stand up before a congregation. If they are correct about his treatise, they need not stand up in church and preach.

To cement his point, he continues with biblical examples. The eunuch in Acts did not understand Isaiah, but he was neither sent an angel nor his mind illuminated inwardly. Instead, Philip was sent by the Spirit because he knew what Isaiah meant: "And to the eunuch, Philip revealed that which was hidden in scripture, with human words and speech" (Prol. 7).[16] Augustine goes on to the example of Moses, who, although he saw God face-to-face, still received advice from his father-in-law with a "good deal of foresight and with little pride" (*maxime providus et minime superbus*) (Prol. 7). It is not as though they are self-evidently prideful; by appealing to divine illumination, in fact, the third group might seem to be the epitome of humility, especially when compared to his prestigious standing as a former rhetor telling Christians what they should do. Nonetheless, Augustine thinks that this vertical appeal to God alone misses out on a fundamental horizontal relationship existing between humans. The inclusion of the double-love command as hermeneutically significant later in the work illustrates this point forcefully.[17] The recognition of humans as bearers of truth is a form of humility. A great many things would be lost if humans failed to learn from one another, not the least of which is everyday speech, which is learned from parents and teachers. Again, these criticisms make the most sense with ministers as the target.

Finally, Augustine turns to the practice of those who claim to have received inner illumination: "Why do they aspire to explain to others and not rather send them back to God, so that they likewise might understand through that inner teaching [*illo intus docente*], rather than through human teaching?"[18] Obviously, he says, they do so because they are afraid of God's judgment. If God grants them understanding and they fail to share it, then they will be judged. And that is precisely what Augustine is doing, he says, sharing what he has been given. He simply goes one step further, telling *how* he understands, not just what he has understood. He, like the intended audience, is a minister. In the same way that they teach what they receive from God, so he does. To put it forcefully, as the prologue seems to do: if these ministers fail to listen to Augustine, they are just as bad as those who cease coming to church because they think they receive divine illumination. Furthermore, if they cannot learn anything from him, why should they dare teach their congregations? The logical conclusion: the church breaks down into individuals alone communing with God. And, further, all truth is from God, and so no one has anything that is not a gift: "For what do we have that we have not received? And if we have received it, why do we boast as though we have not?" (Prol. 8, alluding to 1 Cor. 4:7). Again, the general focus is on pride, and he stresses humility. He is simply the teacher who, rather than reading a book out loud to students, teaches them the alphabet so they can read for themselves.[19] As becomes evident in his delineation of the two sides of interpretation—*modus inveniendi* and *modus proferendi*—especially in light of the fourth book, Augustine thinks a great deal hangs on the delivery of truth to others and the concomitant reception of truth by the hearers. Analogously, the prologue puts him in the place of the teacher in Book 4, the one who has learned certain ways of handling scripture and seeks to pass them on to others. If the opponents are correct in their assertion—that understanding comes from divine illumination alone—then Book 4 would be pointless. And if Book 4 is pointless, so is the entirety of the work. Because no one would argue that ministers should not preach to a congregation, his explanation of these rules is not inappropriate. If, on the other hand, his rules are unnecessary, then the same thing *mutatis mutandis* applies to the delivery of a sermon in the churchly context. Augustine sees ahead to the problems latent within the view he attacks. Not only does it fail to account for the horizontal relationship between humans, but it also, in the end and for that reason, leads to the breakdown of church fellowship. Once a person is cut off from the church, doubt and temptation creep in.

By insisting that appeal to divine inspiration is enough, the third group fails in precisely the opposite manner from the first two by placing all the emphasis on God and none on humans. This failure ignores the double-love command. Augustine thinks their position is prideful because it ignores God's established order. To make the charge stick, he has to appeal to numerous biblical examples to show God's order in action. Augustine does all of this with a specific target in mind: ministers who do not think his rules are necessary. He attempts to gain a hearing, and in the process makes a general charge that applies to his opponents: they are prideful because they do not think they need to hear from a teacher. With Augustine's rules, the student, upon arriving at a difficulty in the biblical text, can figure out what is obscure on his or her own, or, at the very least, avoid falling into horrible error. Perhaps the person could receive divine illumination, but God typically does not work that way. And here he ends, feeling as though he has effectively silenced the potential opponents. If they ignore him, then their congregations can ignore them. And, clearly, they would not want that to happen. They should therefore listen to Augustine.

A few points should be noted. First, the prologue's goal is very specific. He seeks to gain a hearing for a treatise that he thinks might not receive the warmest welcome. He stresses the necessity of vertical and horizontal relationships, striking a balance. The first two groups should keep trying to understand the text and how it connects to scripture; the way to do so is by appealing to God. Augustine knows the treatise will not be the easiest thing for some to understand, but he still thinks it is useful. In contrast, the third group should give Augustine's work a chance because he, like them, is only passing on what he has received. More dangerous is the focus on divine illumination at the expense of the horizontal relationship. Such a move epitomizes pride and fails to take into account the *double*-love command and its vertical and horizontal aspects. Second, in the context of gaining a hearing for the work, the prologue offers a balanced portrait of divine and human agency working in connection. All things come from God (Prol. 8), but this God has condescended and used humans to convey his message to one other. In doing so, he has elevated their status, showing that they are, in truth, his temple.[20] Two things come from God working through humans: (1) no one can be so prideful as to think that he or she has anything not received; (2) humanity is drawn together in a bond of love.

A picture of the kind of community Augustine has in mind begins to emerge from these two points. This ecclesial community seeks to support one another in the unity of love by attending to a specific text in order to understand it together (Prol. 5). The community does not comprise isolated, individual readers. Instead, it comprises people knotted together in love, a community where souls are poured and mixed together. Partly, the focus on the corporate body is pragmatic because solitary people stand in danger of doubting their salvation: "Should we warn those to whom such things [e.g., ecstatic experiences reminiscent of Pentecost] do not occur to consider themselves not to be Christians and to doubt that they have received the Holy Spirit?" (Prol. 5). One need not go very far into Augustine's theology to understand the importance of baptism and unification to the church for his soteriology.[21] This focus on baptism is made explicit in two out of the four scriptural examples concerning God's use of humans to spread his message: Paul and Cornelius. In addition, the story of Philip and the eunuch, the third example, ends with the eunuch's baptism (Acts 8:26–39). Therefore, it seems reasonable to suggest that the presupposed communal practices informing *De doctrina* involve—at the least—baptized believers who support one another in love to help each other on their journey to their homeland (cf. 1.16.15). For Augustine, scriptural interpretation begins within this human matrix. The biblical texts and their exposition stand in connection to the horizontal relationships between humans as well as the vertical relationship between humans and God. Humans learn how to love one another and God by interpreting these texts, that is, by understanding them and sharing that understanding. To fail to account for either the human or the divine aspect in the exposition of scripture fails to do justice to how these texts fit within God's providential order. Interpreting them builds up the double love of God and neighbor. This double-love command is the end of scriptural interpretation—that much the following books make clear—but it is also the beginning— neither the horizontal nor the vertical relationship can be ignored.[22]

Though Augustine is balanced in his approach to these horizontal and vertical relationships, it must be noted that the prologue primarily concerns the importance of the horizontal, the relationships between humans. *De doctrina* concerns scriptural interpretation, and as the prologue has begun to make clear, it is not an individual pursuit (not even if God is included). Rather, it takes place in the church, where people are drawn together in love by telling one another what scripture means. The precise communal location presupposed in this work is one that involves delivery because there is a specific, divine economy of salvation attached to the church and to scripture. In this particular hermeneutics, interpretation does not occur without telling others what one discovers. To suggest otherwise is, for Augustine, the epitome of pride, a failure to understand a fundamental theological point: humanity's status is raised because God considers us integral to the communication of himself.

## THE CANON: REORGANIZED BY THE INCARNATION

The ongoing interpretive practice can also be glimpsed in Augustine's discussion of the canonical books (2.8.12–13). It should be remembered that he locates scriptural interpretation, about which he speaks here, within the seven stages that lead to wisdom. Immediately, then, it can be noted that he intends the person for whom these rules apply to be a believer intent on progressing in wisdom, which begins with fear of the Lord. His first rule for interpreting scripture is to have a working knowledge—if not a complete understanding—of the divine scriptures, at least those that are pronounced canonical (2.8.12). The noncanonical books have a place, but only after the student is equipped with belief in the truth (*fide veritatis instructus*) gleaned from the canonical books, which protects his or her mind from prejudice against sound interpretations and from dangerous falsehoods and fantasies (*mendacia et phantasmata pericula*). He then goes on to explain precisely what he means by canonical.

The student should follow the authority of the majority of churches, especially those that have apostolic seats and received letters from the apostles. Those books that are accepted by all churches should be preferred to those some do not accept. Yet the matter does not stop here; some books can be accepted that all do not accept, as long as the majority of churches accept them, as well as the churches with more authority.[23] These should be preferred to those supported by fewer churches, or by churches of lesser authority. He concludes, before going on to list the books: "If, however, he should find some held by the majority, but others held by the more authoritative—a situation which is not possible to find easily—I suppose they should nevertheless have equal authority" (2.8.12). One is struck immediately not by the weight Augustine places on the authority of the Catholic Church, but on the rather relaxed view he takes concerning which books are canonical.[24] In fact, one is reminded of his earlier proclamation in *Contra epistulam Manichaei* 5.6: "I, however, would not believe the Gospel, unless the authority of the Catholic Church moved me." The community he has in mind is not an authoritative hierarchy, declaring what is canonical from the top down. Instead, his canon comes from an agreement among a number of churches, an agreement rooted in practice, though also based in authority, insofar as the apostolic sees have more authority than other churches. Yet, he does not seem to think of the canon as prescribed only by the authority of the churches. There is some kind of inherent authority within the books as he makes clear in the case of Wisdom and Ecclesiasticus, whose authorship is in question: "Which in any case, because they have earned the right [*meruerunt*] to be received as authoritative, they deserve to be numbered among the prophets" (2.8.13).[25] He says the same thing about the churches that "earned the right" (*merere*) to be apostolic sees and to receive letters from the apostles (2.8.12). The case in both instances is the same: something set these churches and these books apart. Ruling bodies did not arbitrarily choose them. Nevertheless, one can note that the church communities do have some role to play in deciding what books are canonical. This is not to say that the church, in pronouncing them canonical, *makes* them authoritative; the previous citation rules this out. Rather, the churches recognize an inherent authority, an authority that is, apparently, built upon the practice of the more authoritative churches. As in the prologue, it can be suggested that Augustine's view here is balanced: human and divine authority work together.

The ongoing interpretive practice comes straight to the fore. These books have been read in a worship context long enough that they have acquired authority. The churches that are to be looked to are those that received apostolic letters and were apostolic seats. In other words, Augustine ties the canonical selection straight back to apostolic tradition. It is not as though the canon was decreed *ex nihilo*. It arose from continual usage by a vast number of churches.[26] When there is some kind of discrepancy, appeal is made to authority, which is rooted in the apostles. Yet he also allows for other books to be utilized that have less authority. The view here is one of ongoing public reading and interpretation, where biblical books show themselves worthy of the attention concentrated on them. In these books, those who fear God and are tamed (*mitescere*) by their holiness seek God's will (2.9.14). These books have an inherent *telos* because God has established them within the divine economy with the express purpose that they show God's will and, thereby, engender the double love of God and neighbor when they are interpreted, that is, when they are understood and explained.

Augustine's concern with the canon is practical, not theoretical. He gives the canonical list in the context of his discussion of the seven stages in the progression to wisdom. In the context of *De doctrina*—as the discussion above concerning the prologue illustrated and the discussion below concerning Book 4 will illustrate—the interpretation of these books takes place in the context of a church. A person seeks God's will in these books to present it to a congregation. Therefore, Augustine's concern is not with which books should be in the Bible but with which books should be read and commented on in the context of the ecclesial, worshiping community.[27] Evidence for this concern can be seen in his discussion of reading aloud (*pronuntiatio*) in 3.3.6–4.8. Before one dismisses this passage as unnecessary or as referring simply to reading—as most reading in the ancient world was done aloud—the preceding passages should be noted (3.2.2–5). There, Augustine treats punctuation (*distinguo*), that is, the private aspect of reading and figuring out how the passage should be divided. In 3.3.6, on the other hand, he focuses on simple things like how to inflect a question, concerns that have to do with when a passage is read out loud to a group of people. Such a discussion would be unnecessary did Augustine not have in mind an ongoing communal practice of reading aloud for others to understand.[28]

This ecclesial community that gathers to hear the scriptural words has a certain relationship with the books. When discussing the Old Testament, Augustine dispenses with the notion of "the law and the prophets," replacing it with "history" and "the prophets." The Pentateuch, Joshua, Judges, Ruth, "the four books of Kings," the two of Chronicles, all make up one historiographical class—*haec est historia*—which is separate from another: Job, Tobit, Esther, Judith, the two Maccabees, and the two of Ezra. These books are separate from one another and the previous historical class, but are all nonetheless history. Only then does he move on to the prophets, which include the Psalms and the wisdom tradition. This suggests that his interpretive community has done away with the notion of the law as a binding institution. By making it history, the community makes the entire Old Testament point to Christ. What was law is no longer law after Christ.[29] A community that holds to the fundamental rift that the incarnation brings will inevitably read these texts differently from a community that continues to hold to the notion of "the law and the prophets."[30]

*De doctrina* presupposes a community existing in the days after the incarnation (cf. 3.8.12, 22.32).[31] The law stands in a different relationship to the church. There is no more Old Testament, in the sense that Augustine uses it in *De spiritu et littera*: the threatening law given at Sinai is null and void because God has now written that same law on the hearts of his people.[32] This relegates the law to history, severing the prophets from the foundation of the law, and putting them onto a new foundation, Christ. The way the Old Testament books are interpreted in this community, then, will be fundamentally different from interpretation in a community that still views law as fundamental to the scriptures. Yet Augustine does not suggest that the new community applies a different interpretive framework than called for by scripture itself. It is a canonical exercise, where one seeks to understand the will of the one speaking through the human authors:

> The person who endeavors to search the divine utterances should strive to reach the intention of the author through whom the Holy Spirit produced that part of scripture; he may reach this meaning or carve out another from those words which does not oppose right faith, if he has evidence from some other passage of the divine utterances. Of course, that author might have seen the same meaning in those words which we want to understand, but certainly the Spirit of God, who produced this through him, without a doubt foresaw the same meaning which occurs to the reader or to the hearer. Indeed, he planned that it should occur because that meaning also relies on the truth. (3.27.38)

The canon is fitted together both by the human authors and the Holy Spirit. The human author may not have understood his words to mean what the interpreter sees, but that does not negate the truth of the interpretation.[33] There is another who speaks through the author, who has produced the entire canon, and when appeal to the canon brings something to the surface that the author may not have seen, the "new" meaning is just as true, if not more so, than the "old" meaning. As the relegation of the law to history illustrates, what the author might have intended can be superseded by what the Holy Spirit intends through him.

To sum up, the section on the canon reveals that Augustine presupposes a community that centers around a single group of texts that have been recognized as authoritative, seen as the place to hear

God's will. This illustrates that the presupposed community is a worshiping community, where these books are read aloud. As the previous section illustrated and this one bears out, this community has a noncompetitive relationship between the divine and the human; it has ministers who explain what these texts say to a congregation. In addition, the Holy Spirit speaks through humans, using what they say *as well as* the interrelation between what they say and what the other authors say to speak the will of God.[34] Furthermore, an occurrence in history—the incarnation—has relegated what was formerly law to the status of history, and it has therefore raised the prophets from interpreters of the law to witnesses to the Christ event. The community built on this historical occurrence reads these texts differently from one without this foundation. Its members dwell as strangers in a foreign land, but they are aware of the path home, pointed out by the one who became flesh for them. The apostles who heard the Good News from him had seats at certain churches, and sent letters to others. These churches, because of their apostolic links, have more authority than others, and the traditions linked with them help illustrate what books should be read in order to discover God's will. The communal location reveals scripture's *telos*: it engenders the double love of God and neighbor by witnessing to God's will. And this serves to guide interpretation because God's will has not been more clearly shown than in the incarnation. Augustine's hermeneutics, then, stresses the use of these books in the community, but it also stresses their divine origin. God, through the Holy Spirit, through the human authors, has revealed his will in these books.[35] The act does not stop there, though, because another reads these books and finds meanings that may go beyond the intention of the original human authors. This person then turns to deliver what he or she finds in the books to a congregation.

## THE *REGULA FIDEI* AND THE *REGULA DILECTIONIS*

In *De doctrina*, the *regula fidei* is an important tool for the interpretation of scripture. Immediately, then, one is confronted by the fact that this work operates with a certain set of theological presuppositions informed by its communal location. Book 1, as the previous chapter demonstrated, serves as an exposition of the rule of faith. Augustine himself states this in 3.2.2. In Book 1, he moves systematically through the "things" of the faith, in order to make the move finally that all scripture teaches the double-love command, that is, how to relate to the "things" that the *regula fidei* describes. Again, the previous chapter illustrated that, throughout the work, he continually points back to Book 1 in order to aid (or, indeed, to correct) interpretation. In addition to the *regula fidei*, Augustine establishes the *regula dilectionis*: "For this *regula dilectionis* has been established by God: 'You shall love your neighbor as yourself,' but God 'with all your heart, all your soul, and all your mind'" (1.22.21). The *regula dilectionis* corresponds to the appropriate love of the *res* of which scripture speaks. Both *regulae* are authoritative, and it will be useful to illustrate how Augustine views their relationship.[36]

Scripture has two kinds of teachings—commands for living and rules for believing—as he says in 2.9.14: "Then [after one has a working knowledge of the canonical books], those things which are stated clearly in them—whether commands for living [*praecepta vivendi*] or rules for believing [*regulae credendi*]—should be carefully and diligently investigated. The more one investigates them, the greater is his understanding. Among those things that are openly stated in scripture one finds all those things which involve faith and morals for living [*fidem moresque vivendi*] (certainly hope and love, which we handled in the previous book)." These two categories of teaching correspond to the two *regulae* Augustine posits in Book 1. Only one "thing" should be loved for itself, God. The rest are loved for God's sake but loved nonetheless. Love is the *telos* of scripture because correct doctrine—the *regula fidei*—is only the beginning, the proper understanding of God and his creation, to which one must relate with appropriate love. Scripture exists not to avoid heresy per se because heresy is no more than an obstacle to proper orientation to God. Scripture's *telos* is to engender the appropriate love of God and neighbor. The two rules exist always together.[37] Right belief and proper love cannot be teased apart, though love does have some priority.[38]

A most illuminating comment occurs in what might initially to modern eyes seem to be a rather unimportant discussion: how to punctuate the texts one seeks to interpret (3.2.2–3.6).[39] The focus on punctuation is important due to certain heretical ways of reading the text. This, in and of itself, points to the specific, underlying communal location of *De doctrina*. The discussion occurs in Book 3, where Augustine explores how to handle unknown ambiguous signs.

The first step when encountering an ambiguity that arises from the literal usage of words (*verba propria*) is to see if the section has been phrased or pronounced correctly. If, however, this is unclear, then the next step is to refer to the *regula fidei*: "So, once close attention has been given, and it is still unclear how [a passage] should be punctuated [*quo modo distinguendum*] or how it should be pronounced, let him consult the *regulam fidei*, which he learns from the plain passages of scripture and from the authority of the church, concerning which we said enough when we spoke about things in the first book" (3.2.2). Only after the interpreter has determined that several different readings are acceptable according to the *regula* does he or she appeal to the context in order to figure out which of the several meanings the passage suggests are most convincing. Understanding the broad context is important for understanding smaller sections, but here, it is subordinated to the *regula fidei*, which arises out of both scripture and the tradition. Augustine has in view a certain kind of interpretive practice that can be brought to the surface: scripture has clear passages that can be synthesized into a unified whole, the *regula fidei*, which the church hands down. By pointing back to Book 1, he reminds the reader immediately of the scriptural citations he used to illustrate the things of scripture. He is certain that it teaches the *regula*. What remains important is the communal practice presupposed: there is a "mind" of scripture, an overarching framework that comes from the book and also aids in the understanding of it, an overarching framework that the church has some part in handing on.[40]

The *regula* serves as a guide to ambiguities, but it is in this context that it is necessary to highlight that there are clear passages in scripture from which the *regula* derives. Augustine emphasizes the use of the *regula* to clear up potential problems. He is not stressing an aprioristic notion of the *regula fidei* forcing interpretations in a certain direction. Because the *regula* derives at the same moment from plain passages of scripture and from church authority, Augustine yet again balances extremes: text and community, not one or the other. The *regula* derives from scripture, and because it represents the summation of the whole, it usefully pulls the confusing bits into line with the overarching theme of the text. In fact, if the *regula fidei* and the context fail to provide a clue to the meaning of the passage, then he allows for the interpreter to utilize whichever meaning seems best.

When it comes to actual ambiguities due to metaphorical language, on the other hand, he is clear that there is one criterion for determining how to understand the passage, what I have called the "*caritas* criterion": if it does not build up the love of God and neighbor, then the passage must be interpreted figuratively (3.10.14). It is interesting that Augustine's focus on the *regula fidei* and the importance of the church's tradition fades away when it comes to actual ambiguities. He has discussed the *regula* in Book 1, but—as the previous chapter illustrated—it serves to describe the things that are to be loved. The important rule for Augustine in the context of *De doctrina* is the *regula dilectionis* (1.22.21), the double-love command. It is the "mind" of scripture in its essentials, the whole of which there are numerous parts. The focus on communal practice is never far from Augustine's mind: "Now, after ascertaining that a passage is figurative, and after consulting the rules of things [*regulae rerum*] which we discussed in the first book, it is easy to turn it around in several different ways until we arrive at the correct meaning [*ad sententiam veritatis*], especially when the use [of these rules] is aided by the exercise of piety" (3.24.34). The *regulae* that Augustine offers throughout *De doctrina* always occur within a communal context in which the practice of piety takes center stage. The interpreter determines that a passage should be understood figuratively because it does not build up the love of God or neighbor in its literal sense. He or she then applies the "rules" that Augustine gives throughout the book (the *regula fidei* in Book 1, for instance), and those rules *coupled with* the actual practice of piety will result in clearing up difficulties. Augustine's emphasis on the actual practice of love becomes more evident in the fourth book, where he emphasizes that the proper end of scriptural interpretation is not simply connecting one's understanding of the Bible to a nebulous entity called "love," but to the actual, lived, love of the Christian community. Bearing in mind the focus in the prologue on the necessity of human fellowship, it becomes clear that the interpretation of scripture occurs best when located within a community practicing what scripture teaches. Nevertheless, Augustine does not allow the community to override the text. As the previous chapter illustrated by appeal to 3.10.15, he is aware of the human predisposition to pride, which can lead the community to force the text in inappropriate interpretive directions. The text has its own authority, its own voice. It stands over and against the church, while nonetheless the best interpretations occur within this interpretive matrix. In Augustine's portrayal, a delicate balance is achieved, a noncompetitive relationship between the human and the divine.[41]

What remains interesting about his depiction, with its focus on the *regula fidei* and the *regula dilectionis*, is the space he actually leaves open to biblical exegesis and historical inquiry. His appeal to the two *regulae* does not remove the necessity of actually wrestling with the text. One can point to the entirety of *De doctrina* to illustrate Augustine's concern for exegesis, but since this discussion has primarily concerned Book 3, it will be useful to remain there.[42] He begins again with the importance of the *regula fidei* for understanding but does not suggest in any way that because it exists, scripture must be bent to fit it. Instead, he understands the text to have a "mind" that runs through it. Because it is a text, however, some parts are going to be confusing, and that is why the two *regulae* help interpret them. He illustrates how important his rules are for the practice of exegesis by giving numerous examples throughout Book 3.

For instance—and telling for his view of the Old Testament—
he discusses the practice related in the Old Testament of men having
multiple wives (3.12.20, 18.27).[43] One must pay attention to different
times and places and their respective codes of conduct. The men in
those days thought of the kingdom of heaven as an earthly kingdom,
and in order to propagate the race, they took extra wives. Women
could not have more than one husband because that would not help
increase childbirth. When the righteous men took multiple wives,
Augustine argues, they even did so without lust. Hence, scripture
does not censure them. In fact, they could live chastely with many
wives, whereas a man with one wife might live in lust with just the
one (3.18.27). The issue is one of motive. The righteous men looked
to procreation, while such a man with one wife thinks of sexual
gratification. After this extended discussion, Augustine draws the
conclusion that nearly all the actions done in the Old Testament
should be interpreted both literally and figuratively: "Therefore, all,
or almost all, of those deeds which are contained in the books of
the Old Testament, are to be taken not only literally, but also figuratively; nevertheless, also those which the reader takes only literally, if those things which they do are praised, but the practices are
abhorrent to the habit of good morals kept by those who keep the
divine commandments after the coming of the Lord [*post adventum
domini*], let him refer the figural meaning to his interpretation, but
not transfer the actual deed to morals" (3.22.32). Leaving aside the
perhaps naïve view Augustine had of the patriarchs' practices, the
principle here is of importance. The community that reads scripture
now exists after the advent of the Lord, and certain practices not
condemned in the Old Testament cannot be accepted as suitable due
to their incompatibility with the *regula dilectionis*. In other words,
the community in which Old Testament interpretation occurs has
some bearing on what exactly the Old Testament means to them.
And this meaning no longer resides fully in the literal sense, if, by
"literal sense," one intends what the author meant.[44] After Christ,
the church must utilize these passages differently than they were
used before the incarnation. They have been revealed as signs: "On

account of this [the fact that some signs—like idols—do not point to useful things], Christian freedom has liberated those whom it found enslaved to useful signs—those who were not, as it were, that far away [the Jews]—and, by interpreting the signs to which they were subjected, has raised them up to those things of which they were signs" (3.8.12). Therefore, one facet of the presupposed interpretive practice is the location *after the incarnation*. This location restructures the possible meanings that the Old Testament texts can have, but it does not eliminate the Old Testament's importance.

To summarize, when Augustine employs the *regula fidei*, he does so to aid interpretation, but it is not an aprioristic straightjacket to force the text to the church's desires. Instead, the church passes it on, while it is a true representation of what scripture says in its entirety. The *regula* helps determine the validity of an interpretation. In addition, the *regula dilectionis* helps determine whether a passage is literal or figurative. It should be emphasized here once more: the *regula dilectionis* is not simply a rule one applies *to* scripture. It derives from an understanding of the function of scripture. Precisely because the Spirit inspired and established the biblical texts to engender the *actual*, lived, double love of God and neighbor (as Book 4 makes clear), this rule is properly utilized to understand scripture. The two *regulae* work together, one with the focus on doctrine or belief (faith and hope), and the other on ethics (love).[45] Though the church has the *regula fidei*, and though Augustine lays out his own version in Book 1, there is still much importance placed on the actual exegesis of a passage. The *regula fidei* does not supersede interpretation, allowing one simply to return to it. One must come to scripture and engage with it, for there the reader finds out what the will of God is. Yet, as emphasized above, this is a canonical exercise, one where God's will covers the entire corpus, where the whole helps determine the meaning of the parts. Furthermore, the *regula fidei* is not the end; it lays out the "things" to which scripture points, while the *regula dilectionis* teaches one how to relate to those "things." Both *regulae* are necessary because one gives the "what," the other the "how." In addition, this community exists after the arrival of Christ. This structures the way they interact with these books, especially the Old Testament corpus, but actual exegesis is still necessary. Hence, the Old Testament tends to work on two levels.

The *regula fidei*'s importance throughout *De doctrina* and the way the *regula dilectionis* supplements it both point to the *a posteriori* nature of Augustine's interpretation.[46] There is a *regula* that has been handed down through the church that corresponds to the clearer passages of scripture. This tells one what to believe. In addition, there is another *regula* that tells one how to interact with others. This rule arises on account of the incarnation and Christ's reiteration that the end of the law and all of scripture is the double love. Engaging with scripture leads both to right knowledge and correct ethics. This is not an interpretation that exists in a vacuum. The community presupposed in *De doctrina* is necessary. The work would not exist without a community that hands on the tenets of faith and that loves one another. Proper exegesis takes place in this context. *De doctrina* suggests both *regulae* are necessary for good interpretation. Without the *regula fidei*, one does not know to whom or what one's love ought to be oriented. But without the *regula dilectionis*, one does not know in what way one ought to relate to those *res* taught by the *regula fidei*. Both work together, and both require engagement with scripture in order to figure out how they work. Still, achieving the correct meaning takes a secondary role to engendering the correct love. Augustine envisions a theological *interpretation* oriented to faith and ethics through the ecclesial community's engagement with scripture, not just a *theological* interpretation that applies the *regulae* without due attention to the divine words that teach them. Interpretation occurs within this matrix, a matrix that informs the expanded hermeneutics of *De doctrina*. And it must be kept in mind that interpretation involves understanding and delivery, a construction that requires more than one person, that requires a person to love in the course of loving God. The *regulae* are components of interpretation because there is a goal beyond the interpretive act itself: the pouring and mixing of souls together in pursuit of the appropriate love of God and ascent to wisdom.

## DELIVERING (FROM THE PULPIT) WHAT ONE
## DISCOVERS IN SCRIPTURE

As stated in chapter 1, the fourth book of *De doctrina* sometimes falls to the side, relegated to articles strictly about its rhetorical background, or—and a more questionable occurrence—overlooked altogether. But it actually offers several clues concerning the particular audience Augustine envisions for his book, as well as the particular ongoing communal practices he assumes. Hill's thesis—that *De doctrina* was written for preachers—makes more sense of Book 4 than other views because Hill takes into account the communal location that it requires to make sense.[47] To suggest that Book 4 traces back to the rhetorical tradition, or to the ancient *paideia*, misses out on the fact that this book (and therefore the work as a whole) presupposes a specific communal context: the church where ministers stand up and preach to a congregation. Moreover, to disconnect it from the treatise misrepresents Augustine's program altogether. A treatment of scripture involves a double process. One does not simply figure out what the texts mean (or meant); one also has to present to others what has been understood. Whether this should apply to the interpretation of all texts is another matter. In *De doctrina*, interpreting scripture and proclaiming the results of that interpretation are both part of the same unified process that occurs in a specific ecclesial setting, the worship of a church. Failing to grasp this can lead to interesting hermeneutical, semiotic, or even theological discussions, but ultimately, it leads to misunderstanding the role of scripture in the community Augustine envisions.

In Book 4, he states that he will not teach rhetoric in the sense that he taught it in his previous career (cf. 4.1.2, 3.4, 7.20).[48] One might question the level of consistency Augustine maintains with respect to these statements, especially with his focus on Ciceronian rhetoric and its three styles,[49] but since the ex-professional rhetor insists that he is not teaching the same rhetoric as he once did, it seems reasonable to take him at his word and figure out what he is in fact teaching. As I suggested above, *De doctrina* can best be described as an expanded hermeneutics, one that includes delivery.

If by "rhetoric" one means the delivery of what one has understood, then Augustine clearly *is* teaching rhetoric. However, his disavowal of teaching rhetoric as he had done in the past points to the aptness of the suggestion that *De doctrina* be considered a hermeneutics that includes rhetoric, rather than a rhetorical treatise than includes *inventio* (as Press suggests). More succinctly, Augustine's program is not classical rhetoric but something distinct, something adapted for churchly use, to teach the truth found in scripture. It is an indication of the communal location, a manifestation of the *a posteriori* nature of his hermeneutics. In fact, he is clear that professional, classical rhetoric is useful but not strictly necessary:

> Why—when from infancy, speakers are not made except that they learn from the speaking of those who are already speaking—can the eloquent not acquire eloquence without the traditional art, but rather by reading and listening and, as far as he is able to follow, by imitating the speeches of the eloquent? What, have we not experienced numerous examples similar to this? For we have known many who have not learned the rules of rhetoric, and who are more eloquent than a great many who have learned them, but we do not know a single eloquent person who has not read or heard the debates and discussions of the eloquent. (4.3.5)

As in 2.36.54, Augustine thinks rhetoric is one of the human disciplines not established by humans but discovered by them and instituted by God. The activity is useful, and even the teaching of it, but his interest lies not in elaborating how to be a good rhetor, but on how the interpreter of scripture should act. Clearly, some rhetorical devices will come into play, but these are not the focus. Instead, he wants the readers of his book to focus on the end goal of exposition and proclamation: to teach and to persuade: "Therefore, the interpreter [*tractor*] and teacher [*doctor*] of the divine scriptures, the defender of right faith and the conqueror of error, should teach the good and refute [*dedocere*] the bad; and in this process of speaking [*in hoc opere sermonis*], he should win over those who are hostile, rouse the lazy, relate to the ignorant because he delivers what they should expect" (4.4.6).[50] This sentence nicely summarizes the primary thrust of Book 4. The person Augustine addresses is both an interpreter and a teacher, that is, one who holds together the two aspects of *De doctrina*. One might wonder how this description can align with anything other than Hill's suggestion for the target audience of *De doctrina*. The person described here is certainly a preacher. Perhaps centuries later it is possible to say that Augustine's rules in this work paved the way for a Christian culture, but that goes well beyond the ideas present in the text. Augustine brings out his focus in the following paragraphs. Even rhetors who have written works have to say that eloquence without wisdom is pointless, and, he insists, these rhetors do not even know the truth, which is the heavenly wisdom that comes down from God. "How much more," he says, "ought we, who are the sons and servants [*ministri*] of this wisdom, to think nothing else [than that eloquence must be about more than style, i.e., about truth and wisdom]?" (4.5.7). Those to whom Augustine writes are, like himself, children of God as well as those sharing God's wisdom with others. This is a narrowly focused target audience, one comprising ministers who seek to explain scripture to their congregations.

He then responds to some who might claim that the speakers of scripture are not eloquent (4.6.9–7.21). Recalling that Augustine was frustrated by the lack of learning in the Bible (*conf.* 3.5.9), it might be suggested that he makes this response because he knows from personal experience that some people think this way. After making this case, he continues to discuss what the speaker should do. Unlike the biblical authors, who wrote cryptically at times, expositors of the kind he envisions should speak clearly, *opening up* the oft-veiled expressions found in the biblical texts. They are to speak as perspicuously as possible (4.8.22). In addition, the focus is not on beautiful speech, but on clarity of communication, which means that, when speaking to uneducated people, one speaks differently than when speaking to those who know how to speak correctly (4.10.24). To risk an anachronism, Augustine does not want his ministers standing before a congregation and speaking as though they were in a university setting. A sermon (*sermo*) requires more effort to be clear than a conversation (*conlocutio*) because no one asks questions. Therefore, the speaker must be sure to aid the listener (4.10.25).[51] The point is always the same: be clear. Indeed, if it is obvious that the group has not understood, the speaker must continue to approach the topic from every angle until the group understands, but the moment they do, he or she should move on to another topic or stop.[52] Otherwise the crowd will become restless. In fact, enjoyment (the opposite of boredom) is an important tool but only insofar as it aids the proclamation of truth (4.10.25).

Here, he moves to discuss Cicero's three aspects of rhetoric: *docere, delectare, flectere* (to teach, to delight, to sway).[53] Augustine states, however, that the first (teaching) is the most important, while delighting and swaying are not necessary except insofar as they aid teaching (4.12.28). Swaying often occurs when people simply hear the truth, but it is still more important than delighting, as he states later. But before moving on to more Cicero, Augustine stresses the need for his eloquent speaker to pray because he or she speaks the truth of God, and moreover, only God knows the hearts of the listeners. Therefore, God ought to be brought into the speech, as it were:

> And thus, certainly let the one who wishes to know and to teach learn all which ought to be taught, and also let him acquire the ability to speak, as it is fitting for a man of the church [*virum ecclesiasticum*]. At the moment of speech, however, let him consider that what the Lord said is more appropriate for a good mind: "Do not think about how or what you will say; for what you should say will be given to you in that hour. For it is not you who speaks, but the Spirit of your Father, who speaks in you." If, therefore, the Holy Spirit speaks in those who are handed over to persecutors for Christ's sake, why not also in those who hand Christ over to learners [*discentibus*]? (4.15.32, citing Matt. 10:19–20)

Most important for Augustine, then, is this focus at the moment of speaking on God's intervening assistance. This does not absolve the

speaker from studying and from knowing how to speak well, but—
as throughout *De doctrina*—it puts God and the human agent into
close proximity. The human agent acts but knows that, in acting,
God acts through him or her and, without God's gracious action,
nothing would occur. In fact, in the next sentence, Augustine seems
to refer back to the third class of critics from the prologue: "But one
who says that people need no instruction [*non esse hominibus prae-
cipiendum*] concerning what or how they should teach, if the Holy
Spirit produces teachers, can also say that we need not pray because
the Lord says, 'Your Father knows what you need before you ask
him,' or that the apostle Paul need not have instructed [*praecipere*]
Timothy and Titus what or how they should instruct [*praeciperent*]
others" (4.16.33, citing Matt. 6:8). He moves on to rebuke them by
discussing Jesus' command to pray even though the Father already
knows what the disciples need, as well as Paul's advice to Timothy
and Titus to instruct others. In fact, he insists, a person with the role
of teaching in the church (*cui est in ecclesia persona doctoris imposita*)
should keep the Pastorals always before his or her eyes (4.16.33).
This attention to the Pastorals strongly supports Hill's thesis that
Augustine has written *De doctrina* for ministers.[54] Augustine discusses passages from the Pastorals for several paragraphs, focusing
on the role of handing on what has been received that falls to teachers (*doctores*) and bishops (*episcopi*). Surely, his focus is far more narrow than developing a culture, and surely, on this basis, his focus
is not on the rhetorical tradition but on the ecclesial community in
which ministers interpret and preach the Word of God. He turns
again to the issue of the Holy Spirit and the minister. Should it be
assumed, he asks, that the human role is canceled out by his focus
on the Holy Spirit giving the teachers their subject matter (4.16.33)?
Of course not; doctors apply medicines, but it is God who works
through them. "Thus, the benefits of teaching applied through a
human, then, profit the soul, when God—who could have given the
gospel to humanity, and not even by humans or through a man—
makes it so" (4.17.34).[55] The stress should be noted: God *could* have
given the gospel without humans, but he did not. Instead, he raises
them from their humble estate.

Pollmann is correct to point out that Augustine widens the target audience in this context, but such a move can better be described by pointing to the paradigmatic nature of the sermon, rather than to a universalization of his hermeneutics. For instance, he states: "But when we discuss the speech [*eloquio*] of that man [*vir*] whom we want to be a teacher [*doctorem*] of those things by which we are liberated from eternal evil and arrive at eternal good, wherever these are delivered—whether before the congregation or in private [*sive apud populum sive privatim*], whether to one person or many, whether to friends or enemies, whether in a long speech or conversation, whether in treatises or in books, whether in long or short letters— they are important" (4.18.37).[56] Pollmann's case rests on the widening from speaking before the congregation to conversations, books, and letters.[57] But such an expansion is better seen as an extension of the primary act of preaching, a standpoint verified by 4.9.23:

> For there are some things which are themselves not fully understood, or are barely understood, no matter how eloquently and for how long even the plainest of speakers turns them over again and again. In books, though, which are written so that in some manner they might hold the reader to themselves when they are understood, but when they are not understood, do not trouble those who do not wish to read them, as well as in private discussions, this duty should not be forsaken: we should bring the truths which we ourselves have already perceived into the understanding of others, no matter how difficult the truths are to comprehend or how much effort we must make in our argument.

On either side of this quotation, Augustine discusses oral delivery. In other words, his emphasis at this point of the argument is on a sermon: "The expositors [*expositores*] of scripture . . . should make every effort [*primitus ac maxime elaborent*] in every one of their sermons [*sermonibus*] to make themselves understood" (4.8.22). Only after stating this does he move on to the quotation above, after which he immediately moves back to discussing the importance of clarity in public speech, even if one must use incorrect grammar (4.10.24).

The context of this passage, then, leads to the following conclusion: one writes a book because the topic cannot be handled in a sermon. The sermon is the paradigm for all interpretation.[58] I should stress that both words—"sermon" and "paradigm"—are operative. The paradigm is one where the fruits of interpretation are delivered to a certain group of people, the church; the sermon is the model for how interpretation should be done. By putting the matter this way, one can keep in focus Augustine's narrow concern as well as account for his more general statements without downplaying the (initial) target audience of ministers in the ecclesial context. At this point, the theological payoff of keeping a narrow focus on ministers begins to come into focus: if the sermon is the paradigm for scriptural interpretation, several conclusions can be drawn for the study of the Bible and for the study of theology. But I am getting ahead of the argument.

After this section, Augustine moves back to a discussion concerning Cicero's three aspects of rhetoric. By making this move, he has moved systematically from Cicero (human agency) to the Holy Spirit and back again to Cicero. Humans have an important part to play, even dead, pagan ones like Cicero. In this section, Augustine ties the previous three points made by Cicero to three others: when a person is meant to be teaching, he or she should use a subdued style (*genus summissum*), when speaking of intermediate matters a moderate style (*temperatum*) in order to delight, and when speaking of important matters, a grand style (*grande*) to move the audience (4.17.34).[59] But the person Augustine has in mind speaks only of grand matters: the welfare of people, not just on earth, but also in eternity. The teacher speaks of truths that deliver people from eternal evils and conduct them to eternal good things (4.18.37). Yet the grand style should not always be used, as this would be tiresome. Instead, Augustine modifies the point of the three styles. Because the teacher's primary responsibility is to open closed doors and unravel problems (4.20.39),[60] his stress falls on the first, subdued, style for teaching. Second to that is persuasion, for which the tool

of choice is the grand style. Yet the moderate is for speaking beautifully and with flourish. He thinks this is unnecessary. The moderate
style should have its aim redirected; like the grand style, it is a tool
for making people love good morals and shun bad ones. The grand
style persuades people to do something they know they should do,
but do not. The moderate style, on the other hand, is for occasions
when people are not in need of as much persuasion as the grand
style offers. The moderate style helps prod people along a path upon
which they have already started. The grand style, on the other hand,
gets them out of their seats. The insistence on teaching and on persuading people to act ethically points to the underlying community
Augustine envisions: it is a community that needs help understanding what God has willed in the scriptures, a community that often
becomes convinced of something, but more often fails to act on it.
In short, this is a Christian community comprising fallen humans
who need prodding along the way to God, and, in his context, who
can Augustine have in mind to do this other than ministers? Yet, it
must be kept in mind, the preacher does not act on his or her own;
the Holy Spirit speaks through the person by giving him or her the
correct words to sway the congregation. Augustine brings this up
once again in the end, after stressing that the person's life must be
without blemish. The person speaks the truth and seeks to make
it clear to those who listen (4.28.61). He concludes the section on
speaking thus:

> Whether one is about to speak at this moment before a congre-
> gation [populum] or any other group, or to dictate something to
> be said before a congregation or to be read by those who are
> willing or able to do so, let him pray that God would place a
> good sermon in his mouth. . . . Those, however, who are going
> to deliver something they have received from others, should—
> before they have received it—pray for those from whom they
> will receive it; likewise, once they have received it, they should
> pray that they themselves may deliver it well and that those to
> whom they present it might take it up. And they should also
> give thanks for a good outcome to the very one from whom they

know they have received it, so that "the one who boasts" may boast in the one "in whose hand both we and our sermons are." (4.30.63, citing 1 Cor. 1:31; Wisd. 7:16)[61]

Again, the focus is on both God and human agents. There are two kinds of people specified here: those preparing the sermons and those delivering them (whether they prepared them or are reading someone else's). Both groups should pray for God's help, but prayer is not enough. As the section on the prologue demonstrated, the vertical must be accompanied by the horizontal. God speaks to his church through human ministers, the precise (original) target audience of *De doctrina*.

Now to pull together the strands from Book 4, here one finds the second part of Augustine's two-part program for handling scripture, the manner of explaining what has been discovered in the interpretation. The community that he presupposes comes sharply to the surface in this book. It is a community with a certain set of interpretive practices that can be characterized by their focus on God working through humans. Yet this broad application has a more narrow focus. Those through whom God works are ministers, preachers, who stand before a congregation and deliver God's Word to them. Scripture is where God reveals his will, but often he reveals it unclearly, which leaves open the need for human preachers to explain it to their congregations. Thus, God reveals himself through human agents. Furthermore, the communal practice involves prayer, prayer to understand and prayer to be understood. One hears scripture expounded to hear the will of God and to be converted to a holy life. Augustine puts this responsibility on the preacher: he or she exists to unravel ambiguous sections and to explain doctrines and scriptural passages, while also persuading the people to live according to the truths they have learned in the exposition. All of this takes place within the matrix of human prayer and God's gracious action through the Holy Spirit. To be intelligible, then, Augustine's hermeneutics *requires* the ecclesial community insofar as one must present what one finds in scripture to its members, and *De doctrina* makes sense only when the sermon is seen as paradigmatic for all other forms of communicating what has been understood. Before generalizing, one must recognize that Augustine writes first to ministers. The subsequent move to all Christians is a theological move, existing at some remove from Augustine's time, when even some ministers would not have had the training he expects.

## THE CHURCH, HER MINISTERS, AND THE SERMON AS PARADIGM

Several factors have come to the surface, but the emphasis in all of them rests on the identity of the community Augustine presupposes, the worshiping church. More specifically, it has become evident that *De doctrina* intends to be read by ministers first, and only by extension, others in the church. From the prologue through Book 4, the focus has been narrowly on practicing preachers, those whose task is to stand up and teach the ecclesial community. Yet Augustine handles this narrow focus often in general terms, ones that are useful in broader discussions about biblical interpretation. But the focus must always remain on the interpretation of scripture and its presentation to a certain body of people, the church. This community comprises humans who are fundamentally unable to do what they should do. For that reason, there is a continual focus on the necessity of prayer and the concomitant activity of the Holy Spirit in interpretation and proclamation. One interprets the divine books in a prayerful, humble mode. This practice of prayer is crucial for all scriptural interpretation. While the preacher—and more generally, the interpreter—seeks to understand what God communicates, he or she must be humble, fearing God, and seeking to know his will in these texts. To interpret otherwise—for Augustine—cannot happen. This suggests the crucial focus on the *telos* or "mind" of scripture, which informs his thought. Scripture has a fundamental point, an overarching unity, which can be summed up in the divine command to love God and love one's neighbors, the *regula dilectionis*. From this basis, interpretation springs. It is not as though he narrows all interpretations to this; instead, this is the field, as it

were, in which interpretation takes place. Because scripture's end is
to engender the double love of God and neighbor, it should be interpreted in light of this end, precisely because it is an instrument in
the divine economy to be used to aid people in their ongoing quest to
live in accordance with God's self-revelation in Christ. If, at the very
least, an interpreter does not find a meaning that either encourages
the love of God or neighbor, then the interpretation is necessarily
incomplete. That Augustine stresses the need to get to the author's
intention (whether the Holy Spirit or, say, Moses) shows he does not
think of scripture as dispensable, something that can be put aside
in exchange for the double-love command.[62] In addition, scripture is
not only about ethics, though ethics are crucial to the program. Piety
is necessary for interpretation, but it is not the entirety. This focus
on an ongoing pious life demonstrates the practices that inform the
hermeneutics of *De doctrina*.

Interpretation takes place within the context of two relationships:
the interpreter's relationship with God and with other humans. The
relationship with God forces the person to a status of humility, in
which he or she recognizes that nothing is possessed that has not
been given. Yet this relationship elevates the person because God
considers humans important enough to become one in the incarnation. The bond with humans is fundamental to the treatise. One
cannot interpret scripture except in community. This is not just
suggested but actually required by the fourth book. Throughout the
discussion, I have highlighted how *De doctrina* intends to be read
initially by ministers and preachers. If one fails to take into account
this ecclesial context, the ensuing description of the work will prove
one sided. The ecclesial, worshiping community is required in the *a
posteriori* hermeneutics espoused here. Though the work does seem
to have ministers as its intended readers, it nonetheless allows for
more general application, as Augustine handles many of the issues
in general terms. For instance, the prologue seems at first to be a
general discussion about three potential groups of objectors. In point
of fact, however, a close reading reveals that Augustine is attempting
to gain an ear for his work, a work intended for ministers. Only after
this has been noted can one make the move to a broader application

for general readers of scripture; to make the move too early would risk ignoring the bipartite structure of the work, a structure not just important but essential. Therefore, an interpretation of *De doctrina* that fails to take into account the fourth book misses the entire focus of the work. Without the delivery described in Book 4, the process of interpretation is incomplete. In order for Book 4 to make any sense, there has to be an ongoing gathering where a person stands up and explains difficulties in the text, where people listen and learn. The person teaches and exhorts, challenging his or her listeners to act in a manner that accords with what they learn. Yet these people, at times, cannot act; they require persuasion. For that reason—and because only God can persuade people of the truth—the speaker must pray that God would give words congruent with the needs of the gathering people. Once more, scriptural interpretation cannot be separated from the actual, lived response to scripture, which is why the preacher must exhort his or her listeners to act in accordance with what they hear taught from scripture. Again, the focus is on prayer and on God's activity, but as was noted several times, God's action does not preclude human action. In fact, God's action is the presupposition for any human action. This is a noncompetitive notion of the relationship between divine and human agents.

Within this community—where scripture is expounded by a person who has read and figured out what the difficult passages mean—people come together for mutual encouragement and support. They need this support because they recognize that they are living in an odd era, one that exists between the incarnation and the eschaton when they will see God face-to-face, when all will be made clear, when they will arrive home. Because of this location, the texts they interpret are interpreted in a fundamentally different way than at another point in history. One might say that, after the incarnation, the status of the *res* of the Old Testament has changed. No longer does the church read scripture as the Israelites did. Canaan cannot represent Canaan anymore because that is not where the church is heading. Indeed, when God commands his people to slay another nation, he can no longer mean this because, when he came in the incarnation, he taught a different way of living: the way of the double love. In other words, the *regula dilectionis* forbids this interpretation for the church. Its existence after the incarnation fundamentally changes the interpretive practices of this community, forcing them to read in certain directions, ruling out reading in other directions. The previous chapter addressed Jeanrond's worry that a reader's ideology would override the text, and this chapter provides a theological answer to his worry over certain ideologies of the text overriding the reader: the incarnation and the *regula dilectionis* do in fact restructure what one might find to be disconcerting portions of scripture without eliminating their ability to teach us something. Still, Jeanrond might respond that this move simply allows the ideology of the reader to override the text. However, when held in tension with the previous chapter's discussion and what follows in the next chapter, I would suggest that there are theological resources to address both worries precisely by holding text and community in their proper locations: God's providential ordering of the economy of salvation.[63]

Yet none of this rules out the practice of exegesis and knowledge of history. For Augustine, these can only aid in understanding what God wills through the divine books. God and humans are not in competition; he has raised them up and given them a task. They must determine what his will is and share it with one another. This can occur only in the context of a church that agrees on the reality of Christ's incarnation, that interprets the same books that have been handed on by the majority of churches, that seeks to love one another and God. All of this finds its summation in the *regula fidei*, which tells what the things of scripture are.

Interpretation for Augustine occurs within the church, where ministers help the congregation understand what God's will is. As this chapter has unfolded, it has become clear from a focus on the text that Hill's thesis has much to commend itself. Primarily, his attention to the ecclesial context makes his reading more persuasive than others that fail to take this context into account. This ecclesial focus can usefully be supplemented by the view that sees in *De doctrina* a hermeneutics, though, as I have suggested, it is an expanded hermeneutics, one that involves delivery to another. It has been helpful to keep in mind that *De doctrina* can, and does, have broader applications than just to preachers. As Pollmann points out, there are universalizing aspects to several of the discussions. While Augustine certainly is indebted to the rhetorical tradition, and while *De doctrina* might very well have aided the establishment of a Christian culture, the point of the treatise is far more narrow: there is a church of people who are bound in love, with ministers who must communicate God's will to them. They support one another, and they seek to know God's will together. God, rather than beaming his message into the brains of each individual, has chosen to have his will revealed first in the divine writings, and second, through the interpretation of those writings in the context of a community of Christians who live after the Christ event. Scripture and the church are vehicles in the divine economy, tools in God's providential ordering of the world. *De doctrina* focuses on interpreting scripture in this context, with due weight on the importance of human community. The focus on preachers throughout only highlights this communal location all the more forcefully. One can note this emphasis in the prologue and again at the end of the treatise, when Augustine discusses the explanation of scripture in terms of teaching, that is, clearing up ambiguities for others and prodding them on their way to living as God would have them live. The sermon—that is, the oral delivery to the church of what one finds in scripture—becomes paradigmatic for all delivery.

By focusing narrowly on the intended recipients, one is able to arrive at this conclusion, especially when taking into account the fact that—when compared to Jeanrond—Augustine's hermeneutics presupposes a specific community. By taking the sermon as the paradigm for biblical interpretation, one can hold together the two-part act of interpretation: understanding the biblical text and delivering that understanding to a certain group of people. In this day and age, there are certainly theological reasons for not restricting biblical interpretation solely to the clergy. Indeed, Augustine's text itself gives several useful rules that one can imagine applied to anyone even in the fourth and fifth centuries, but, as I have argued, the primary focus of the work is on teaching preachers how to preach. To some degree, that could have been an accident of history, but the insight that the sermon is the primary avenue of biblical interpretation will prove—as the next chapter will demonstrate—to be a helpful paradigm that strikes both ways in the contemporary climate: not only must our understanding of the biblical text be impeccable but also our presentation of this understanding to others in the church. That is, biblical exegesis must receive due attention; persuasive preaching must receive due attention; and, as an extension of preaching, theology—books, lectures, or debates—must be handled skillfully.

The problem could potentially be raised of how one discusses those outside the church. Augustine himself dealt on numerous occasions with those he considered to be on the outside. Perhaps the best way to treat this issue is to think in terms of speaking *through* the church *to* the world. As Paul says: "If, therefore, the whole church comes together and all speak in tongues, and outsiders or unbelievers enter, will they not say that you are out of your minds? But if all prophesy and an unbeliever or outsider enters, he is convicted by all, he is called to account by all, the secrets of his heart are disclosed, and so, falling on his face, he will worship God and declare that God is really among you" (1 Cor. 14:23–25, ESV). Here, the church is the place of conversion. In this passage, Paul insists that the Corinthians focus more on being intelligible to build up the church than on the outward manifestations of the Spirit, and he ends with a focus on the unbeliever. Thus, too, for biblical interpretation and the sermonic paradigm: the primary target audience is the church, and through it, the world.

To sum up, the portrait of the community that arises in *De doctrina* is a worshiping community, one led by ministers who interpret scripture to find God's will, and who then present what they have found to it. This is an ongoing practice, and Augustine's hermeneutics does not require him to step back in abstraction from it to formulate logically prior constraints to a subsequent practice to guard interpretation. Rather, his rules serve as an aid to the ongoing tradition of worship within the Christian community, personified most narrowly in the preaching ministers who are the original recipients of the treatise. Therefore, with this image of a worshiping church and its preachers, it becomes clearer just how Augustine's hermeneutics is, in fact, *a posteriori*. He has engaged head-on with those who were occupied in the practice of reading scripture and explaining it to congregations in worship. He does not view interpretive practice as fraught with misunderstanding. There are misunderstandings, certainly, or else he would not need to write this treatise, but his hermeneutics is more low level than the ones surveyed in the previous chapter. His rules are not prior constraints on a subsequent practice, as one might find in an *a priori* hermeneutics; they are more like helpful mid-flight correctives. His book comes into an already existing situation and seeks to assist it. Even his more general comments remain firmly rooted in the ongoing ecclesial practices of the worshiping church, where people read and share what they learn from scripture. To offer a brief description, then, of Augustine's *a posteriori* hermeneutics: it exists in the worshiping church, where the practice of piety takes center stage, where two rules structure the reading, the *regula fidei* and the *regula dilectionis*, one focusing on the true faith, the other on correct living. His hermeneutics has a balanced view of the human and the divine; both operate together; neither supersedes the other.

# *De doctrina christiana*
# and the Theological Interpretation
# of Scripture

The preceding discussion regarding the presupposed communal context of *De doctrina* means that Augustine can now be placed in dialogue with a contemporary theologian who presupposes a similar communal context, who, in other words, has an *a posteriori* hermeneutics. In a recent work, Daniel Treier argues that the "essential theme" in contemporary appeals to a more theological engagement with scripture—a "new movement" he labels "theological interpretation of Scripture"—could be seen as a concern for the church.[1] If Treier is correct, then Augustine could be placed into dialogue with any number of current practitioners. Treier suggests there are four basic strands of theological interpretation stemming from Karl Barth:[2] the canonical approach, which is broadly associated with Brevard Childs;[3] the narrative approach, of which David Kelsey, Hans Frei, and George Lindbeck stand as prime examples;[4] the communal approach, which is associated with Stanley Hauerwas in particular, and which may also be linked with Stephen Fowl;[5] and an eclectic approach, which Treier suggests is personified by Francis Watson.[6] This is not to mention the other strands of theological interpretation stemming from the Roman Catholic Church and Evangelical circles.[7] If the goal is to let Augustine set the parameters for dialogue, then it makes sense—in light of the previous chapter's discussion—to place Augustine into dialogue with the position that Treier describes as "Reading with Others."[8] Still, if Treier's diagnosis is correct—that the core proposal of the "movement" "theological interpretation of scripture" concerns the church—then there will inevitably be overlap with the other positions.

Because of his nuanced position, Stephen Fowl represents a good theologian with whom to place Augustine into dialogue. By doing so, the distinctiveness of Augustine's approach will become visible, and in the course of discussion, it will become apparent that his program helps balance some potential weaknesses in Fowl's. But as the introduction stated, this is not an exercise in using Augustine to criticize a bad example of theological interpretation. The goal is for Augustine's example to make a strong program stronger.

Throughout the preceding chapters, it has become increasingly clear that Augustine's treatise is not intended to guard his practice from the start in a theoretical sense; that is, De doctrina represents an a posteriori hermeneutics because its goal is the training of ministers who will read scripture to find out what God's will is so that they can turn to deliver this message to a congregation. This congregation comprises people who need to hear a message from outside, who need to be persuaded to act in accordance with God's will. Yet Augustine's hermeneutics cannot simply be labeled "local" because he makes use of several rather general discussions in order to elucidate the ongoing practice of interpreting scripture for delivering its message to a congregation. I have described De doctrina as an expanded hermeneutics, that is, a hermeneutics that—in contrast to hermeneutics since Schleiermacher—includes a turn to rhetoric. To reiterate, De doctrina does not represent a hermeneutics and a rhetoric. Further, it is not just a hermeneutics influenced by rhetoric. Instead, it is a hermeneutics that encompasses rhetoric. Within any act of theological interpretation, a turn to delivery is involved. Without this turn to delivery, the interpretation is necessarily incomplete. For Augustine, the delivery envisioned is paradigmatically that of the sermon to a congregation. Other forms are assumed, but these are only extensions of the primary act of preaching. The dual focus on understanding and delivery will become important as the current chapter progresses.

Fowl perhaps comes closest to Augustine in the dual focus on the relationship between scripture and the ecclesial community.[9] Fowl's program is by all appearances Augustinian, though he ends up making moves that Augustine would not.[10] For Fowl, scripture has an extrinsic *use*. In other words, scripture is important insofar as it is a tool put to a particular use by a specific community. To interpret scripture is to use it to move closer to God. This construal stands in contrast to Augustine, whose language is comparable but who thinks scripture has an intrinsic *telos*. It is itself, on the basis of its internal structure, a vehicle that moves readers closer to God and to one another. The programs are similar at first because they both construe scripture in functional terms, but differences begin to emerge upon closer inspection. Likewise, both interpreters are interested in a "virtuous community," but they approach this concept from opposite sides. For Fowl, the primary concern is how the community's existing virtue affects how well or how poorly it reads scripture. In other words, a preexisting virtue is necessary for proper scriptural interpretation. Augustine, on the other hand, speaks more about virtue being produced by scriptural interpretation. The church needs to be taught and persuaded to live in the double love of God and neighbor. Both interpreters also address the way in which the Old Testament remains authoritative for the church. For Fowl, it is not theologically helpful to argue over a text's "meaning." He is especially concerned with equating "meaning" with "authorial intention" because too close an association between the author's intention and the Old Testament's normative "meaning" will render the Old Testament unsuitable for Christians. For Augustine, however, what the authors meant is theologically important. After comparing the two, some conclusions can be offered for contemporary theological interpretation. Though Augustine's program looks different than Fowl's, they share many of the same interests, as the conclusion will demonstrate. By offering significant correctives to Fowl's program,

Augustine's ideas will help define more precisely what a theological hermeneutics should be. *De doctrina* highlights the necessity of both the text and the community; neither exists without the other. In other words, neither biblical theology nor theological interpretation (as defined by those surveyed in this chapter) is entirely correct. One needs theology as well as resources for reading. One needs a theological hermeneutics that includes rhetoric.

## THE *SENSUS COMMUNIS*

Again, many theologians have recently stressed how important the ecclesial community is for scriptural interpretation. In fact, some of the ones discussed in the third chapter who argue for a local hermeneutics draw the conclusion that the church is indispensable.[11] Even those whose main interest does not lie in theological hermeneutics per se want to stress how necessary the church is for biblical interpretation.[12] Those espousing such a need for the church tend to see themselves in reaction against the predominance of more historical forms of interpretation.[13] One way to combat such a focus on history is to argue for the privileging of "interpretive communities."[14] One community is the academic, scholarly community that utilizes more objective and historical methods of discovering what the Bible means (or meant). The other is the ecclesial, worshiping community.[15] Depending on which community does the interpreting—so the argument goes—the results will be wildly divergent. Some have sought to bridge the two communities by developing what has become "biblical theology," where the tools of biblical criticism are put to theological use.[16] Others see this exercise as futile and want to limit, if not fully excise, such methods from their repertoire.[17] The majority, however, want to find some form of middle ground.[18] In each instance, the point remains: the Bible is the church's scripture and can (must) be read as such.

For example, in an influential article, Frei argues that there are dangers in utilizing general hermeneutical theory in anything more than an ad hoc way.[19] Instead, the literal sense (in Frei's terminology, "the established or 'plain' reading") is the way that a religious community reads its sacred text.[20] The *sensus literalis* is tied strictly to the community that interprets the text.[21] Though this is a slightly odd and perhaps unhistorical use of the term "literal sense," Frei is not alone in stressing the connection between the literal sense and the ecclesial community.[22] Robert Jenson emphatically argues that its ecclesial location should norm scriptural reading: "There can be no churchly reading of Scripture that is not activated and guided by the church's teaching. But to go back to an earlier point, there can be no reading of the Bible that is not churchly. Therefore there can be no reading of the unitary Bible that is not motivated and guided by the church's teaching. We will either read the Bible under the guidance of the church's established doctrine, or we will not read the Bible at all."[23] For Jenson, the Bible exists because the church assembled it.[24] For that reason, one cannot simply go and read this unitary book in any way because it only exists as a product of the church. If one fails to recognize this ecclesial location, the book can and does break into its constitutive parts.[25]

Such interpretive proposals view themselves as alternatives to the standard practices of biblical interpretation that occur in the academy. It is not my intention to provide yet another summary account of what is wrong with biblical interpretation after the Enlightenment,[26] or even to argue that theological interests are (or are not) corrosive to biblical interpretation.[27] Rather, I want to fill out what theological interpretation looks like. The adjective "theological" requires some appeal to the ecclesial community. For instance, *The Scripture Project* states in its sixth thesis: "Faithful interpretation of Scripture invites and presupposes participation in the community brought into being by God's redemptive action—the church."[28] Indeed, even John Barton feels compelled to address such attempts to relocate biblical interpretation in an ecclesial context: "There is a battle going on at the moment between those who believe that biblical criticism is too much in the grip of a secular and skeptical spirit and those who think it has still not managed to escape the hand of ecclesiastical and religious authority. My sympathies lie on the whole more with the second group. . . . I believe it is high time for biblical critics to stop arguing defensively that their work does, after all, little real damage to faith, and to start claiming firmly that a faith uninformed by it is, at this point in the history of Christian thought, simply an ostrich."[29] Though from an opposing position, Barton's statements show there is a movement within contemporary biblical interpretation that focuses on the need for an ecclesial focus when engaging with scripture. And because of resonances from *De doctrina*, it is this movement with which I am concerned.

Barton's worry—that theological interpretation might overwhelm the meaning of the text—is helpful when trying to narrow down the particular scholar with whom to place Augustine in dialogue.[30] Failing to grasp the meaning of the biblical text is by no means impossible. It could take the form of a christological overlay of the Old Testament, as one finds in the oft-criticized Wilhelm Vischer.[31] Or it might take the form of a reader not addressing the history of the text at all.

For example, Hauerwas argues forcefully for the necessity of locating biblical interpretation within the church.[32] He states: "Of course the Church creates the meaning of Scripture, but that does not invite an orgy of subjectivist arbitrariness. Rather the Church must continue to return to the Scriptures because they are so interesting, given the Church's task to live as a people of memory in a world without memory. The Church returns time and time again to Scripture not because it is trying to find the Scripture's true meaning, but because Christians believe that God has promised to speak through Scripture so that the Church will remain capable of living faithfully by remembering well."[33] Hauerwas wants to discuss not the meaning of scripture but its usefulness.[34] When one turns to his commentary on Matthew, the question can be posed: How important is the gospel for his interpretation? Hauerwas is, he says, retelling the story that Matthew tells as "a ruminative overlay."[35] His primary focus is not writing *about* Matthew but writing *with* Matthew. He assumes that "the gospel was written for us."[36] In light of these comments, it is not surprising that Hauerwas, at times, interprets the text in a way that many readers will find difficult to follow, and in ways that add weight to the force of Barton's arguments against locating reading in the church.

For instance,[37] in his chapter on Matthew 14–15, Hauerwas discusses the feeding of the four thousand.[38] He describes the early church's allegorization, which, he says, interpreted the seven loaves as the seven Christian virtues and the two fish as the law and the gospel. He then states: "It may be objected that there is nothing in the text to suggest that Jesus is using the seven fish to represent our need for courage, temperance, justice, practical wisdom, faith, hope, and charity, but neither is such a reading excluded by the text. Such readings are always possible. *The crucial issue is whether such a construal builds up the body of the church.*"[39] The point, Hauerwas argues, is not whether the text of Matthew says what one claims but whether what one says on the basis of the text builds up the church.[40] How this happens exactly is never fully taken up. Hauerwas does think a reading can be deemed wrong because the text excludes it, but how such a negative criterion can exist without the concomitant positive ability to argue that a text says *something* seems never to be addressed. The text is secondary; the interpreter should be more concerned with building up the community than detailing what the text says. In the terms I am using, the focus should be on rhetoric— on the location of interpretation within the ecclesial community— even if that is at the expense of hermeneutics.

Though Hauerwas is perhaps more interested in the use-value of the Bible for the ecclesial community than with the actual interpretation of the biblical texts, there are more nuanced proponents of theological interpretation. Fowl represents one of the better options, with attention both to interpretation and to the necessity of the community. I have already described in the previous chapter some of what makes Augustine's program ecclesial. In this chapter, the dialogue with Fowl will bring out other aspects of *De doctrina* that have not yet been addressed.

## IN DIALOGUE: STEPHEN FOWL AND AUGUSTINE

For several years, Fowl has been a significant voice in the debate concerning the role of theology in biblical interpretation. Rather

than describing his project as "biblical theology,"[41] Fowl prefers
the description "theological interpretation."[42] Biblical theology, he
argues, searches for unity within the biblical text. In his opinion, this
is a futile quest philosophically: "[T]he notion of texts having properties that can be mined by anyone using the appropriate method
is deeply problematic on philosophical grounds."[43] For Fowl, one
should not come to the text in order to excavate its meaning because
"meaning" itself is a question-begging term. Instead, one should
discuss the "interpretive interests" of a certain community of readers, in this case, the church.[44] Throughout his work, Fowl offers several definitions of theological interpretation of scripture:

> I take the theological interpretation of scripture to be that prac-
> tice whereby theological concerns and interests inform and are
> informed by a reading of scripture.[45]

> I treat scriptural interpretation as a practice which both shapes
> and is shaped by Christian convictions and practices and which
> both calls forth and relies upon the presence of a community
> manifesting a certain common life.[46]

> Commenting on Scripture is a theological discipline in that one
> expects that by attention to the words of Scripture one will hear
> the voice of God. . . . More generally, then, one of the aims of
> theological commentary must be to allow others to hear God's
> voice.[47]

> In short, I no longer think that a general theory of textual mean-
> ing is crucial to interpreting Scripture theologically. If one's
> exegetical practice is governed by some sort of general herme-
> neutical theory, then it is very hard to avoid the situation where
> theological interpretation of Scripture becomes the activity of
> applying theological concerns to exegesis done on other, non-
> theological grounds. One of the points I have tried to argue per-
> sistently over the past several years is that the key to interpreting
> theologically lies in keeping theological concerns primary to all

others. In this way, theology becomes a form of exegesis, not its result.[48]

Christians interpret scripture as part of their ongoing struggle to enter into deeper communion with God.[49]

[T]heological interpretation of Scripture will involve those habits, dispositions, and practices that Christians bring to their varied engagements with Scripture so that they can interpret, debate, and embody Scripture in ways that will enhance their journey towards their proper end in God.[50]

Several things can be noted. First, Fowl stresses the need for theology to influence and be influenced by reading scripture. As one scholar says, there is a "bi-directional movement between the biblical texts and Christian doctrine and practice."[51] Second, one attends to scripture not as any other text; rather, through the words of the biblical text, God speaks.[52] The theological interpreter seeks to help others hear what God says through those words. Third, one can note the way that Fowl disparages general hermeneutical theory. Again, this text is not like every other text. Theological interpretation is not a two-stage process where one first seeks to grasp the meaning of the text and in a subsequent move applies this meaning theologically.[53] In fact, Fowl's stance on "meaning" precludes such a process from the start. Theological interpretation is itself a form of theology,[54] and by "theological," he has in mind a connection to a certain community, the church. Precisely in connection to this community theological issues are raised. Further, one reads scripture so that it impinges on the community's corporate life: "Christian friends read Scripture so that they can engage each other about how to fit their stories into the economy of salvation. At the same time, they must learn to order and direct their reading of Scripture in the light of the economy of salvation. . . . The deeper one drinks from Scripture's well, the better one is equipped to fit one's own life and the lives of one's friends into the ongoing drama of God's saving purposes. The better one grasps the movements of this drama in its past, present, and future episodes, the better one can then read Scripture."[55] Again, one can note the dialogical nature of Fowl's program. Scripture and community (more precisely, its beliefs and practices) both form and are formed by the other. God speaks through these texts to a certain community that uses the texts in order to move closer to him. How well the community has been formed in the past affects how well it can read scripture: "When Christians' convictions about sin and their practices of forgiveness and reconciliation become distorted or inoperative, then Christians will find that they cannot discuss, interpret, and embody scripture in ways that will build up rather than tear apart the body of Christ."[56] From the preceding, it is clear that Fowl and Augustine have much in common. Both stress the community in which interpretation occurs. Both stress the need to embody one's interpretation of scripture. Both speak of God's voice coming through scripture. Both assume scripture helps the reader move toward his or her proper *telos*, fellowship with God. Both actually interpret scripture in the context of their discussions. In the details, however, it will become evident that the two diverge in somewhat significant ways.

### The Telos of Scripture

In later articles and essays, Fowl stresses the need to think theologically about what exactly scripture's role in the economy of salvation is. Another way to frame this issue might be to focus on the ontology of scripture,[57] but Fowl is similar to Augustine in exactly this manner. He does not talk so much about what scripture *is* as about how scripture *functions*.[58] Often, he notes, discussions about what scripture *is* tend to employ a christological analogy that focuses on scripture's status as the word of God and the work of human hands.[59] Admittedly there are many ways to utilize such an analogy, but his main concern is scholars who employ the christological analogy precisely to legitimate (and at times to require) the use of historical-critical tools.[60] Fowl summarizes such a view by emphasizing that one's convictions need not play a role in the interpretation: "Biblical interpretation becomes an end in itself whose goal is either the unearthing or the construction of textual meaning(s)."[61] Whether or not his depiction of such a stance is too dismissive, his point remains: "scriptural interpretation is not an end in itself for Christians."[62]

In order to specify the proper end of interpretation, Fowl pushes back beyond the text of the Bible to the revelation of the triune God:[63]

> In creation God freely wills not simply the existence of humans created in the image of God, but God also desires fellowship with humans, offering them a share in the divine life. This is both the intention with which God created and the end for which God created. Given this, God's self-presentation or self-communication is an essential element in establishing the fellowship God freely desires to have with humans. Thus, God's self-revelation to humans is both the source and content of a Christian doctrine of revelation. . . . In this light, the written text of scripture is subsidiary to and dependent upon a notion of revelation that is itself directly dependent on God's triune being. . . . This recalibrates the relationships between God, scripture, and Christians in several interesting ways. For Christians, the ends of reading, interpreting, and embodying scripture are determined decisively by the ends of God's self-revelation, drawing humans into ever deeper communion with the triune God.[64]

Because of the triune God's desire to reveal himself to his creation, and because scripture is one vehicle God utilizes to accomplish this—it is "the result of God's condescension to human sinfulness"—scriptural interpretation has a goal.[65] One reads scripture in order to draw nearer to God, and this objective provides "an overall set of aims and purposes" that should inform a Christian reading of scripture.[66] For Fowl, therefore, scripture is a vehicle that, when interpreted, brings Christian readers to their proper end, fellowship with God. When coupled with Fowl's dismissal of the term "meaning," it can be suggested that scripture is an inanimate object, awaiting an external agent—whether humans or God—to use it in order to accomplish a certain act. That is, scripture has an extrinsic *use*, one that arises when the church utilizes it in a certain way.[67] Scripture is a vehicle because scriptural interpretation has an end: drawing closer to God. In describing scripture as a vehicle, Fowl explicitly invokes Augustine.[68]

As he approaches the end of Book 1 of *De doctrina*, Augustine stresses that the end of all scripture is to engender the double love of God and neighbor, and continues: "Therefore, this entire temporal dispensation was established for our salvation by divine providence so that we might know this truth and have the ability to act on it; and we must use it, not with such permanent love and enjoyment, but rather as transitory means, as our vehicles or other such instruments (there may be a better way to say this) so that we love that by which we are born on account of that to which we are born" (1.35.39). Scripture has a two-part function here: it teaches the truth and, by doing so, gives the ability to act on it. One can already note a distinction between this definition and Fowl's. For Fowl, God does somehow speak through scripture, but one does not approach it to find a meaning. For Augustine, however, there is a meaning—the love of God and neighbor—that must be discovered in scripture and its discovery engenders it. Scripture, in other words, has an intrinsic *telos*. It is established by God in such a way that its internal structure points to this end. Worded differently, the *regula fidei* and the *regula dilectionis*—the two rules used to norm scriptural interpretation within the ecclesial community—arise from the communicative intent discovered through the scriptural texts. That is, for Augustine, there is something within scripture, while for Fowl, the issue is how an external agent uses it. As further exploration will demonstrate, Augustine thinks the discovery of what the authors mean becomes the basis for the ability to act. Precisely because *De doctrina* is a hermeneutics, one can note the necessity of interpretive practices to ascertain what the intrinsic meaning of the text is. Scripture is here defined within a larger framework: it is the vehicle that moves its reader on a trajectory to God. One does not love scripture for itself; rather, it is transitory, loved only because it is taking the reader to God. This is Augustine's summary of Book 1; he has been working up to this point through credal statements, as the third chapter demonstrated. For him, scripture has an intrinsic *telos* connected to what the reader finds in it. In contrast to Fowl, he can say not only that the text should be used in a specific manner, but also that the text, because of its inherent structure, operates in this manner. He fills out just how scripture does this in light of God's relationship with humanity.

It should be kept in mind throughout that his express purpose in writing *De doctrina* is to teach ministers how to interpret scripture. The flow of Book I then makes sense: he defines what one can expect to find in scripture by describing just what its *telos* is. Throughout the first book, he utilizes the metaphor of a journey and the need to recognize that the journey itself is not the point; rather, the destination is most important, and that destination is God:

> Therefore, since that truth, which lives unchangeably, should be enjoyed to the full [*perfruendum sit*], and since in it, God the Trinity, the author and creator of the universe, looks after the things which he made, the mind must be purified, so that it might be able to see that light and to hold fast to what is seen. Let us consider this purification to be like a walk or a voyage to our homeland. For we are not moved to him who is present everywhere by moving in space, but in good devotion and virtuous character. We cannot do this, except that Wisdom itself condescended to adapt itself to our great weakness and provided us with an example for living, not in any way other than as a human [*homine*], because we are also humans [*homines*]. . . . Therefore, although Wisdom is our homeland, it also made itself the way to our homeland. (1.10.10–11.11; cf. 1.34.38)[69]

At this point, scripture has not entered Augustine's formulation. Instead, the point is that the triune God wants to bring humanity to himself and has done so by becoming human.[70] Humanity cannot reach God because of weakness; therefore, God becomes both the destination and the road. The similarity with Fowl's characterization can be noted: both focus on the inability of humanity to make it to God and the concomitant necessity of God's condescension, and both highlight the fact that scriptural interpretation is located within the economy of salvation.

As he continues in his credal discussion, Augustine locates the necessity of the church firmly in its relationship to Christ's death, resurrection, and ascension. His death removed the barriers of humanity's return to God (1.18.17). This return, however, takes place in the ecclesial community: "He has therefore given keys to his church, so that whatever it looses on earth might also be loosed in heaven, and whatever it binds on earth, might also be bound in heaven. So that for whoever does not believe his sins are forgiven in God's church, they are not forgiven. But whoever does believe, and in correction, turns from these sins, is established in the bosom of the same church and healed by the same faith and correction" (1.18.17, alluding to Matt. 16:19). Here, Augustine continues to describe humanity as on a journey to God; this journey has been aided by God's descent in the form of Jesus Christ and is now aided by membership in the ecclesial community. Scripture—the interpretation of which is the very subject under discussion—has not yet entered the picture. So far, Augustine has spent his time discussing how one should relate to certain *res*, either by using (*uti*) them or by enjoying (*frui*) them.

Now, however, he begins to bring in scripture:

> Therefore, because there is no need to command someone to love himself and his body; that is, because we love that which we are and that which is below us but relates to us nonetheless, according to an unshakeable law of nature, which is seen even in animals (for even animals love themselves and their bodies), it remains for us to receive commandments concerning that which is above us and that which is next to us. "You shall love," it says, "the Lord your God with all your heart, all your soul, and all your mind. And you shall love your neighbor as yourself. The whole law and all the prophets hang on these two commandments." Thus, the end of the commandment is love, and it is twofold, that is, of God and neighbor. (1.26.27)[71]

Scripture exists to instruct people how to love God and their neighbor. That does not mean that scripture simply exists to promote ethics, but it does mean that the end of all scriptural interpretation is embodiment. Scripture exists to bring people into a properly ordered love of God and neighbor: "The one who lives a just and holy life, who is a sound judge of things, is one who has a properly ordered love" (1.27.28).[72] One loves God in himself, but one loves one's neighbor as a way of loving God: "God shows mercy to us on account of his own kindness, and we show it to one another on account of his kindness; that is, he has compassion on us so that we might enjoy him, and we have compassion on one another so that we might enjoy him" (1.30.33). Again, Augustine leaves scripture behind to talk about loving one's neighbor. Before he reaches the concluding section with which this discussion began, he stresses that Christ is the way to God, but even he did not want humanity to pay attention only to his flesh: "Instead, he wants us to cross over, not clinging weakly to temporal things—although they were undertaken by him for our salvation—but rather let us eagerly run through them, so that we might approach and draw near to him who has liberated our nature from temporal things and placed it at the right hand of the Father" (1.34.38). The Incarnation, in other words, was meant as a bridge to get humanity to God. The ascension itself demonstrates for Augustine that Christ wants us to move through the temporal order toward communion with the eternal God.

Finally, at this point, Augustine can state that the entire temporal dispensation has been established as a means of transport to God.[73] In this context, the temporal dispensation Augustine has in mind is scripture: "Anyone, therefore, who thinks he has understood the holy scriptures, or perhaps a certain part of them, in a way that his understanding does not build up that double love of God and neighbor has not yet understood them" (1.36.40). Scripture exists to bring about a certain response, which is progress in loving God and neighbor, and it does so in connection with its communicative intent. He has spent the entirety of Book 1 talking about *res* and how one should love the *res* and has, in the process, subordinated the *signa* of the scriptural words to the *res* beyond them. It will become clear, however, that this subordination is not as dichotomous as it might seem. Scripture is a vehicle, nothing more. This even leads him to state that scripture can—in a sense—be dispensed with: "A person, therefore, who relies on faith, hope, and love, and clings to them unshakingly, does not require the scriptures except to instruct others" (1.39.43). This emphasizes scripture's subordinate status— as the entirety of Book 1 has done. Scripture finds its location in the context of the triune God's gracious condescension to humanity. It is a vehicle to bring them to him. Even those who might not need scripture themselves need it to teach others. Indeed, they have only gotten to where they are by learning from it: "*By these mechanisms* [the scriptures], so to speak, such instruction of faith, hope, and love has arisen, that holding to something perfect, they do not seek those things which are only partly perfect, 'perfect' of course referring to what is possible in this life" (1.39.43).[74] Scripture plays a secondary role in the sense that it refers beyond itself. Again, scripture's *telos* is not simply a function of the community's use. Scripture itself exists to deliver humanity to a certain (metaphorical) place. Only after establishing this fact does Augustine state: "Wherefore, when someone has learned that the end of the commandment is love 'from a pure heart and a good conscience and genuine faith,' he will relate every understanding of the divine scriptures to these three [faith, hope, and love], and he may then approach the interpretation [*tractatio*] of these books without fear" (1.40.44, citing 1 Tim. 1:5). Scriptural interpretation, for Augustine, occurs within the context of understanding who God is—the triune God—and what he has done to bring creatures to himself—come in the person of Jesus Christ. Scripture teaches how to relate to God and neighbor in love. In spite of the claim that scripture can be dispensed with, it is clear that Augustine wants to stress the need to interpret it well, as the subsequent books stress.

Scriptural interpretation takes place within a certain network of relationships: God and sinful humans, Jesus Christ and humans, the church and humans, scripture and humans, individuals and other humans. Scripture's character is defined precisely by its function within this divine economy. The church is also defined in relation to Christ's death, resurrection, and ascension. This is not just any interpretive community. Rather, it is a community called into being for a specific purpose. The scriptural texts are also utilized with a certain aim because of how they are located in the divine economy. One can note a more precise definition of the scriptural books in the later sections of *De doctrina*, when Augustine's topic is the actual practice of interpretation.

One's aim when reading scripture is, he says in 2.5.6, "to find nothing other than the thoughts and desires of those by whom it was written and through them the will of God, according to which we believe such men were speaking." God's utilization of this text to bring humanity to him is linked somehow to those who wrote it. This will become important later, but for now it is enough to note that the scriptural books have a *telos*—they are a vehicle bringing people closer to God and one another—and this is connected to the revelation of God's will in these texts through the human act of communication through human words. God has made scripture a vehicle precisely by speaking through human authors. After defining the canon in 2.8.13, he states: "In all these books, those who fear God and are tamed by their piety seek the will of God" (2.9.14). This is a reference back to the first two stages of Augustine's seven-staged ascent to wisdom. One reads the scriptural texts to find God's will and, in doing so, one is brought nearer to him. Book 1 has made clear that God's will is the double love of God and neighbor, but Augustine here specifies "commandments for living" (*praecepta vivendi*) and "rules for believing" (*regulae credendi*), which correspond to the *regula dilectionis* and the *regula fidei*, as the previous chapter argued. God's will is somehow found in scripture through the words of those who wrote the texts. And the discovery of his will in the human words of the text is intimately connected to scripture's nature as a vehicle to God.

At this point, one can note a distinction between Augustine and Fowl. For Fowl, it is not helpful to try to resolve interpretive disputes by appealing to the "meaning" of the biblical text. As I will outline below, Fowl thinks such a move leads to question-begging polemic, and he suggests the argument should take place at the deeper level of what the aims of scriptural reading are. To a certain extent, Augustine would agree, but he thinks that the communicative act of the scriptural authors is theologically necessary. For Fowl, the quest for meaning within the biblical texts is theologically (and philosophically) problematic because it abstracts the interpretation of the text from its location in the ecclesial community.[75] Augustine, on the other hand, holds the two together. The text is at the same time a vehicle that is used by the ecclesial community and a collection of human texts through which God speaks *by the means* of the human authors' words. There is no dichotomy between the two. The text's status as vehicle to God is located precisely in its connection to the human authors who wrote it. Fowl allows that—at times— one might decide that authorial intention is important to theological interpretation, but he argues that this becomes seriously problematic when utilizing the Old Testament.[76] Augustine, in contrast, locates the quest of the interpreter precisely in determining what the authors say (1.36.40). He thinks the text intrinsically has a *telos* that is connected to uncovering the meaning of the human authors, while Fowl thinks the text moves people closer to God when used correctly in the appropriate network of practices. For Fowl, humans have a *telos*, and they use scriptural interpretation to reach it. The agents who interpret scripture do so with a certain goal in mind. It has an extrinsic *use*. In contrast, Augustine construes the text as having an intrinsic *telos* due to the way God speaks to humans through humans.

For Augustine, scripture is a vehicle to God, and while Fowl says something similar, the way he completes the picture differs fundamentally. When reading his works, it often appears that scripture's existence—albeit connected to the triune God's self-revelation—is an a priori. Scripture just *is*. If it is defined in any specific way, it becomes a function of community self-identification: "Most importantly . . . I have tried to show the integral connections between Christian scriptural interpretation, Christian doctrine and practices, and Christians' abilities to form and sustain a certain type of common life."[77] In addition, the community seems simply to exist. For all of his talk about the importance of the Christian community, Fowl seems to lack a precise definition of just what this community looks like. Because he does not locate scripture and the community in the divine economy as fully as Augustine does, Fowl runs the risk of describing scripture as a vehicle not because it is established as such by God, but because the already-existing community uses it, an already-existing text, in a certain way. Augustine, on the other hand, locates the community first in relation to the Incarnation, which is in turn located in God's self-revelation to sinful humanity. One might categorize the difference in these terms: Fowl seems to have a self-contained community, while Augustine has a community of radical dependency. A prior divine reality grounds not just the scriptural texts (as perhaps with Fowl), but that prior reality for Augustine grounds both scripture and the church. By locating scripture and the community in it, Augustine conceives of scripture as having an inherent *telos*. Scripture moves humanity closer to God and to one another because of its own internal structure. It and the community find their being in the triune God's relationship to humanity. God establishes both with certain intrinsic ends.

At this point, Fowl might retort that it was possible for Augustine to hold a view of scripture that assumed that the entity named "scripture" contains something like a *telos*, but in this day and age, such a position is untenable. "Texts," Fowl says, "don't have ideologies,"[78] and, presumably, if they do not "have" meanings or ideologies, they cannot—strictly speaking—be said to "have" a *telos*. At least insofar as Fowl insists that scriptural interpretation requires more tools than those arising from philosophical hermeneutics, Augustine would agree. And, indeed, in the contemporary context, Fowl is correct to insist that scriptural interpretation cannot be abstracted from a network and range of practices, all of which Augustine could presume when he wrote *De doctrina*, especially considering he wrote it, at least initially, for priests. And Augustine is nuanced; he does not think the text "contains" something called a *telos*. Rather, he thinks the text has a *telos* in connection with the communicative intentions of the authors, who were inspired by the Holy Spirit. The text contains their words, thus it itself can and should be seen as, in some sense, "having" a meaning and a *telos*, but again, for Augustine, interpretation is a two-part process that requires turning to the text from within the community, in the context of the seven-stage ascent, and then turning from the text to the community to deliver what one understands God to be saying through the words of the prophets and apostles.

In our contemporary context, it seems reasonable to suggest that both Fowl and Augustine need to be heeded. Fowl is perhaps too quick to dismiss the very specific role Augustine gives to scripture itself, but Fowl is correct to note that the text is not activated, as it were, until it is interpreted. As both theologians point out, this interpretation must occur in the proper context for it to accomplish its divinely ordered goal of engendering the double love of God and neighbor. Fowl makes explicit the communal practices Augustine could presume, while Augustine reminds Fowl—as I will argue below—that authors need not be dismissed when making just such an appeal.

Both Augustine and Fowl talk about the function of scripture before they talk about how to engage in the actual practice of interpretation. Both view scripture as a vehicle that brings humanity closer to God, but Augustine describes scripture and the community as both being radically dependent on God, while Fowl—because of his rightful insistence on the interconnected nature of the two—seems to take both the community and the text as *a prioris*. For Augustine, the triune God reveals himself to sinful people. He does so by coming himself as a person, and calling the church into being, giving it keys to bind and loose. Only when Augustine has established all of these things does he then fill out scripture's role, and he does so by highlighting the text's own inner structure. Scripture's *telos* is that it brings the specific community of the church closer to God and to one another when they approach this text to hear the will of God as he has revealed it in the words of the prophets and apostles. Because his is an *a posteriori* hermeneutics, the theological location of the church and scripture and their relationship with one another are the presuppositions underlying the practice that he supplements with

*De doctrina.* His hermeneutics can utilize general discussions—as the preceding chapters demonstrate—but always within this theological matrix.

## The Virtuous Community

Like their descriptions of the biblical text, Fowl and Augustine initially appear to offer similar descriptions of the ecclesial community, but this similarity gives way to a profound disagreement. In the previous chapter, several conclusions were drawn concerning Augustine's presupposed interpretive community, and a few notable conclusions should be recalled. Crucial to the discussion was his focus on the church as a group of people knitted together in love. Because God values humanity, he does not transmit his will directly into individual brains. Rather, he speaks through the writers of scripture; by doing so, he creates a need for interpreter-preachers. They must turn to scripture to discover what God's will is, but this is only done with the aim of sharing with others what they discover. I described this two-part structure as an expanded hermeneutics. Another crucial conclusion in the previous chapter was the aim of the rhetoric described in Book 4—to move the listeners to practice piety. Piety, as *De doctrina* sees it, is the act of putting into practice what one learns from scripture: "And for this reason, teaching is necessary. For people can either do or not do what they know. But who could tell them that they ought to do something that they do not know? For that reason, persuasion is not necessary, because it is not always useful, such as when the hearer consents simply from teaching or even from delighting. Persuasion is a victory because a listener may be taught and delighted, but still not give assent" (4.12.28). In other words, for Augustine, persuasion is secondary to teaching because the very act of learning the truth can in fact prompt correct action. Furthermore, simply persuading someone to act cannot be disconnected from the act of teaching him or her the truth, which the reader of *De doctrina* knows from Book 1. The order is teaching the truth, then if necessary persuading, and finally acting. This suggests that piety comes as a result of biblical interpretation.

*De doctrina*, therefore, stresses the need for a virtuous community, a church that puts into practice what scripture teaches her through her ministers.[79]

Fowl also stresses the need for a virtuous community. In his case, however, the virtuous community exists on the opposite side of the equation, as it were. Above, I quoted his contention that a church without the proper convictions cannot interpret or embody scripture in an edifying way.[80] In that context, his concern is the necessity of such ecclesial practices as repentance and forgiveness for scriptural interpretation. He fills out the picture of a virtuous community in *Engaging Scripture*.[81] For Fowl, to prevent a slip into interpretive anarchy, one appeals to the idea of a virtuous community (in his terminology, the "vigilant community and the virtuous reader"). Having dispensed with textual meaning, he argues that this need not imply relativism.[82] He states:

> If Christians are to read and embody scripture in ways that result in lives lived faithfully before God, they will need to recognize themselves as sinners. Moreover, they will need to train and form new members so that they, too, can identify themselves in this way.
>
> Recognizing that one is a sinner must be done within the context of a community that engages in the practices of forgiveness, repentance, and reconciliation if that recognition is to result in lives manifesting single-minded attention to God. Further, recognizing oneself as a sinner is necessary but it must lead to growth in virtue, particularly growth in virtue as an interpreter of scripture.[83]

Two things should be noted: the community is the location of formation, and scriptural interpretation is the result of this formation. Fowl is primarily concerned here with providing tools to prevent communities from interpreting scripture in such a way as to underwrite sinful practices. Rather than appeal to the question-begging term "meaning" as the locus of authority, Fowl thinks it is better to appeal to the "vigilant community" as the place where virtuous readers are formed.

In *De doctrina*, the community is also the location of formation—it occurs in the interaction between text, interpreter-preacher, and congregation—but it is primarily a result of interpretation, not the other way around. That is, the interpreter-preacher comes to the text with the express intention of discovering what God's will is for his church. Understanding the biblical text alone does not constitute an interpretation; what is understood must be communicated to the community so that its members can act correctly by loving God and neighbor. They need to hear how they should act. The underlying presupposition is that the community may well not be virtuous prior to coming to the text. For Fowl, in contrast, the community's right standing provides the proper context to interpretation. He agrees with Augustine that biblical interpretation can build up the double love of God and neighbor, but this is not his focus; rather he wants to look at "how the development of charity might manifest itself in biblical interpretation."[84] This move is crucial. He does not dispense entirely with the idea that biblical interpretation brings about virtue. As has been noted, Fowl stresses the need for interpretation to influence *and* be influenced by theological interests. Nonetheless, it is at this point that a difference between Fowl's and Augustine's programs can be noted. One is interested in the effects of interpretation upon the community, while the other is primarily interested in the effects of the community upon interpretation. One need not go so far as to say that Fowl's program is suspect because of this focus on the community's virtue.[85] One need only note the importance Fowl places on the community's *already-existing* piety. The same problem that became evident in the previous section comes to the surface here: Fowl's program tends to construe the community as self-contained, a given. Because it exists, one should look at its effect on interpretation. In the contemporary context of academic theology, such a focus on the community's identity is important, but one need not downplay the *effect* of interpretation in order to place the focus on the ecclesial community. Because Fowl does not think that hermeneutical theories can provide the proper "regulative structure" for scriptural reading, he must appeal to the community.[86] There is, he notes, no guarantee that the church will not interpret scripture to underwrite sinful actions, but if the community has certain practices in place, these will help theological interpretation go forward in a more productive way than an appeal to hermeneutical theory.[87]

For both interpreters, scripture is a vehicle that conveys humanity to God. It is an instrument in the divine economy, used by humans in their movement toward God (and concomitant movement toward one another) and established by God for this very purpose, but the similarity stops here. Fowl stresses the need for the community to have certain practices in place before proper interpretation can go forward. In other words, the function of scripture is something created when the community reads it; it comes from a human agent using the text. Augustine, on the other hand—while presupposing certain practices—puts the weight on the subsequent effects that interpretation has upon practice. Scripture, because it has an inherent *telos*, brings about certain effects. Their positions appear alike at first, but their respective emphases betray a fundamental divergence.

Fowl—because he has dismissed "meaning" as the location of authority—appeals to the preexisting virtue in the community to prevent a slip into interpretive anarchy. One learns to read by watching others who are further along in their Christian lives: "In regard to the interpretation of scripture, Christians will need to mark, remember, and attend to those who preceded them in the faith and who were accomplished interpreters of scripture."[88] For that reason, Fowl stresses the importance of premodern biblical interpreters. Yet he means more than simply looking to the early church: "Christians seek to form their members into practically wise people—people who can deploy the skills, virtues, and dispositions needed to live holy lives, growing into deeper communion with God and others. In this light, the formation of practically wise interpreters cannot be separated from issues involved in the process of Christian formation more generally. Such formation takes place in a variety of ways and contexts, and Christians and Christian communities must attend to them all."[89] Being able to interpret scripture well is a product of learning the correct habits; it is a matter of catechesis, he goes on to say, which is linked to baptism. For Fowl—in spite of claims otherwise—the primary focus is on the proper location of scriptural interpretation. In the confessing church that has certain practices in place, proper interpretation can occur. That is, while Fowl theoretically espouses a bi-directional program, in practice, he seems to privilege the community above the text.[90] Such a conclusion can also be drawn from the manner in which Fowl describes the Spirit's relationship to interpretation. For Fowl, "Spirit-inspired interpretation" is driven by communal practices, the Spirit being immanent in the community: "To be able to read the Spirit well, Christians must not only become and learn from people of the Spirit, we must also become practiced at testifying about what the Spirit is doing in the lives of others."[91] In other words, "reading" the Spirit is more about discerning the Spirit's presence in the community than it is about recognizing the Spirit's voice through the words of the prophets and apostles.[92]

As helpful as such a focus on community is—it mitigates the force of certain arguments for the necessity of academic biblical criticism—it perhaps puts too little weight on scripture, and the Spirit speaking through it. If the community does not manifest appropriate virtues, then scriptural interpretation can only go forward in a partial way: "Division is seen as a form of resistance to the Spirit of God. It dulls believers' abilities to hear and respond to both the Spirit and the word, which, in turn generates further unrighteousness."[93] Interpreting in the divided church is one of Fowl's primary concerns, and he helpfully notes that interpretation will be affected by the division. Augustine would undoubtedly agree, but only to a certain point. Fowl's construal focuses more on scripture's instrumentality; scripture is more like a tool that can be used—whether by God or the church—than a vehicle. The extrinsic *use* of scripture depends upon the community, not the community upon an intrinsic *telos* that the biblical texts have. Though Fowl describes scripture as a vehicle conveying humanity to God, his intense focus on the community's use of the text obscures the force of his appeal to Augustine's vehicle metaphor.

In *De doctrina*, Augustine describes how exactly scripture operates as a vehicle: it moves the church into a proper relationship with God and with one another through interpretation. And, as Fowl also states, this only happens when there is an interaction between theology, community, and text. For Augustine, scripture engenders the love of God and neighbor because it tells us in *signa* about certain *res*. The interpreter-preacher has to read the holy books to determine what God says there. He or she then turns to tell a congregation what God's will is in order to prompt them to action. For Augustine, faith and love belong inextricably together: "For if someone lapses in his faith, he inevitably lapses in his love as well, since he cannot love what he does not believe to be true. If on the other hand he both believes and loves, then by good conduct and by following the rules of good behavior, he gives himself reason to hope that he will attain what he loves" (1.37.41).[94] Love, the focus of Book 1, indeed the end of all biblical interpretation, cannot exist without faith. Again, the two rules—the *regula fidei* and the *regula dilectionis*—are interacting. One cannot love what one does not understand. The two *regulae* cannot be separated. Scripture exists to teach these two things: what we are to believe and how we are to relate to it. Again, the focus cannot stop here, however, because there is more to Augustine's hermeneutics than just figuring out what the biblical text says. *De doctrina* is a hermeneutics that includes rhetoric; one has only interpreted when one explains this understanding to another. Each *tractatio* involves both a *modus inveniendi* and a *modus proferendi*. So scripture is a vehicle precisely because it describes who God is, who our neighbor is, and how we should relate to them. First, one turns to scripture to determine what it says (*modus inveniendi*); only then does one turn to deliver that to a congregation (*modus proferendi*).

Throughout, I have stressed the bipartite structure of *De doctrina* and how this structure is crucial to any understanding of Augustine's text. It also helpfully distinguishes his project from Fowl's in the way it holds together the relationship between scripture and community. Scripture indeed operates as a kind of tool within the community. It becomes active, as it were, when the interpreter-preacher approaches it with the goal of communicating to the ecclesial community what

God says to them so that they might act accordingly. Fowl's close attention to the way that a community's virtue affects its interpretation does not satisfactorily stress the purpose for which scripture is used: to change the way people act. Throughout his work, Fowl highlights the negative impact that a breakdown of love has on interpretation, but the positive corollary of this description is that proper love is needed for proper interpretation. That is, Fowl's position requires the stance that the community is (or can be) inherently virtuous. When the community—with a properly ordered love—approaches the text and uses it, proper theological interpretation occurs. Augustine, in contrast, has a more pessimistic view of human nature: even those within the church need grace to order their love.[95] That is, the church itself comprises sinful humans. Scripture has an intrinsic *telos*, put there by God, which engenders a properly ordered love. For Fowl, love holds scriptural interpretation in its right place. For Augustine, scriptural interpretation engenders love, but love can never be separated from the things of faith. This occurs paradigmatically in the sermon.

The difference between the two can perhaps be described as a difference in their doctrines of grace. When discussing the three styles of Ciceronian rhetoric, Augustine states:

> It is the universal office of eloquence [*eloquentia*]—in whichever of these three styles—to speak suitably in order to persuade; the aim, however, that which you intend to persuade when speaking, in whichever of these three styles, the eloquent speaker indeed speaks in order to persuade, but if he does not persuade, then he has not arrived at the end of eloquence. In the subdued style [*genus summissum*], he persuades people that what he says is true; in the grand style [*grande*], he persuades them in such a way that they are driven to do what they know they should do even though they have not done it yet; in the moderate style [*temperatum*], he persuades them that he speaks beautifully and elaborately. But what is the point of that for us? . . . We should refer this style to another end, namely, that what we aim to do in the moderate style is the same as when we speak in the

grand style (that is, that good morals might be loved and bad ones avoided) if they are not so distant from that action that they might seem to need urging to it with the grand style of speaking, or if they already do it, so that they are made more eager and persevere steadfastly in it. (4.25.55)

Here, he collapses the three Ciceronian aims into two: teaching and persuading. Earlier I quoted him saying that persuasion is not strictly necessary because sometimes knowledge of truth itself brings about the appropriate response. Yet there are times when the congregation is at such a point that they cannot even fathom how to begin to live in accord with what the preacher tells them God wants. At this point, *De doctrina* states, the interpreter-preacher should utilize the rhetorical devices culled from Cicero in such a way as to inspire his or her listeners to act well. In other words, sometimes the knowledge of the *res* of scripture is enough to bring about the proper relation to them, that is, the love of God for himself and the love of neighbor on account of God. Sometimes, however, knowledge alone does not prompt properly ordered love, and at this point, the preacher has a responsibility to persuade his or her congregation to act correctly. Crucial, however, is the fact that teaching is always necessary, and teaching is nothing more than telling the church what the *res* of scripture are and how to relate to them. For Augustine, scripture and preaching are *addressed to* the community. Certainly, scriptural reading and preaching occur within the community, while they also address the community with a message from God, that is, from the outside. Such a construal implies that scripture has a certain function within God's prevenient grace. It is not the community's use that is of utmost importance; of consequence is the fact that the Holy Spirit speaks through the text and the sermon, bringing about the proper double love of God and neighbor.

A few things should be noted. Scripture's end is to bring people closer to God and one another, and this occurs primarily within the ecclesial community's worship. Both Fowl and Augustine operate with an *a posteriori* hermeneutics. Both presuppose a certain community with certain practices, and they both seek to supplement the ongoing practices with their programs. Neither envisions his theory to serve as a theoretical safeguard existing before interpretation begins. Furthermore, both focus on the necessity of a virtuous community. The similarities, however, end there. Augustine pictures a community whose virtue is potentially in need of drastic repair, hence the necessity of the grand and moderate styles. It needs God's prevenient grace. Indeed, even the interpreter-preacher himself is not envisioned as necessarily virtuous: "The life of the speaker is more important for people to hear with obedience than any grandness of speaking. For the one who speaks wisely and eloquently, but lives wickedly, certainly teaches many who are eager to learn, although 'he is useless to his own soul,' as it is written. For that reason, the Apostle says, 'Whether with pretext or with truth, let Christ be proclaimed.' Christ, though, is the truth, and yet truth can be proclaimed even by untruth. That is, things which are right and true may be proclaimed by a crooked and deceitful heart" (4.27.59, citing Phil. 1:18).[96] To stress the point, for Augustine, interpretation is part of the participation in God's temporal dispensation, but it is neither the community's nor the interpreter's virtues that are important for scriptural interpretation. Instead, the truth, Christ, the *res* of scripture, brings about change and can do so even within a context fractured and broken by sin; indeed, it can heal such divisions. While Fowl is clear that one should not wait until the ecclesial community's practices have been repaired, his concern for the community's (negative) effect on interpretation comes at the expense of a trust in the Spirit's use of scripture to heal the very divisions that threaten that interpretation.[97]

As in the previous section, Fowl's project helpfully highlights issues in the current context: scriptural interpretation—which should be fitted into a network of practices that lead to fellowship with God—is affected by the community's standing before God. Augustine suggests that Fowl's project could usefully be supplemented by an appeal to the Spirit's use of the biblical text. Thus, the church must become adept at reading the Spirit's presence in the gathered community *and* at hearing the Spirit's voice through the words of the prophets and apostles. The *meaning* of scripture, the *res*, must be grasped prior to delivering what God's will is. That is how divisions and lapses in love are healed. Only then can proper action occur, either simply through knowledge or through the additional means of being persuaded. In the end, it is a work of God, as Augustine's focus on prayer suggests.

At this point, however, I have begun to describe Augustine's project in a manner that goes directly against Fowl's program. Augustine does have something to say about meaning and authors. How it compares to Fowl's distrust of a hermeneutical concern for authors, however, should be explored before any conclusions are drawn.

### Interpretive Interests or Authorial Intention?

As mentioned earlier, Fowl argues on numerous occasions that a search for "meaning" is not philosophically or theologically helpful; rather, one should discuss "interpretive interests" and, on the basis of these, use the text to move closer to God.[98] Fowl's primary theological reason for this move is the Christian interpretation of the Old Testament: "Any attempt to tie a single stable account of meaning to authorial intention will put Christians in an awkward relationship to the OT."[99] His philosophical reservations can be traced to Stout's article, "What Is the Meaning of a Text?": because "meaning" means different things to different people, and because there is no straightforward way to navigate these differences and further the discussion about interpretive disagreements, one should simply give up the term and be clear about what one wants do with the text. This would shift the conversation to the things that really matter. Fowl sees only two options available to those who want to keep authorial intention as the definition of determinative meaning: either they will have to give implausible arguments regarding the communicative intention of the Old Testament writers, or they will have to view a christological reading as subsidiary or parasitic: "A single meaning determined by authorial intention will either force Christians into rather implausible arguments about the communicative intention of Isaiah, for example, or lead them to reduce the christological aspect of these passages into a subsidiary or parasitic role."[100] The Old Testament, however, is not the only part of scripture that would suffer; even the Gospel of John could be interpreted in an Arian direction without something at work other than authorial intention.[101] Furthermore, the moment someone asks the question, "Why should something like the author's intention count as the meaning of a text?" two things can happen: either there is an outpouring of "question-begging philosophical polemic," or there is an arbitrary exercise of power by those authoritative interpreters who can do such a thing.[102]

If one accepts the dichotomies Fowl here delineates, then surely it makes sense to dispense with all talk of authorial intention as "meaning," or even "meaning" as something important to seek.[103] If the choice is between getting rid of authorial intention and losing the Old Testament, or between getting rid of meaning and an arbitrary decree by an institution, then there would be no question; we can all stop arguing over what Paul meant or what deutero-Isaiah intended by writing.[104] Instead, the reader of scripture can assume that there are numerous different "meanings," each with a claim to authenticity, or in the words of a later essay: "to the extent that we today share in [Thomas's] views about God, the church, Scripture, theological study, and the proper end of human life . . . we should also consider holding a similar notion of a many-sided literal sense of Scripture."[105] For Fowl, the most one can say for appealing to authors is that the Holy Spirit is the primary author of scripture; in fact, "The human authors under the Spirit's inspiration are significant though secondary in this respect."[106] Yet again, it must be kept in mind that Fowl's driving concern is to prevent an overreliance on hermeneutical methodology, and to encourage a reading of scripture that is firmly located in the ecclesial community, which keeps the proper ends in place. An ever more forceful insistence on authors will not settle interpretive disputes and, in fact, runs the risk of making interpretation an end in itself and making theological concerns subsidiary to hermeneutical ones.[107]

At first glance, Augustine might seem to agree that authorial intention is only important up to a certain point: "Therefore, although all, or almost all, of those deeds which are contained in the books of the Old Testament are to be taken not only literally, but also figuratively; nevertheless, also those which the reader takes only literally, if those things which they do are praised, but the practices are abhorrent to the habit of good morals kept by those who keep the divine commandments after the coming of the Lord [*post adventum domini*], let him refer the figure to understanding, but not transfer the actual deed to morals" (3.22.32). Like Fowl, Augustine is clear that the Old Testament does not mean for Christians just what the author meant. Nevertheless, he does not dispense with authorial intention altogether. Augustine's move is connected to scripture's center, the incarnation of Jesus Christ. He still thinks discovering the author's intention is extremely important:

> Anyone, therefore, who thinks he has understood the holy scriptures, or perhaps a certain part of them, in a way that his understanding does not build up that double love of God and neighbor has not yet understood them. Anyone who draws such a meaning from them that may be useful for the building up of this love but does not say what the author can be shown to have meant in that place, has not erred disastrously, and he is certainly not being deceptive. . . . [H]e is mistaken in the same way as someone who departs a path by wandering but nevertheless goes on through a field to the place where the path also leads. But he must be corrected and shown how it is better not to leave the path, so that the habit of deviating does not compel him to take a crossroad or go the wrong direction altogether. (1.36.40 – 41)[108]

Augustine, in other words—as Book 1 attests—thinks scripture in its entirety points to and engenders the love of God and neighbor. The interpreter, however, cannot simply make a passage say this; he or she must instead discover what the author meant and how this connects to the double-love command. His metaphor at the end, of a person losing his or her way in a field, emphasizes the great importance that Augustine attaches to discovering the author's meaning. A forced interpretation every now and then could lead to faulty interpretation and even to bad theology. He thinks, therefore, that authorial intention is intricately connected to proper interpretation and, consequently, proper theology.

How, Fowl might ask, does Augustine then avoid falling into the trap of claiming that any given passage only has one meaning?[109] There are two aspects to Augustine's move. First, the reader him- or herself plays a significant role in determining meaning:

> It often happens that someone who is (or thinks he is) at a higher level of the spiritual life considers statements to be figurative, which are commanded to those at a lower level. So, for example, if a person has embraced the celibate life and castrated himself for the kingdom of heaven, he contends that anything the sacred books command concerning loving and directing a wife should be taken not literally, but figuratively. . . . This should therefore also be in the observations about the interpretation of scripture: we should know one thing can be commanded to all in common, while another to different classes of people, so that the medicine reaches not only the entire situation of health, but also the special sickness of each member. For what cannot be raised to a higher level must be cured on its own level. (3.17.25, alluding to Matt. 19:12)[110]

At this point, Augustine begins his discussion of not taking literally all the practices of the Old Testament, a section discussed in the previous chapter. He is clear that the location of the reader has an effect on the text's meaning. The second aspect to his move is the *res-signum* distinction from the first book.

After Christ, those *res* which appeared under the old covenant to be themselves *res* have now been revealed to be *signa*. Here is the utility of Augustine's preliminary distinction: signs point to things, which can then become themselves signs.[111] The Old Testament is, for Augustine, full of examples of such things:

> So Christian liberty has freed those whom it found under useful signs . . . by explaining the signs to which they were subjected and lifting them up to those things the signs signified. Out of

these people, the churches of the holy Israelites were formed. . . . For one is enslaved under a sign when he serves or venerates a signifier [aliquam rem significantem] without knowing what it signifies. But the person who serves or venerates a useful sign that is divinely instituted and understands its strength and significance does not venerate that which is seen and passed over, but rather that to which all such signs are referred. Such a person is spiritual and free, and in the time of servitude, when the time was not right to reveal those signs to carnal minds, under whose yoke they needed to be tamed. The patriarchs and the prophets were such spiritual people, as well as all the people of Israel through whom the Holy Spirit furnished us with the help and consolation of the scriptures. Certainly at this time, after the resurrection of our Lord, when a most clear proof of our liberty has been illuminated, we are not burdened with heavy service, even of those signs which we now understand. (3.8.12–9.13)

He has in mind here the sacrifices and cultic worship of Israel, and he compares them to the sacraments of baptism and the eucharist, "those signs which we now understand." For Augustine, Christ reveals these things for what they have always been: signs. He thinks those who wrote the Old Testament saw them as signs of a heavenly reality, but the majority of people would not have seen past the signs themselves.[112] After Christ's resurrection, however, these signs were revealed as signs to all. So when one turns to the Old Testament, one must bear in mind that the words—*signa*—refer to things and practices—*res*—that in light of Christ become *signa* themselves. Christ has reconstituted the Old Testament's meaning.[113] *Res* cannot be disconnected from their *signa*, however: "Once that is clear [whether a passage should be taken literally or metaphorically], the words in which it is expressed are found either to come from some similarity of the things, or from some connection between them" (3.25.34).[114]

The point of the preceding is simple: Augustine need not dispense with authorial intention because he has—for theological reasons—reconfigured how the author's *signa* relate to the *res*, to which scripture as an entire canonical work points. Augustine has provided a theological way of avoiding a single, determinate meaning, while also emphasizing the communicative intention of the authors of scripture.[115] It is a canonical exercise, however, as his emphasis on the center demonstrates. For example:

> He who endeavors to search the divine utterances should strive to reach the intention of the author through whom the Holy Spirit produced that part of scripture; he may reach this meaning or carve out another from those words which does not oppose right faith, if he has evidence from some other passage of the divine utterances. Of course, that author might have seen the same meaning in those words which we want to understand, but certainly the Spirit of God, who produced this through him, without a doubt foresaw the same meaning which occurs to the reader or to the hearer. Indeed, he planned that it should occur because that meaning also relies on the truth. (3.27.38)[116]

The Holy Spirit uses the human authors' words and their connection to the entirety of scripture to bring about meaning. Indeed, for Augustine, the writers were following the Holy Spirit as they wrote (2.5.6). The Holy Spirit, then, is active in the production of the texts *as well as* in the interpreting and preaching of the texts. Theologically, Augustine ties the Holy Spirit's activity into the entire process of scriptural production. The Spirit is present in the original writing, in the canonical ordering, even in the translation into Greek,[117] and finally in the interpretation and delivery to a congregation. None of these can be held apart from the others. Augustine's program is theologically robust, brimming with theological rationale. I have shown how the Holy Spirit is active at the instantiation of scripture. Now it remains to demonstrate that the Spirit is active in the interpretation of scripture and preaching. It will then be clear why Augustine's theological reasons for keeping "meaning" are critical and why they overwhelm Fowl's more philosophically driven criticisms of the term.

As I have argued throughout, Augustine's program has two parts: understanding what scripture says, and communicating that understanding to others. Behind this bipartite structure is a theological rationale, one pointed out in the discussion of the prologue in the previous chapter. God wants to tie humanity together in fellowship: "Then, if humans learned nothing from one another, love itself, which binds people together in the knot of unity, would not have any means of pouring and, as it were, of mixing souls with one another" (Prol. 6). The very act of teaching draws people into the bonds of fellowship, into the fulfillment of half of the double-love command. As I said in that chapter, there are vertical and horizontal aspects to Augustine's thinking. Neither exists without the other. This can be seen in another place, where he discusses humanity being bound (*vincire*) and cemented together (*agglutinare*). Coming to the human Jesus Christ is also to come to God. In the process, "the Holy Spirit binds and, as it were, cements us together so that in him we might remain in the highest and unchangeable good" (1.34.38). In other words—as these two quotations demonstrate—people teach one another in order to draw closer together and this occurs in connection with the Holy Spirit. Teaching is therefore part of the way God works to knit his church together; it is one place the action of the Holy Spirit can be seen.

As discussed above, Fowl, too, has moments where he discusses the Holy Spirit's role in the community. But he and Augustine differ in just how they locate the Spirit in the community. For Fowl, the Spirit's activity is immanent in the church. The Spirit is not tied to scripture, but to the community: "[I]f Christians are to read with the Spirit . . . then they must also become adept at reading the Spirit's activity in their midst."[118] This occurs when Christians form friendships with others. "Spirit-inspired interpretation" gives "innovative re-readings of scriptural texts in light of the life, death, and resurrection of Jesus."[119] This definition comes close to an understanding of the "center" of scripture, but Fowl has something else in mind: the Spirit's work within the community comes about as the community's members partake in friendship with one another. In the context of such friendships, the activity of the Spirit can be seen in such a way as to legitimate a new reading. For instance, Fowl discusses the way in which Christian readings of the Old Testament go against the "plain sense" of those texts that demand circumcision for Gentiles to be included in the people of Israel. His conclusion: "It does, however, raise again the sharp issue about how compatible a static notion of the 'plain sense' of scripture, a plain sense located in the text rather than the believing community, is with Christian theological approaches to the Old Testament."[120] Again, he thinks that a notion of "meaning" gets Christian readers in trouble with respect to the Old Testament. In order to provide warrant for "re-readings," he invokes the Spirit's involvement in the community. Augustine, however, has the Spirit at work from the origination of scripture right up to the moment an interpreter-preacher delivers to the congregation what he or she has discovered in the divine books. Fowl, in contrast, locates the Spirit in the friendships formed within the community. It seems, then, that he has a truncated notion of the Spirit's connection to the biblical texts. For Fowl, the scriptural texts simply *are*; he does indeed discuss what they *do*—move people closer to God and one another—but unlike Augustine, he does not address how they, as a collection of works by human authors, find themselves taken up into the divine dispensation. For this reason, when Fowl dispenses with authorial intention, he has to appeal to the Spirit's activity within the community. Even when Fowl speaks in later writings about the Holy Spirit as the author of scripture, he does so precisely to limit the appeal to the human author's communicative intent.[121] Scripture itself has no agency, no intrinsic *telos*. It is used by the community and by the Spirit (within the community) to bring about certain actions. This happens in an interaction between practices, theology, and scriptural interpretation. His very helpful appeal to the necessary location of scriptural reading leads him to downplay hermeneutical concerns too far. For Augustine, on the other hand, scripture—located in the divine economy—drives the theology and the practices precisely because the Spirit speaks to the ecclesial community through the human authors' communicative intentions.

The turn to delivery cannot happen without the first move of interpretation, understanding. Rhetoric—delivery *in order to produce a certain effect*—as Augustine has it, only works when it is the product of a preceding act of understanding. His reason: the Holy Spirit was at work in the production of the texts. The Spirit does not simply come into play in the contemporary context. There is a prior move made by God in the production of the texts and, most importantly, in the incarnation. The interpreter seeks the meaning of those who wrote scripture because the writers followed the will of God as they wrote. In order to find it, the interpreter-preacher must pray:

> Students of the venerable books should be admonished so that they might understand the styles of speech in Holy Scripture, and they should pay diligent attention and commit to memory in what way things are customarily said in them. And especially—this is particularly and absolutely compulsory—they should pray so that they might understand. In these very books of which they are students, they read, "The Lord gives wisdom and from his face is knowledge and understanding," from whom also they have received the desire to study itself, if it is provided with piety. (3.37.56, citing Prov. 2:6)

Familiarity with the books of scripture and prayer go together to help understanding, which precedes delivery, which is also driven by prayer:

> Whether one is about to speak at this moment before a congregation or any other group, or to dictate something to be said before a congregation or to be read by those who are willing or able to do so, let him pray that God would place a good sermon in his mouth. . . . Those, however, who are going to deliver something they have received from others, should—before they have received it—pray for those from whom they will receive it; likewise, once they have received it, they should pray that they themselves may deliver it well and that those to whom they present it might take it up. And they should also give thanks for a good outcome to the very one from whom they know they have

received it, so that "the one who boasts" may boast in the one "in whose hand both we and our sermons are." (4.30.63, citing I Cor. 1:31; Wisd. 7:16)

Prayer and therefore the Spirit exist both in the interpretation (the understanding and the delivery) and in the reception by the congregation. The Spirit is thus at work throughout the entire process, from inspiration straight through to illumination and proper action. Augustine assigns a wider range of roles to the Holy Spirit than Fowl does. The Spirit is not simply immanent within the community; the Spirit also takes part in the origination of scripture and so in that which is addressed to the community from outside. And, for that reason, what the authors say in these books is extremely important. Augustine demonstrates that Fowl's dichotomies—between meaning and losing the Old Testament or between giving question-begging answers to the question "Why authorial intention?" and authoritative command—are too black and white. Augustine keeps both the Old Testament and authorial intention. He answers the question "Why authorial intention?" not with question-begging arguments, but with a demonstration of the Holy Spirit's activity throughout the production of the biblical books. He need not use the weight of his authority to make this so.[122]

## Summary and Evaluation

Both Fowl and Augustine discuss scripture more in terms of its function (its extrinsic use or intrinsic *telos*) than in terms of its ontology. For Fowl scripture and the community simply seem to exist. The community, in some regards, is an already-existing entity. For Augustine, on the other hand, it has an explicit relationship of radical dependency on God. Fowl supposes that "meaning" is an unhelpful, question-begging term, while "interpretive interests" of a community should be the location of discussion. Augustine does not operate with such a dichotomy. For him, the community and scripture are caught up in the divine economy. In contrast, Fowl's focus on the community as the locus of authority, rather than on the text's meaning, leads him to concede too much authority to the community.[123]

This concession becomes visible when one places Augustine's notion of the virtuous community up against Fowl's. For Fowl, a community that has "distorted or inoperative" convictions and practices will have difficulty reading scripture.[124] Augustine, on the other hand, presupposes that the community will have difficulty understanding some parts of it, but the bulk of difficulty is on the side of living appropriately, something scripture helps repair, first because it has difficult parts that break down pride, and second because it teaches the church whom and how to love. Hence, he writes a hermeneutics that includes a turn to rhetoric. Augustine's community needs interpreter-preachers who will read the holy books and tell it what God wants it to do. Sometimes, its members will do what they should simply because they have been taught what God says. Sometimes, however, they are so captive to sin that the preacher must persuade them to live in accordance with what he or she hands on to them from God. Fowl and Augustine, therefore, place virtue on opposite sides of the process. For Fowl, the emphasis is on how virtue affects interpretation; for Augustine, the emphasis is the other way around. For Fowl, a breakdown in love leads to problems in interpretation; for Augustine, interpretation leads to proper love. Fowl describes the fractured church thus: "Doctrinal or scriptural differences cannot divide the church unless there is this prior failure of love."[125] Love, as it were, cements the church together. Augustine has a similar notion, but for him, love is the product of interpretation. The community is knit together precisely in the act of interpreting and preaching; this knitting together in love is a product of the Holy Spirit, which, as he stresses time and again, "is given to us."[126] For Augustine, this is the logic of grace: interpretation is not an achievement but a moment of God's gracious interaction with his creation. Augustine fills out his notion of love with his focus on the objects of faith. One cannot love what one does not know. Scripture plays a fundamental role in teaching what the *res* are to which one responds in love by either using them or enjoying them.

The community also plays an important role for both interpreters. It provides the context in which interpretation occurs. Both hermeneutical programs are *a posteriori*, yet for Fowl, scripture is collapsed into the community. In the end, it is located more within the community and its use than within God's divine economy. This conclusion arises from the ways in which Fowl describes the Spirit's relationship to the text and to the community; the Spirit is located more within the community than in the words of the human authors of scripture. For Augustine, however, scripture has been given to the community as a vehicle. Its role is temporal, related to the community, but never to be identified with the community. It is instead identified with God's gracious act of condescension to sinful humanity. For Augustine, therefore, and in contrast with Fowl, the community does give the direction to interpretation—one reads scripture precisely to teach a congregation how to relate to God and one's neighbor—but it does not give the direction in the sense that interpretation becomes a matter of identifying the community as *this* community. Scripture—by definition—has to stand outside the church because it is a vehicle moving her to God. I do not mean to imply that it is not, on some level, within the community. In fact, even those who composed it can be said to be members of the Body of Christ, and moreover, for Augustine, the canon arises because of communal agreement. Here, I mean something different: scripture stands outside of the community because it stands between the community and God as a means of transport to move it closer to him. Scripture is subordinate to God, but not to the community. It is activated, as it were, when the interpreter-preacher comes to it to hear what God's will is *so that* he or she can turn and tell this to a congregation in order that they may live accordingly, but God's will is still intimately connected to the words of scripture, to the *res* to which they point. Fowl misses out on this aspect of scripture—that it itself points to God's will—and Augustine's construal highlights this weakness.

Connected to it is the unnecessary dismissal of "meaning" for "interpretive interests." Both interpreters are keen to avoid losing the Old Testament as a witness to God. But they go about this in fundamentally different ways. Fowl decides that "meaning" begs too many questions. It is not normative. Normativity resides in the community. Augustine, however, thinks the interpretive interests of the church are skewed. He, in contrast to Fowl, appeals to the center of scripture: Christ reveals the *res* of the Old Testament actually to be *signa*. One might argue that this is not that different from Fowl. Has Augustine not just redefined "meaning" or even "authorial intention"? Yet that is precisely the point. Because Augustine thinks the Holy Spirit is at work throughout time in relation to the holy books, he cannot dispense with authorial intention *for theological reasons*.[127] If one were to dispense with authorial intention, one effectively rules out the human component within the divine dispensation that Augustine holds to be so crucial. That is, throughout the prologue of *De doctrina*, as I have demonstrated, Augustine stresses that God does not want humans to deal only with him. There is a horizontal and a vertical dimension to love. In Book I, the same comes to the fore: God himself became a human person to reveal to humans that there is something outside the created order so that they can turn their attention home (1.12.12). The entirety of *De doctrina* is an exercise in humans teaching humans in order that they might be caught up together in the love of God. How much more, then, would removing the human authors of scripture damage the human aspect of God's revelation of his will to humans?

Fowl runs the risk of making God's revelation of his will contingent on something other than the understanding and delivery of what God says through the writers of Holy Scripture, that is, contingent on something other than God's chosen way of communicating to humanity: *through* humans themselves.[128] Augustine assumes that ordinary human communication is essential to God's revelation of himself: "God could have given the gospel to humanity without using humans [*non ab hominibus neque per hominem*]," but he did not (4.16.33). It is part of the way God raises humanity up, part of the way he binds them together in the unity of love, which is poured into their hearts by the Holy Spirit. This focus on human community does not simply apply to the present ecclesial community as it appears to do in Fowl's program, it applies also to the human writers of scripture—to the great cloud of witnesses. Augustine's reasons for stressing authorial intention are therefore immensely theological.[129] The only reason one would go against what the author intended is because the author's meaning has—in light of Christ—become a *signum* for something else, not because the author's meaning is unimportant. The situation is exactly the opposite.

Fowl suggests that authors, readers, and texts are philosophical concerns: "The different aims and purposes that Christians bring to theological interpretation raise different sets of questions that do not really bear on the *philosophical concerns* of authors, readers, and texts."[130] Augustine's example, however, has shown that authors, readers, and texts are theologically important.[131] The issue here is that the philosophical ideas override the important theological reasons for keeping a focus on meaning and on authors. Precisely because *De doctrina* is an *a posteriori* hermeneutics, Augustine can take on board philosophical ideas without them overriding his theological concerns.

It must be reemphasized: Fowl writes at a time when the academy and the church need to be reminded of how crucial it is to grasp the *telos* of scriptural interpretation. He helpfully reminds theology that understanding is not an end in itself. The primary conclusion of the preceding discussion can be summarized as follows: because Fowl is so concerned to highlight ecclesial concerns, he runs the risk of overemphasizing the community at the risk of underemphasizing the text. By putting him into dialogue with Augustine, a path out of the current impasse—does authority reside in a better, hermeneutical definition of "meaning" or in the ecclesial community—can be suggested. Augustine speaks into the contemporary discussion and suggests that the key is to understand the divine economy of salvation: the Spirit speaks through the human words of scripture to the ecclesial community, the Body of Christ, called into existence after the resurrection and Pentecost.

"Long ago," the writer to the Hebrews says, "God spoke to our fathers by the prophets, but in these last days he has spoken to us by his Son" (1:1–2, ESV). As the church confesses, the Spirit, the Lord, the giver of life, speaks through the prophets. So, Augustine is correct to emphasize the human writers and their meaning, and Fowl is correct to emphasize the Spirit's connection to the community. "Now we have," says Paul, "received not the spirit of the world, but the Spirit who is from God, that we might understand the things freely given us by God" (1 Cor. 2:12, ESV). The two sides cannot be teased apart—a statement with which Fowl would agree—and Augustine serves to balance out a potential imbalance, by providing theological reasons to emphasize hermeneutics, texts, and authors.

## COMMUNITY AND TEXT IN THE DIVINE DISPENSATION

I began the chapter by suggesting that Fowl's program stood amongst a host of other proposals, all seeking to locate the reading of scripture within the ecclesial community. Meaning, as it were, is what the community agrees upon. Fowl, as I have argued, has a more nuanced position. He certainly stresses the bi-directional relationship between the community and its scriptures. In comparison with Augustine, however, it became evident that Fowl's privileging of the community does in some ways override his attention to the text. This focus on Augustine's attention to the historical authors of scripture might sound similar to what some would describe as "biblical theology." That is, Augustine's attention to authorial intention comes close to what Fowl and others claim the proponents of biblical theology seek.[132]

For instance, Childs speaks often of the "discrete voice" of the Old Testament: "In order to hear the voice of the Old Testament's witness in its own right, it is essential to interpret each passage within its historical, literary, and canonical context."[133] Is this, then, what Augustine has in mind when he claims authorial intention has a major part to play in interpretation? The answer seems to be no; nowhere in *De doctrina* does Augustine even hint that the Old Testament has some kind of independent voice from the New Testament.[134] Rather, when Augustine discusses the canon in Book 2, he depicts the entire collection of books as the place where people seek the will of God. In fact, vast amounts of the Old Testament, for Augustine, seem to fall into the category of metaphorical signs (*signa translata*). The section I quoted above regarding the advent of Christ reconstituting the *res* of the Old Testament into *signa* falls within Book 3, where he discusses how to interpret metaphorical statements. In other words, determining the meaning of the Old Testament has less to do with understanding the history and the languages than with grasping the fundamental significance of the Christ event. For Augustine, the Old Testament has been made clear precisely in its relationship to the New Testament. There is no discussion of "discrete" voices; rather, the discussion concerns the theological reality of Christ. In other words, Augustine utilizes something akin to the "center" of scripture. This is not to say, however, that language and history are unimportant:

> An important remedy against unknown literal signs is knowledge of languages. Latin speakers—whose instruction we have now undertaken—need to know two others to understand the holy scriptures, Hebrew and Greek, so that they might have recourse to the original text if the infinite variety of Latin translators causes any doubt. (2.11.16)

> Therefore, whatever the subject called history indicates concerning the order of past times helps us a great deal in understanding the sacred books. (2.28.42)

One should note, however, that both of these passages occur in Book 2; they are therefore concerned with *signa ignota*, unknown signs. Book 2 handles the literal level of scripture, the clear portions. Augustine is not handling metaphorical sections, which—as I stated—he finds much of the Old Testament to be. For that reason, he handles the Old Testament primarily in Book 3, where Christ has revealed the *res* to be *signa*; all (or almost all) of the deeds in the Old Testament are interpreted historically and figuratively due to the church's existence after the advent of Christ (3.22.32). For Augustine, then, the theological understanding of the Old Testament as reconfigured in light of Christ supersedes the weight that one can put on language and history. They are important, but not as important as the theological rationale. Fowl's program is much closer to Augustine's than is Childs's.[135]

Furthermore, for Childs there is a concern for "critical criteria."[136] The turn to a more homiletic mode worries him: "Many modern interpreters would probably agree that it is legitimate for a Christian interpreter at some penultimate stage in exegesis to move into a homiletical mode of discourse to accommodate a church audience, and from a subjective, confessional stance join the witnesses of the two Testaments into a kind of Christian biblical theology. The effect of this personal construal, however, lies outside all critical criteria and can be neither proven nor disproven by rational argument."[137] Rather than this "flight of creative exploration," Childs has in mind something more rational. For him, theological exegesis is a two-staged process. First, "one seeks to hear the historic voice of Israel in its literal/plain sense."[138] This is "exegetically crucial" because it reveals how obscure the nature of God's messianic promise was. Only then does the interpreter use scripture "as an authoritative collection of sacred writings which has assumed a unique shape and been given a special role within the Christian community of faith as the continuing vehicle of divine manifestation."[139] The purpose of this second stage is to invoke praise and thanksgiving. The subject matter of the two discrete witnesses—the Old and New Testaments—is the same, God. The biblical text itself forces the reader to unite the two "critically."[140] It is precisely at this point that one can see how Augustine stands closer to Fowl than Childs. For Childs, appeal to the Christian community is only made in the second stage.[141] For Augustine, however, the community is *always* presupposed. The church provides direction to the exegesis. Perhaps this presupposition does open up the possibility of uncritical reading, but this worry seems more theoretical than actual. It can appear at times that Childs gets stuck in history. Augustine, on the other hand, sees history as a small part of the way that God speaks through scripture to his church in the present.

*De doctrina*, therefore, does not represent a pure appeal to a more critical reading, seeking to provide warrants by appeal to authorial intention. Rather, as argued in the previous chapter and as has been presupposed throughout this chapter, the community always plays a crucial role in Augustine's hermeneutics because the interpreter-preacher should always read scripture with the goal of presenting to the congregation what God says to them through scripture. Still, as I have been at pains to show, this communally focused reading is not as communally located a project as Fowl's runs the risk of being. Instead, it is better to view the community as providing direction for Augustine's interpretation. The goal of interpretation is, as Fowl states, to move closer to God and one another. Yet that *telos* cannot be reached without a more immediate aim: preaching to the community. More precisely, scripture exists to bring humans to God—that is its intrinsic *telos*—and it does this when humans come together and listen to what God says through the prophets and the apostles. In other words, Augustine locates authority neither in the community nor in the text, but in the *interaction* of God revealing his will to humans who write books that are read by others in order to teach and persuade God's church to do his will.

The focus shifts from where the weight of authority lies—in the community or in the text—and on to making certain that the *telos* of scripture is grasped. Scripture is a vehicle and, as a vehicle, it is of utmost importance. The community provides the direction for interpretation while the text moves the community closer to God and to one another. Augustine's model of interpretation, then, precisely because it is a hermeneutics that includes a turn to rhetoric, balances out the shortcomings inherent in a program like Fowl's while also not surrendering to the more critical and rationalistic tendencies inherent in a program like Childs's. Augustine does not, however, walk a middle line; he is certainly closer to Fowl's program than Childs's because his theology and his ecclesial location are not secondary to the historical, analytical reading of a text. The reality of Christ and the church that he calls into being do not allow Augustine to see the text as merely a text. This text is a vehicle. To interpret it is to move the church closer to God. That fundamentally alters the way one can read the Old Testament, which is after all Childs's main concern.

The ecclesial location, while of crucial importance, does not override God's voice speaking through the text. Scripture stands, as it were, outside the community. It stands between God and humanity. This is implied by the vehicle metaphor. Scripture does not knit the congregation together, that is, does not serve only as an identity marker. Instead, the *interpretation* of scripture knits the community together and moves them together to God. This occurs because every act of interpretation includes both discovering what the authors (and God through them) say and delivering this to others within the church. There is no interpretation without delivery and there is no delivery without proper action. Thus, the rubric of an expanded hermeneutics helps clarify what exactly Augustine's interpretive project looks like: it locates both text and community in relation to God and, in doing so, puts them into an interlocking relationship with one another. The text is not simply a function of ecclesiology, and the church is not just a creature of scripture (*creatura verbi divini*). Instead, both arise out of God. The church is a creature of Christ (*creatura christi*) and scripture is a vehicle to move this creature closer to God in the same way that Christ, the wisdom of God, came down in the flesh but ascended again to the Father (1.10.10–13.12): text *and* community, hermeneutics *and* rhetoric. Scripture exists for the community to discover what God says so that they might live in the manner he commands. There is no interpretation unless the interpreter-preacher delivers what he or she discovers in scripture to the church.

Augustine's program describes readers and interpreters, texts and words in theologically important ways. This reveals that one need not be so dismissive of such "philosophical" concepts as Fowl is on the surface. The issue is not whether one should use philosophical notions or not; rather, it is how one utilizes philosophy in one's theological interpretation.[142] This in turn demonstrates yet another benefit of describing Augustine's two-part hermeneutics as *a posteriori*. He can take on such general philosophical notions as writers and texts, but because he continually has the ecclesial community in mind and seeks only to supplement an ongoing interpretive practice, he can utilize these general philosophical notions without capitulating to their often inappropriate foundational anthropologies.[143] His program is therefore extremely robust. There is no hesitation to employ useful philosophical notions or certain disciplines that exist outside of the church. This demonstrates that truth—no matter where it is found—should be utilized to aid biblical interpretation. The ecclesial community provides the direction to interpretation, and the act of interpreting-preaching draws the community together in the bonds of love. Love is the *result* of interpretation, not the grounds for it. As the community reads and discusses what God says in the divine books, its members are drawn together into the unity of the Holy Spirit, journeying together toward God until at last they behold him in all his glory when "sight of the visible reality will replace faith, and that blessedness to which we will eventually arrive will replace hope. Love, on the other hand, will actually be enlarged when these things pass away. For if through faith we love what we cannot yet see, how much more will we love it when we actually begin to see! And if through hope we love that which we have not yet reached, how much more will we love it when we finally reach it! . . . However high one's expectations when on the journey, he will find it more impressive upon arrival" (1.38.42).[144] When combined with Augustine's notions of the *telos* of scripture and the importance of the ecclesial community, this emphasis on the eschatological movement of the readers toward God brings out the primary points to take from the preceding dialogue.

Reading scripture requires an understanding of what scripture does: it engenders the double love of God and neighbor when interpreters come to it in order to share with others the will of God as it is expressed in the words of the prophets and apostles. But more than that, it requires an understanding of the persons who read scripture. It requires a theological anthropology: fallen humans who need to be formed into the image of God, whose sin has tainted this image and prevents them from loving God with all their hearts and their neighbors as themselves. As Fowl points out, the reader of Scripture has his or her own *telos*. Scripture is established—by the God who condescended and took on human flesh—to be an instrument his Body uses to move ever closer to one another and to him, and this occurs through the interpretation of the human words bound together as scripture. The ecclesial community comprises fallen humans and thereby remains only partially what it will be in the eschaton. The Spirit knits us together in love through the interpretation of scripture in the context of the Body of Christ. That is the high calling of biblical interpretation: to move in the direction of God's unification of all things under Christ. Those separated by sin can be joined in love through interpretation in the Spirit. Union with God and with one another is an eschatological reality, one toward which we ought to strive, though we will never reach it this side of the new heavens and the new earth. Now, we see a fractured Body; then we will see a glorious Body with "radiance like a most rare jewel" (Rev. 21:11, ESV).

# Conclusion

The previous chapters have allowed Augustine to be a living voice in dialogue with contemporary theological hermeneutics. During the course of the investigation, a number of points were highlighted, both with respect to Augustine's *De doctrina christiana* and with respect to contemporary theological hermeneutics. As emphasized at the outset, theology engages with the past in order to move beyond the problems of the present, an exercise performed in faith that the Holy Spirit spoke and continues to speak through the saints who engage with scripture. This dialogue has proven fruitful, and it remains now to draw out the implications more generally. The preceding pages are an example of the kind of work that should occur when engaging with a text from the past in order to allow the past theologian to speak to present theology. At least two general conclusions can be drawn from this dialogue.

1. *The past theologian should be allowed to set the parameters for discussion.* There is no shortage of theologians appealing to church fathers in order to further their own theological proposals. The introduction mentioned Work and Levering, both of whom appeal to *De doctrina* in order to develop, respectively, an ontology of scripture and a theology of the instrumentality of scriptural reading. Both theologians develop helpful theological accounts of scripture by appeal to Augustine, but neither one fully grapples with what Augustine himself says in the entirety of *De doctrina*. Such a practice is not in and of itself wrong, but Augustine's individual voice runs the risk of being lost in the process. A theological engagement with the past looks in faith to learn from it and not simply to mine a

text for citations, and such a stance necessitates a thorough engagement with the text (or texts) in question. As the previous pages have demonstrated, certain questions are currently being asked about how one should interpret scripture. A logical text to utilize was *De doctrina*. As easy as it is simply to look at the first three books (or even the first one alone)—assuming that these are about interpreting the Bible while Book 4 is about something else—the discussion has shown that paying attention to the entirety of *De doctrina* offers numerous insights for a theology of biblical interpretation, not the least of which is that theological interpretation has the sermon as its paradigm. Without the close reading of Augustine's text, this conclusion would not have been reached.

Ayres is correct, then, to insist on engaging with contemporary historical scholarship on the text and person in question.[1] Part of the theological work of performing a dialogue with a past figure is understanding what the text says. Historical work is necessary, but it is not an end in itself. The theological work has not been accomplished simply by understanding what Augustine meant, as though it were even possible to do so from a neutral, ahistorical position. The historical work is the gateway to the contemporary theological work. To allow the ancient author to set the parameters for dialogue helps prevent a forced reading by working to keep the contemporary context from framing the discussion in such a way as to obscure the voices of past figures. Only by paying close attention to what they say can any real dialogue go forward.[2]

2. *The past theologian can be put into close dialogue with contemporary interlocutors.* In immediate connection to the previous point, the historical work and attention paid to the text or figure in question is but one half of the dialogue. It is precisely the location of theology in a specific time and place that drives the theologian back into church history. The current situation is such that another perspective may well provide insight that is missing in the discussion. The past figure does not speak into a void. While one can imagine a philosopher engaging with the ideas of *De doctrina*, Augustine is very explicit: *De doctrina* is a book about biblical interpretation. It is a theological

hermeneutics. For that reason, when one wants to connect theology and biblical interpretation, and when one seeks a different perspective from what is currently on offer, this work begs for a rereading. And conversely, when reading the entirety of De doctrina with the goal of seeing what Augustine says there, one is forced to look to theology and biblical interpretation as the touchstone of dialogue. The argument is circular, certainly, but that is not a weakness; it is the way things are. In nearly any theological conversation, the past can offer much needed perspective on the present, but it is precisely in the context of the present conversation that one looks backward. The present has its own concerns, biases, and blind spots. Still, the goal is not simply to understand everything a church father ever said, or to create a comprehensive survey of a specific text. The purpose is particular; the turn to the past has a point.

For this reason, the form of a dialogue is helpful. By assuming at the outset that what the historical figure says will have relevance for the present, the theologian can allow the figure to interact fairly closely with current theological discussions. In the previous pages, I suggested that two specific discussions bore some relationship to what De doctrina says. Because there is a discussion regarding theological hermeneutics and how it relates to philosophical hermeneutics, and because De doctrina is a hermeneutics, one can look to this ancient text to see what it says to the present. And there can be little doubt that this dialogue moved the current debate forward. The argument—so the example of Augustine showed—is not really about the relationship between general and local hermeneutics, but about how theory and practice actually relate. Precisely because of the questions Jeanrond poses in his works, the engagement with Augustine brought out the ecclesial aspects of his program, which sent the investigation back to the text to seek answers to Jeanrond's questions about ideological distortion. And, once more, Augustine's reflections in De doctrina began to sound very similar to contemporary discussions about the importance of the ecclesial community for interpretation, moving the discussion toward proponents of such a view. The second dialogue brought out specific points regarding the theological interpretation of scripture itself. Both dialogues went forward under the assumption that Augustine's voice is strong enough to engage fruitfully with the current discussions.

One need not, therefore, assume that the past needs to be protected by setting it apart from current considerations. The temptation exists to hold the historical discussion at some distance from the theological one; if the two are too close together, the present has the potential to override the past. We are, after all, wedded unconsciously to the thoughts and ideologies of our historical context. For that reason, the theologian must spend more time putting the ancient theologian into context than he or she does placing contemporary thinkers into theirs. Their context is our context, which is precisely why the turn to the past is necessary.

If the first thesis above is held in tension with this one, the theologian can worry less about the present overriding the past or, indeed, the past overriding the present. Allowing past and present to interact closely in dialogue with one another can lead to profitable insights. And, as the preceding discussion has shown, the benefits of the dialogue apply to both sides. Without putting Augustine into dialogue with Jeanrond and Fowl, the term "expanded hermeneutics" might not have arisen, and as the discussion has demonstrated, this term is particularly useful for describing Augustine's project in *De doctrina*. In addition, the notion of an expanded hermeneutics led to the idea that the sermon is the paradigm for theological interpretation. Such terminology allows for the precise focus of Book 4 while at the same time accounting for the universalizing tendencies that are present.[3] Perhaps Augustine's theological ideas were not themselves questioned as much as some contemporary theologians might like, but that is not because Augustine's ideas are flawless. It is, instead, because the very nature of a dialogue means the less helpful ideas remain muted, left in the background, as the horizons of past and present are fused into one.

In addition to the new terminology gained for discussing *De doctrina*, positive theological contributions were offered to the current context. It might have been possible to draw principles from Augustine's text and then go and find theological interpreters who did or did not exhibit these principles, thereby allowing Augustine more authority than he was arguably granted here. In such an exercise, the church father would be presumed to offer the correct way of going about interpretation, while the current discussion may not have anything to offer back to him. By putting him into close proximity with other theologians, Augustine was—in a sense—forced to defend his viewpoints.[4] Certainly a measure of authority was granted to him by the very fact that I turned to his text and not to, say, Origen's *De principiis*. But other theologians were given their say in direct connection to Augustine, questioning him, arguing with him. The dialogue is fruitful, then, because it allows an actual engagement between two different times, the dialogue providing insights that go both forward and backward.

In addition to these general, historical theological points, placing Augustine into such a dialogue with contemporary theology also led to a number of conclusions for contemporary theological interpretation. On the basis of the previous chapters, I would suggest the following basic requirements for theological hermeneutics and the practice of scriptural interpretation:

1. *Theology should not be afraid of using philosophical tools when engaging with scripture.* Scripture is not simply literature. It is not only a classic text. It is these things and more. Scripture is an instrument in the divine economy, sanctified by God, set apart by the Holy Spirit's "hallowing of creaturely processes" to point to the revelation of God in Jesus Christ.[5] This is the reality, and theologians must bear it in mind, must remember that certain tools are indispensable for reading the text: prayer, humility, and dialogue with past and present interpreters, for example. But these things do not negate the possibility for theologians to utilize tools present within the contemporary philosophical context. At this point, one finds the theological reward of the *a priori–a posteriori* hermeneutical distinction. Christian theologians cannot escape the philosophical currents of their intellectual context, but they can use them flexibly and eclectically within an *a posteriori* hermeneutics. One need not create an *a*

*priori* hermeneutics by stepping back from practice and developing a theory to constrain a logically subsequent practice, but one also need not create a specifically local hermeneutics that attempts to avoid philosophical ideas altogether. The theologian must be on guard, must submit the dominant philosophical systems to theological critique, but one cannot dismiss a scriptural reading simply because it uses, say, Heidegger's language of "authenticity" or Marxist categories. Likewise, one cannot dismiss a hermeneutical system just because it appeals to speech-act theory, or to Ricoeur's hermeneutical description of "distanciation." To be dismissive of theology on these grounds is to commit the same error as one who rejects Augustine on the grounds that he is, in actuality, a Neoplatonist rather than a Christian. Each theological use of a philosophical concept must be judged on its own merits. The previous pages have demonstrated how deeply theological Augustine's program is, even while it seems at times to venture beyond theology into other disciplines, like Stoic philosophy, or Neoplatonic notions of ascent, or forensic rhetoric. By paying attention to the text, one sees that Augustine's theology holds his philosophy in place. One need only compare his early appeals to philosophy to his later usage of it to grasp the point.

In the same way, contemporary theology need not fear the use of certain philosophical concepts if they are deemed suitable on theological grounds, if they are used in an *a posteriori* hermeneutics. One might, for example, suggest that an appeal to the "critique of ideology" is a helpful way to discuss a reader's sinful proclivity for reading what he or she wants in a text and the necessity instead to be open to the enlarged world proposed by the text,[6] but the move here is crucial: one does not begin with a general notion of what a generic reader does with any given text and then apply that to scripture. Instead, the move goes in the opposite direction: God's will is revealed through the human words of scripture and comes to fruition in the delivery of that message to others, but because humans are sinful, we tend to ignore or allegorize those parts that question what we think, and for that reason, the reader must recognize such a tendency, must resist projecting him- or herself onto the text and instead "expose [him- or herself] to it."[7] The key point is that theology owes no answers to philosophy; rather, theology recognizes its relation to the church, the body of Christ that bears witness to the truth. Practically speaking, this means that a theologian can utilize philosophy when it serves his or her theological agenda.

Moreover, while Augustine does change Cicero to some degree, what he does is recognizably indebted to Cicero. He does not use Cicero's language simply to give authority to his own ideas. Rather, he uses Cicero because what Cicero says is useful. When he does shift Cicero's focus, he does so explicitly. There is a further practical ramification of such a practice. Following the example of Augustine, one would not want to use, say, the language of deconstruction as though it has no connection with Derrida.[8] Rather, a theologian uses philosophy when it makes a good point, one that is consonant with what the theologian wants to say on the basis of the biblical witness. In other words, the Christian theologian seeks to proclaim the gospel to the church and through it to the world, and, to do so, he or she can appropriate any useful concepts or tools that are present in the prevailing philosophies of the day. Within an *a posteriori* hermeneutics, the fear that philosophical concepts might override theological ones becomes less of a worry.

2. *Theological hermeneutics should be expanded to include rhetoric.* There is no scriptural interpretation without the communication of what one has understood from scripture. For that reason, any theological hermeneutics that focuses simply on understanding what the text says is deficient.[9] It cannot—to state the matter as forcefully as possible—even be considered a theological hermeneutics. It may be a good hermeneutics; it may even have very good insights about how one goes about the act of understanding what scripture says, but—theologically speaking—it must be considered deficient if it does not include rhetoric. To reiterate: rhetoric is here defined loosely as the delivery of what has been understood to the church and through it to the world with the goal of persuading people to the double love of God and neighbor. Interpreting scripture is not an activity for individuals. Scriptural interpretation always has as its end the communication of what has been understood in order to bring about the appropriate response. For that reason, a theological

hermeneutics must also have some discussion of the communication of what has been understood. The question of such a hermeneutics is not only, "How does one understand scripture?" but also,
"How does one go about sharing this understanding with others to
bring about the appropriate response?"

Any theological hermeneutics that does not pay attention to this
double concentration has failed to understand just what scriptural
interpretation involves. Certainly, there are two exercises: interpretation and communication. For practical reasons, they can be
separated. Even Augustine (loosely) separates them. Still, the link
between the two is indissoluble: one cannot go forward without the
other. Splitting the theory of scriptural interpretation from the theory of homiletics in too rigid a manner leads to misunderstanding
both of them. There should be no scriptural interpretation that does
not lead naturally to a delivery of some kind. Conversely, there is no
proper delivery without a prior understanding of scripture. Theory
must match practice, and if the argument of the preceding pages is
correct, then theological hermeneutics, like biblical interpretation,
must include rhetoric, a discussion of the turn to delivery with the
goal of bringing about proper action.

Practically speaking, this viewpoint draws into question numerous practices current in theological hermeneutics.[10] Discussions
focus so intently on proper understanding that little time is spent
explaining how to express that understanding to others. Indeed, *why*
one would even want to express that understanding to others does
not even seem to be an issue. But as I have argued, the *why* and the
*how* are inextricable. One understands to explain; one explains to
persuade; these processes are done because God speaks to humans
through humans to bond them together in love, which is poured
into our hearts through the Holy Spirit. Understanding scripture is
not an end in itself, and a theological hermeneutics must make this
point explicit.[11]

*3. Theology must have an understanding of scripture's telos, which
involves a theological anthropology of the reader.* Scripture is an instrument in the divine economy. Such a statement necessitates an
understanding of the one who reads it: "Understanding scripture's

place in the economy of salvation is inseparable from understanding the place of the soul in the triune soteriological action."[12] One
comes to scripture to understand the will of God in order that one
can deliver this understanding to the church so that its members
can live accordingly. When a reader understands the words of the
prophets and apostles and communicates to others that understanding, this twofold act of interpretation engenders the double love
of God and neighbor. An Augustinian understanding of scripture
necessitates a certain understanding of the church and the reader
of scripture. In fact, the two cannot in actuality be teased apart: the
implied reader is a member of the church and the two are mutually
constitutive.[13]

The church exists in the in-between; it "is precisely an event
*within the event* of the new age's advent."[14] The church is called into
being by Christ and sustained by the power of the Holy Spirit. In the
church, the Spirit works to bring renewal to creation. In the church,
Jews and Gentiles are made one body through the cross, the great
divide in humanity removed in Christ as the baptized gather around
the one bread, drink from the one cup. Through this body, the wisdom of God is made known to the rulers and authorities in the heavenly places (Eph. 3:1–12). The church is sent by Christ in the power
of the Spirit into the world to bring peace: "'Peace be with you; just
as the Father sent me, so I send you.' And when Jesus had said this,
he breathed on them and said, 'Receive the Holy Spirit. If you forgive the sins of anyone, they are forgiven; if you do not forgive them,
they are not forgiven'" (John 20:21–23).

This is the church's mission, the proclamation to creation that
God in Christ and through the Spirit has reconciled it to himself.
But the church comprises sinful humans. One need only read the
letters of the New Testament to grasp the point: from the start, the
church has not lived up to its best insights, to its high calling. For
this reason, scripture exists. Such a description is not only theological; historically, this is the case. Because God deals with humans
through humans, these historical documents are sanctified and are
vehicles for God's revelation of his will to the church. But again, the
church is sinful. It is dependent on hearing the word of God, spoken

through the prophets and apostles. The church exists in the power of the Spirit, but because God speaks to humans through humans, the Spirit inspired the authors of scripture. Whatever one means by "inspiration," the point is the same: God does not operate outside of history. And because the church is sinful, ever in need of God's gracious guidance, scripture exists: "it is—or ought to be—a knife at the church's heart."[15] Scripture and church belong inextricably together. Scripture exists to engender the double love of God and neighbor; it does so in the context of the church—the gathered body of those baptized in the triune name, those who in the power of the Spirit go forth in love to share the message of God's grace and peace. The church, in need of instruction in how to love God and neighbor, turns attentively to scripture to hear the will of God spoken through the historical words of the prophets and apostles, turns to hear so as to act in accordance with what is heard.

But the church is not a nebulous entity. The church is the body of Christ, a new polity, a *family*. Paul constantly appeals to his *adelphoi*, his brothers and sisters; the author of 1 John writes to his *tekna*, his children. The church is a community of individuals, individuals who have been forgiven their sins and restored to a proper relationship with their Father, individuals who have been put into a new relationship with one another, enabled to pray "*Our* Father," to pray "Our *Father*." These individuals are in need of God's grace; they are sinful. The community known as the church is the Body of Christ, knit together by the Holy Spirit in love. But its members are still human, mired in sin, unable to love as they ought. The reader of scripture is located here, in this context. This person is one in the church who fears God and wants to know what must be sought or avoided. The person then turns to scripture in order to discover what God commands, with the intention of sharing this with the church, with his or her family gathered around a table. The turn to scripture is a turn to hear the will of God, which one knows is the *double* love of God and neighbor. For that reason, one never turns to hear what God says for "me," but what God says for "us." The kind of reader such a hermeneutics demands is one who recognizes his or her sinfulness, but who recognizes it as what it really is: a breach of love between humans and their creator and between themselves. Scriptural interpretation is one of the means by which God pours his Spirit into believers and mixes their souls together. Because humans are sinful, God has to tell them what they ought to do, and because God reveals himself to humans through humans, he has given them scripture. The interaction between such a reader and such a text in the power of the Spirit creates fellowship.

That is the *telos* of scripture: the reestablishment of fellowship between God and humanity, fellowship between humans and their neighbors, in other words, the creation of the double love of God and neighbor, the restoration of fellowship sundered by sin. Such a *telos* requires an understanding of the reader as one who lacks this double love and who needs to be shown how to love appropriately. The reader, then, has his or her own *telos*: the proper relationship with God and with his or her neighbor, a relationship that will not be perfected until the eschaton.[16] The church holds people together in love. The church turns to hear God's will in the words of the prophets and apostles by understanding and sharing together. The eucharist becomes crucial at this point: the words of scripture intersect with the visible unity of the church—"We are all one body for we all take of one bread." The reader of scripture reads in the church, for the church. When done in the power of the Spirit, scriptural interpretation creates community, engenders love, precisely because God has revealed his will to the church through the human words of the prophets and apostles. Without an understanding of scripture's *telos* and the concomitant theology of the reader, scriptural interpretation will never be theological.

4. *Theology must pay attention to the christological center of scripture.*[17] Holy Scripture comprises two parts, the Old Testament and the New Testament. One does not exist without the other, and the relationship that obtains has at its core the person of Jesus Christ, the incarnate Word of God. If God is fully revealed in Christ, and if the same God revealed in Christ is the God of Israel, then how one reads the Old Testament is necessarily changed from how one would have read it before the advent of Christ. As Barth says in a slightly different context, the apostles made certain interpretive moves in

relation to the Old Testament, not because the biblical scholarship of the time did so, but "because the Old Testament (Lk. 24:27f.) was opened up to them by its fulfillment in the resurrection of Jesus Christ, and because in the light of this fulfillment Old Testament prophecy could no longer be read by them in any other way than as an account of this subject."[18] One does not read the Old Testament as though it were simply a buildup to the denouement that is the New Testament. The God revealed there is the God revealed in the New Testament through the resurrection of Jesus of Nazareth from the grave and through the gift of the Spirit at Pentecost. God's interaction with Israel has its own integrity, but it is the triune God who interacts with Israel, who calls Abram from Ur. It is not exegetical gymnastics to insist that the Spirit hovering over the face of the water in Genesis 1:2 is the Holy Spirit, though one is certainly reading into the text more than the author meant. It is the result of the full revelation of God in Christ and through the Spirit, a revelation that has recalibrated the significations of the Old Testament.

Augustine helpfully utilizes the language of *signa-res*. For Augustine, the Old Testament represents history, and while one might not want to subscribe to all such a viewpoint entails, his insight remains valid. To utilize John David Dawson's terminology, one might refer here to Augustine's methodology as "figural" rather than "figurative": "Scripture's *figurativeness is not nonliteral*; its figurative character is an extension rather than obliteration of the literal sense of texts."[19] Because of Christ, certain meanings cannot apply any longer, but that is not to turn the Old Testament into a system of non-referential language. The *res* to which the Old Testament points are taken up into God's economy of salvation, themselves becoming *signa* for something deeper.

For example, when one reads the account of Achan's sin in Joshua 7:1–26, one is immediately struck by just how "unchristian" Israel's response seems. Achan takes some silver and other spoils from Jericho that have been consecrated to the Lord, bringing defeat on the Israelites in a later battle. When Joshua finally confronts him, Achan confesses that he has sinned against God. Joshua then takes Achan, the spoils, his sons and daughters, his livestock, and all of his possessions outside the camp, where all of Israel stone him and burn the rest. In light of Christ, such a passage throws up numerous, obvious problems. One would want to read Israel as in some way connected to the church—whether typologically, historically, or in another manner can be left aside—but what one would certainly not want to do is suggest that the church stone every member who confesses to sinning against God.

I would suggest, on the basis of the foregoing pages, that a few points would need to be noted in the interpretation.[20] If one grants that the theological interpretation of this text is connected—in some sense—to a liturgical context (more on this below), certain aspects of the narrative will be suggestive. For instance, the reader will likely notice that the eucharistic celebration begins at a point very similar to the one at which Achan's fate, not to mention his family's, is sealed: the confession of sin against God (Josh. 7:20–21).[21] Likewise, and in line with the location of the reader after the event of Christ's earthly life, death, and resurrection, he or she might also remember that the Christian who lives after Christ's sacrifice has been called to be a *living* sacrifice (Rom. 12:1). These two points draw the reader's attention to the fact that all of Jericho was devoted to destruction except for the silver and gold, and the vessels of bronze and iron; these were put into the treasury. The reader could then note that the passage seems to be emphasizing that everything—in one way or another—belongs to God. Because Achan takes from the devoted things, his life is forfeit, as are all of his possessions. The point is simple: one's failure to respect those things that are God's is fatal.

Once more, the ecclesial location of theological interpretation forces the reader to recognize that the Christian baptized into Christ has been devoted to God; his or her body, his or her entire existence belongs to Father, Son, and Holy Spirit. Such a recognition drives the reader once more to the text, where he or she notes that failing to present one's body wholly to Christ brings judgment on the community, who will be unable "to stand before her enemies" (Josh. 7:13). And once more, the christological center of scripture, recognized by the church after Christ's ascension, reminds the reader that the enemies of the church are not flesh and blood (Eph. 6:12).

Finally, he or she need only look to the current state of the church, to the fracturing disagreements that lead to division, to see that the church is under judgment.[22] Like Achan to Joshua, only confession can turn the situation around. The church cannot follow Joshua and stone and burn the person and his or her belongings; such a practice is forbidden by the *regula dilectionis*. Instead, the church understands that this is a sign for a deeper thing: *everything* belongs to God, who will turn from his burning anger when it is all given to him. The church—who is at war with the forces holding creation from its proper course—is under judgment here, not the world.[23] The church is judged for failing to render to God what is his, for failing to take the message of peace to the damaged creation, which needs to hear what God in Christ has done. Until the church turns and repents, its ability to stand before the forces opposing creation will be hindered. Having noted these points as they arise from the interaction of the ecclesial location, the christological center, and the *regula dilectionis*, the reader might then turn to a commentary to help fine-tune the reading, but it should be noted: the meditation on scripture in light of the christological center and in connection with the ecclesial location of reading norm the interpretation more seriously than a critical commentary.

The preceding reading may not convince everyone, but it does provide a brief example of the way in which a christological center affects the reading of scripture. The Old Testament is read in the church because Christ has given it to the church: "From the standpoint of Christian faith, it must be said that *the Old Testament comes to us with Jesus and from Jesus, and can never be understood in abstraction from him.*"[24] The Old Testament is not simply a history book used to find out the background to Jesus' life and religion. It is the living word of God to the church, established to engender the double love of God and neighbor. But it is this only in recognition of the christological center of holy scripture. Failure to recognize it leads to an incomplete understanding of scripture's role in the economy of salvation.

5. *There is no* regula fidei *without the* regula dilectionis. Scriptural reading must bear in mind the rule of faith, handed on with

scripture by the church. "Guard the good deposit," Paul writes to Timothy, "through the Holy Spirit who lives in us."[25] The charge is directly connected to the "sound words," the healthy teaching that Paul himself passed on to Timothy (2 Tim. 1:13). From the beginning, the church has handed on the rule of faith with scripture. The *regula* and the canonical collection arose together; in the words of Robert Jenson, they "match like conversely notched puzzle pieces."[26] The rule of faith, however, must be combined with the rule of love. In recent discussions about the interpretation of scripture, much emphasis has been placed on the rule of faith.[27] For instance, one proponent of such a view states: "a theological reading of Scripture is the primary practice of a diverse community of faithful interpreters who together apply the church's Rule of Faith to the biblical text to lead all believers toward theological understanding."[28] While such a view is important, it does not provide the full picture. There is an emphasis on the ecclesial background, but the rule is applied primarily to promote "theological understanding."[29] And if the preceding pages are correct, scriptural interpretation is a more complicated enterprise. The rhetorical turn of an expanded hermeneutics demands proper action, and because communication is an indispensable aspect of scriptural interpretation, no biblical text is properly understood until it results in that action: the double love of God and neighbor.

Because of scripture's role in the economy of salvation, one must supplement the rule of faith with the rule of love. In line with its *telos*, reading scripture is ultimately about living in the here and now on the way to proper fellowship with God *and with one another*. The *regula fidei* establishes the overarching narrative of scripture, the specific things one finds there about God and his creation. But again, the Christian faith is about more than intellectual assent. At its most basic level, there are always two aspects to faith—understanding and relationship. For that reason, scriptural interpretation operates with a second rule, the *regula dilectionis*, understanding how a passage connects to love, the primary driving force of the Christian life. That is, the rule of love, like the rule of faith, norms the reading of scripture. The Christian theologian must always ask: "On the basis of what I know scripture does—it engenders the love of God and neighbor—how does this passage connect to the life of those professing faith in God, Father, Son, and Holy Spirit?" Another way to gloss this idea is to speak of revelation.

"God is," says Barth, "he who in his revelation seeks and creates fellowship with us."[30] Revelation is nothing other than God's *self*-revelation in Jesus Christ. Scripture points us to who God is, the God who is fully revealed in Jesus Christ, the triune God, Father, Son, and Holy Spirit. But revelation, as Barth insists, cannot be separated from the creation of fellowship. That is, understanding cannot be separated from love. We do not learn who God is unless we learn how to relate to him. Faith and love are inseparable. Because scripture is an instrument in the divine economy of salvation, it cannot but be structured by these two rules. They are not applied *to* scripture; they arise *from* the divinely ordained text and its location in the economy.

It is not enough, therefore, simply to read scripture theologically in light of the rule of faith; one must also read it in light of the rule of love. Of course, one must not press this idea too far in the opposite direction where biblical interpretation becomes simply ethics, rendering scripture's connection to reality unimportant and emphasizing only living ethically in the present. But to emphasize, there is no rule of love without the rule of faith. The way things are dictates the way we live. Because the triune God is the kind of God who prevents his creation from spiraling into chaos, and because God the Son himself suffered for creation in order to restore the fellowship lost in the fall, love is a response in the Spirit to what we know to be the case. Who God reveals himself to be is who God is, a God who seeks and creates fellowship with his undeserving creation. Faith, then, is the prerequisite for love.[31] One cannot love what one does not know.

And herein lies the gospel—the God who knows and loves us has revealed himself to us by establishing saving fellowship with him in Christ through the Spirit. Because this is the reality, how things *actually* are, and because the Spirit has inspired scripture to engender in us the proper love of God and neighbor, scripture teaches how this love should look, the persons to whom this love should be directed. A theology that fails to take into account this dual aspect of scripture is deficient. It may say correct things about love, or it may say correct things about God and creation, but without a proper emphasis on both, the interpretation of scripture is only partial. For precisely this reason, Augustine continually emphasizes the rhetorical turn of interpretation, that moment where the interpreter turns to tell the listener what scripture says in such a way that the listener acts in accordance with what God says through the words of the prophets and apostles. Scripture does not exist simply to speak *about* God, or simply to tell us how to relate *to* God (in love). Instead, scripture's end is to engender the double love of God and neighbor through the act of interpretation. Because one has to know whom to love, scripture must be understood. Because one has to know how to love, scripture must be interpreted. Because one actually has to love, scripture must be understood and communicated one to another.

6. *Theological interpretation has the sermon as its paradigm and must interpret accordingly.* The preceding points can all be summarized beneath this one. Indeed, they are but extensions of this primary conclusion. I have insisted on the necessity of an expanded hermeneutics for theological interpretation, which leads to the necessity of the paradigm of the sermon. To reiterate, a "sermon," simply put, is the rhetorical delivery of what one understands from scripture in order to evoke the proper response; "paradigm" means that any other engagements with scripture also have this end. Such a stance fundamentally requires the ecclesial community, the body of Christ. The emphasis is on ongoing practices, on the relationship between theory and practice. The sermonic paradigm only really works within an *a posteriori* hermeneutics. Scripture has a certain function because of its *telos*—it engenders the double love. The ongoing practice of interpretation within the church is presupposed, and theological hermeneutics is an aid to this ongoing practice, a mid-flight corrective as it were. Scriptural interpretation is located in a theological web where two rules govern the reading: the rules of faith and love. Understanding the *res* of scripture does not mean that interpretation ends. Instead, one must respond to the *res* with

the proper love, and this requires the ecclesial community, where one loves one's neighbor and where the results of understanding come to fruition in delivery, another act of love wherein souls are poured and mixed together. Thus, scriptural interpretation is not an end in itself but is part of the process by which humans are drawn together and drawn into relationship with God. By operating within this broad horizon, the theologian can utilize concepts from contemporary philosophy and culture without needing to fear that they will overwhelm his or her theological agenda. Such freedom arises from the ecclesial community's relationship to God. Because God established the church and gave it the keys to bind and loose, it represents the place of his presence through the Holy Spirit, and because all truth belongs to God, the church need not fear utilizing anything useful because everything is fundamentally changed—its true nature revealed—when put in close proximity to Christ. In addition to philosophical tools, one can note that theological hermeneutics need not fear that oft-dreaded specter biblical criticism. When used within the theological context of the *regula fidei* and the *regula dilectionis*, when used in the interpretation of scripture following the paradigm of the sermon, when used to interpret scripture on the way to loving God and our neighbor, biblical criticism can be plundered and put to theological work.[32] Augustine deploys the metaphor of plundering the Egyptians, a possibility brought about by his *a posteriori* hermeneutics. Scripture exists to engender the double love of God and neighbor. It does this by presenting the will of God in the human words of the prophets and apostles. The Spirit brings scripture into being and illuminates the one interpreting the text. The theologian understands scripture through prayer in the power of the Spirit, understands in order to communicate to others what God says to them. The Spirit fills the listeners and prepares them to hear the message from God, enables them to live appropriately. Such a description does not simply apply to a sermon presented to a congregation on a Sunday morning; it applies even to biblical commentaries. At the very least, an interpretation comprises two parts: understanding the text and communicating that understanding to the church to elicit the proper response—love of God and neighbor.

Failing to keep the church in mind misses out on the purpose of scriptural interpretation.

Because the church is assumed, one can do more with the biblical text than simply interpret it to find out what it means—as necessary as this is. For instance, in a sermon it is often the interaction of texts and practices that drive conclusions more than the meaning of the individual passages. And while the hermeneutics developed in the preceding pages necessarily would emphasize the importance of paying attention to the individual passages, it would also stress the need to remain open to other aspects of the texts. Indeed, one can turn a final time to *De doctrina*, to a passage not yet examined, to see how such a practice might look. When Augustine takes Song of Songs 4:2 as a poetic image of the elders of the church bringing people to the pools of baptism, he states after discussing the concept in plain terms:

> Why is it then that if someone says these things, it delights
> [*delectat*] the hearer less than if it were explained to him in the
> sense of that passage from Song of Songs where it is said of
> the church, when she is praised like a beautiful woman: "Your
> teeth are like a flock of shorn sheep ascending from the pool,
> all of which give birth to twins and there is not a barren one
> among them"? Does a person learn anything different from
> when he hears it in plain words without the aid of this image?
> And nevertheless—I do not know why—I consider the saints
> more pleasant [*suavius*] when I picture them as the teeth of the
> church cutting men off from errors and transferring them to its
> body, softening hardness, as biting off and chewing. Also with
> the greatest joy [*iucundissime*] I recognize the shorn sheep, with
> worldly loads like fleeces being put aside, ascending from the
> pool (that is, from baptism), all to bear twins (that is, the two
> commandments of love [*praecepta dilectionis*]), and I see not one
> of them lacks that holy fruit. (2.6.7)

One can easily argue that this is not an *interpretation* of the passage in the more modern, strict sense of the term. Rather, it is more like

the *use* of scripture to make a point. Such a distinction would probably not have occurred to Augustine, and it is precisely here that he
can be of help. Scripture—because it is an instrument in the divine
economy—does more than simply sit there as a voiceless text from
which to excavate meaning. Its *telos* is not disconnected from the
author's intent because God has chosen to speak to humans through
humans, but scripture's function nonetheless allows for a more
relaxed view of the use of the text than is often assumed. As Byassee
states, "[a]n Augustinian aesthetic in exegesis would shift interpretive debates from simply being about the rightness of one's words
according to the letter and toward the promotion of the flourishing
of lives."[33] Because it is a canonical book, authorial intent is only
one aspect of scripture's meaning. There is a christological center,
pulling the meaning of passages in certain directions. Thus, when
Augustine uses the image of the shorn sheep, he is clear that it says
nothing more than can be found elsewhere in the canonical witness (2.6.8). Because he is certain that Song of Songs is a love song
between Christ and his church, he thinks he does follow the author's
intention insofar as it is possible to find it and insofar as it melds
with the overall communicative intent of scripture.[34] Such a use of
examples need not be feared, though it often is. What is even more
striking is Augustine's appeal to delight. Scriptural interpretation
should be a joy, a pleasure. Part of scripture's purpose is providing
puzzles that need to be solved by the interpreter, who feels delight
when he or she figures out what God says through that obscure portion of scripture.

By taking the sermon as paradigmatic and insisting on the
importance of the ecclesial community, one can recognize that such
a use of scripture still exists today, though it is perhaps disappear-
ing more and more. For instance, Ruth 1:16–17 has been used as
part of the liturgy in marriage ceremonies: "Do not urge me to leave
you or to return from following you. For where you go I will go,
and where you lodge I will lodge. Your people shall be my people,
and your God my God." Though some might frown at such a bla-
tant "misinterpretation"—this is a daughter-in-law speaking to her
mother-in-law!—the use of these beautiful words in a marriage

ceremony is like Augustine's use of Song of Songs: the utilization of a passage as an example of a more detailed point that can be derived from the entirety of scripture. One can take another example from a liturgical reading at the thirteenth station of the cross, "The Body of Jesus is Placed in the Arms of His Mother": "All you who pass by, behold and see if there is any sorrow like my sorrow. My eyes are spent with weeping; my soul is in tumult; my heart is poured out in grief because of the downfall of my people. 'Do not call me Naomi (which means Pleasant), call me Mara (which means Bitter); for the Almighty has dealt very bitterly with me.'"[35]

These words are placed into the mouth of the Blessed Virgin Mary, and the discerning reader will note that the first sentence comes from Lamentations 1:12, the second from 2:11, and the last from Ruth 1:20. That is, the passage has taken verses concerning the fall of Jerusalem and the words of a woman who has lost her husband and two sons, and put them into the mouth of a woman who has watched her son die. Such a use of scripture would not seem at all strange to Augustine, but it would indeed seem odd in academic biblical criticism and even in some deployments of theological interpretation. It nonetheless continues to exist in certain liturgical contexts and is at least one area where theological interpreters in the academy might do well to pay attention to the church and put a little practice before theory. If one wants to follow the example of Augustine demonstrated in the preceding pages, it is just this kind of delightful scriptural "interpretation" that should be encouraged. It takes seriously the practices of the church as found in its liturgy, and—because the authorial intention of the canonical Bible cannot be dismissed—it takes seriously the text.

One might object that such a close association of hermeneutics, the practice of interpretation, and the ecclesial practices in which interpretation occurs might lead to an ideologically distorted reading, but an *a posteriori* hermeneutics need not be so threatened by practice. The biblical text does have its own voice, the voice of the prophets and apostles through whom God speaks. Thus, there is no reason for the church's liturgy and practices not to interact with a theological interpretation that engages with the text. Scripture is a

vehicle to God and interpretation is the way of using it. This interpretation includes understanding and delivery to the ecclesial community. Scripture and the church cannot be teased apart, and if that
is the case, liturgy and ecclesial practices such as baptism and prayer
also have a role to play in interpretation.

One can therefore turn to the liturgy of the church to provide an
image for what theological interpretation can be.[36] That is, the practicing ecclesial community may well have something to show academic theological interpretation. On a Sunday morning, churches
around the globe gather to celebrate the eucharist.[37] The sermon
occurs within this context, spoken to a community gathered in the
triune name celebrating the life, death, and resurrection of their
Lord and Savior. Indeed, the sermon is not even the focal point;
numerous other things occur before and after it that are of equal
or greater importance. For example, hymns are sung, prayers said,
absolution granted, and a blessing received. Such a fact does not
downplay the importance of the sermon but insists upon its location
within a network and range of other activities all meant to draw the
community into fellowship with God and with one another. This
fellowship occurs, respectively, in the absolution and the passing of
the peace, and finally in the celebration of the eucharist. In the midst
of these activities, several passages from scripture are read—often
from the Old Testament, the Psalms, the New Testament, and the
Gospels—and then commented upon. The sermon should engage
with the readings, should engage with the people of the congregation where they are. In other words, it is an interaction between a
number of scriptural texts, the congregation, the liturgy, as well as
the world. It cannot simply replicate the texts. The church has after
all already heard them read aloud. The preacher must instead ask
a question of scripture: *What should I say to this congregation on the
basis of these texts at this point in history in such a way as to persuade
them to act accordingly?*[38] For obvious reasons, scriptural interpretation involves two parts—understanding the texts and delivering
that to the congregation. Understanding the Bible involves an active
dialogue between the minister and the range of canonical texts,
between the contemporary world and the world of scripture. Then,

the congregation hears what God says to them through scripture and the preacher. It is precisely in the interaction of the texts and their interaction with the congregation that the sermon arises.

Again, however, it should be noted that the sermon is only one part of the service. At that moment, the preacher speaks to God's people on the basis of the words of the prophets and apostles. But afterward, the people recite the Nicene Creed, recounting the faith they believe as well as the context in which the sermon can be comprehended. Later, the congregation passes the peace. The sermon is preparation for this moment where people demonstrate their love to one another before they turn and offer themselves to God as living sacrifices and go forward to commune as one body with their Savior by taking the bread and wine, the body and blood. At this point, and in a way that only occurs in the eucharist, the church is drawn into the love of God and neighbor, becoming one body for they all share in one bread, receiving the body and blood of Christ, praying that the Father send upon them his Holy Spirit. The sermon is preparatory for this moment, a step in the process along the way to the celebration. Yet again, the eucharistic celebration is not the end. The congregation is then sent out to the world in peace.

Several things can be noted: the interpretation of scripture—the sermon—occurs in the midst of a network of prayers, hymns, recitations, and eucharist. Theological interpretation can therefore be seen for what it is: part of an integrated set of theological activities that culminates in the love of God and the love of neighbor. The church gathers together to hear what God says through the words of scripture, but this is not enough: the preacher must proclaim on the basis of these readings what God says to them in their time. Theological interpretation must for that reason be self-consciously concerned with questions currently facing the church and use scripture to answer them. The sermon is embedded in the flow of a service leading to the celebration of Christ's death and resurrection and its continuing effects for the church. Thus, theological interpretation takes the incarnation, death, and resurrection of Christ seriously, necessitating a christological center of scripture that affects, for instance, the way one reads the Genesis account of creation. In the sermon, the interaction of the canonical books and the issues currently facing the church help the preacher determine what God says. Two or more readings interact to bring out the message for the church on that particular day.[39] Theological interpretation is therefore canonical, taking account of the entire range of scripture. No one verse, book, or testament determines a theology. An interaction of both the church's current situation—the questions it asks of the biblical texts—and the words of the prophets and apostles further indicates that a running commentary on the text is not enough; the sermon—and therefore theological interpretation—must declare what the church should do now on the basis of these texts. The theologian therefore reads scripture to declare something to the church and through it to the world. But even that is not the end: the church must profess what she believes, partake in the holy mysteries, and then go forth into the world loving her neighbors as she loves herself.

Scriptural interpretation is therefore neither the end nor the beginning of theology. Rather than downplaying its significance, such a move reinvigorates it, for in the twofold act of interpreting the Bible, the God who came to earth to save humanity interacts once again with his people. And as in the Incarnation, he speaks to humans through one of their own, and as then, so now he himself takes part—this time in the person of the Holy Spirit. Humans are bound together in love as they gather to hear God's words through the human words of the Bible and the human interpreter. Theological interpretation recognizes that God established scripture as a vehicle to move people toward him and toward one another. It recognizes that God speaks to humans through humans in the midst of a network of theological practices that themselves interact with the interpretation. It comes to scripture with a question to which it seeks an answer to deliver to the church, and it need not be afraid of utilizing insights from outside the church because it trusts that all truth is God's. It can be flexible and eclectic. It should be delightful. And as its end, it should engender the double love of God and neighbor.

# Notes

## Introduction

1. My theological work here owes much to the following: Ayres, *Nicaea and Its Legacy*; Watson, *Text and Truth*, 305–329; Webster, "Theologies of Retrieval," 583–599; R. Williams, *Why Study the Past?*

2. Certainly much can be gained from relating the theoretical ideas of *De doctrina* to Augustine's actual interpretive practice, but for the sake of space, I must relegate these comparisons to footnotes.

3. Van Fleteren, "Principles of Augustine's Hermeneutic," 2. Van Fleteren also has an article investigating Augustine's exegesis apart from *De doctrina*: "Augustine's Principles of Biblical Exegesis, *De doctrina christiana* Aside," 109–130. For similar judgments, see Byassee, *Praise Seeking Understanding*, 62 n. 20, 262 n. 41; Brock, *Singing the Ethos of God*, 106–108.

4. Pollmann, "To Write by Advancing in Knowledge and to Advance by Writing," 136.

5. In fact, as Plumer, "*Expositio epistulae ad Galatas*," points out, Augustine completed only one commentary on a biblical book that was not initially composed as a set of sermons: *exp. Gal.*

6. *ench.* 31.117, NPNF 1/3 (adapted).

7. FC 81, 17–30. The letter dates from late 426, early 427, or even 428.

8. *en. Ps.* 54.4 (LXX; Psalm 55 in MT). The passage in its entirety is well worth reading.

9. Though I think Byassee, *Praise Seeking Understanding*, is unnecessarily dismissive of *De doctrina*, his reflections on *en. Ps.* are excellent and the entire book well worth reading to gain insight into how Augustine's interpretive practice might be helpful in our current context.

10. Cf. *en. Ps.* 54.20.

11. For example, Toom, *Thought Clothed with Sound*; Pollmann, *Doctrina Christiana*; Arnold and Bright, *De Doctrina Christiana*.

234 NOTES TO PAGES 6-7

12. Toom, *Thought Clothed with Sound*, covers only *doctr. chr.* 1.1.1–3.25.35. A good examination of the entire work in English is Jackson, "Semantics and Hermeneutics." Jackson, though, focuses more on the sign theory than the entirety of the work.

13. Ayres, "On the Practice and Teaching of Christian Doctrine," 88. Ayres provides four criteria for the treatment of all theological texts: the part of a text addressed must be related to the whole; the "conceptual idioms" of the author's logic and expression must be grasped, along with the traditions and immediate context from which the text arises; developments in contemporary scholarship on the text must be explored even if they are rejected; and the dead should be shown the same respect as the living. Ayres here modifies the seven criteria for judging a historical interpretation of a text given in Barnes, "Rereading Augustine's Theology of the Trinity," 150–154. To witness Ayres put theory into practice, see *Nicaea and Its Legacy*.

14. Aside from the two works I survey in the following paragraphs, I should also mention Jacobs, *A Theology of Reading*, esp. 9–35. Jacobs uses *De doctrina* as a starting point to develop a general theory of reading. Strictly speaking, such ideas—though interesting—do not necessarily arise from a careful consideration of what Augustine himself says, but that is not to say that they are unrelated to his text.

15. Athanasius, *De Incarnatione*.

16. Work, *Living and Active*, 50–67. It should be noted that Work bases his reading of *De doctrina* primarily on three texts: Burns, "Delighting the Spirit," 183–194; Cavadini, "The Sweetness of the Word," 164–181; Jordan, "Words and Word," 177–196.

17. Work, *Living and Active*, 64.

18. Ibid., 64, emphasis original.

19. For dangers associated with the deployment of the christological analogy, see Ayres and Fowl, "(Mis)Reading the Face of God," 513–528.

20. Work, *Living and Active*, 216.

21. For example, Work maps Augustine's seven stages of ascent to wisdom in 2.7.9–10 on to the Beatitudes and the *ordo salutis*. As he is forced to admit, "[t]he correspondences are not perfect" (*Living and Active*, 307), and that is because the stages are actually from Isaiah 11:2–3, though their order is inverted on the basis of Psalm 111:10 (LXX: 110:10). While there are hints of the Beatitudes in this list, and while Augustine has a similar description of ascent in *s. dom. m.* 1.3.10–4.12, the two versions are distinct.

22. Levering, *Participatory Biblical Exegesis*, 66–70.

23. Ibid., 67.

24. For another "redefinition" of the term "history" along similar lines, see Rae, *History and Hermeneutics*.

25. Levering, *Participatory Biblical Exegesis*, 69.

## 1. Augustine's *De doctrina christiana*: History and Context

1. Origen, *On First Principles*; Tyconius, *The Book of Rules*.

2. I use "handbook" and "treatise" interchangeably as generic terms. For a discussion regarding *De doctrina*'s relationship to these terms in the education system of antiquity, see Pollmann, *Doctrina Christiana*, 89–104.

3. Translations of *retr.* are the author's unless noted.

4. For example, Kannengiesser, "The Interrupted *De doctrina christiana*," 3–13, argues that Augustine stopped because of his struggle to understand Tyconius's *Liber regularum*, a constant theme in Kannengiesser's writings on the subject. Steinhauser, "Codex Leningradensis Q.v.I.3," 33–43, argues that Augustine fell ill. Toom, *Thought Clothed with Sound*, 220–221, argues that Augustine ceased because he ran into a problem he could not solve, how to tell the literal from the figurative. Others suggest Augustine was simply overwhelmed by his clerical duties and perhaps the composition of *conf.*

5. Moreau, "Introduction to *La Doctrine Chrétienne*," 13–14, suggests that the unfinished work was in circulation and that this would have given Augustine an additional motive for finishing his work: so its true scope could be understood.

6. For instance, *Gn. litt. inp.*, for which Augustine points the reader to *Gn. litt.* (*retr.* 1.18); *ep. Rm. inch.*

7. *retr.* 2.4.1, citing *doctr. chr.* 3.25.35, Luke 13:21.

8. R. Green, "Introduction to *De doctrina christiana*," xii. Kannengiesser, "Augustine and Tyconius," 151–152, states, however, that the thirty-year hiatus is "one of the most neglected aspects of the study" of *De doctrina*. The subsequent discussion will demonstrate that the intervening period is not as important as he suggests.

9. Opelt, "Doctrina und Doctrina Christiana," 5–22, argues that the rules of Tyconius do not really fit; Babcock, "*Caritas* and Signification," 162–163 n. 30, thinks Tyconius's rules are more a "dissipation" of themes than a "culmination." But see Sieben, "Die 'Res' der Bibel," 87, and the discussion below.

10. Opelt, "Doctrina und Doctrina Christiana," 5–8, argues that the theology in the beginning and the end are different. Lettieri, *L'Altro Agostino*, argues for a "Ddch-A" and a "Ddch-B" (beginning at 3.25.36), the

latter influenced by Augustine's new ideas on predestination, the former by his original Neoplatonic ideas. But see R. Green, "Introduction to *De doctrina christiana*," xii–xiii.

11. For example, Jordan, "Words and Word," 177–196; Opelt, "Doctrina und Doctrina Christiana," 7–8, 21–22.

12. Unless otherwise noted, translations of *De doctrina* are the author's. All in-text citations are to *De doctrina* unless otherwise specified. See the bibliography for translations consulted. I utilize the text of R. Green's edition in comparison with the texts of W. Green (CSEL) and Martin (CCL). I use the older, more common numbering system, in spite of the precision of W. Green's system.

13. For more on chronology, see Andrews, "Abbreviations of Aug.'s works."

14. For more on Augustine's ordination (and life in general), see in particular Lancel, *Saint Augustine*, 147–161; Brown, *Augustine of Hippo*, 131–197; TeSelle, *Augustine the Theologian*.

15. For more on the manuscripts of *De doctrina* and text-critical issues, see Martin, *Praefatio*, xix–xxxvii; W. Green, *Praefatio*, xiii–xxix; W. Green, "Textual Notes on Augustine's '*De doctrina christiana*,'" 225–231; Schäublin, "Zum Text von Augustin," 173–181; Gorman, "The Diffusion of the Manuscripts of Saint Augustine's 'De doctrina christiana' in the Early Middle Ages," 11–24.

16. Quoted in W. Green, "A Fourth Century Manuscript of Saint Augustine?," 191. See also Mutzenbecher, "Codex Leningrad Q.v.I.3 (Corbie)," 435–437. Mutzenbecher argues, on the basis of the designation "*episcopus (a)eclesiae catholicae*," that the codex is probably from North Africa, where the designation of "catholic" would make sense because of the Donatist church's influence.

17. W. Green, "A Fourth Century Manuscript of Saint Augustine?," 195. See also Moreau, "Introduction to *La Doctrine Chrétienne*," 13–14.

18. For more on the book's dating, see Martin, *Praefatio*, vii–xix, who argues the first part of the work was finished no later than 397, though perhaps as early as 396, while the second part was completed in 426 or 427; R. Green, "Introduction to *De doctrina christiana*," xii, who argues the work had to be completed up to 2.40.61 by April 397, on account of Ambrose's death and the fact that Augustine does not list him among the departed saints, while the works in *retr.* surrounding *De doctrina* suggest a later date because Simplician (Ambrose's successor) was bishop when Augustine sent *Simpl.* Still, R. Green opts for the work's completion in 397, hence my practice of writing 396/7. Some suggest a date as early as 395, but that does seem too early. There is a consensus that the work was completed in 426 or 427, but with no firm evidence either way, I have opted for 426/7.

19. See *retr.* 2.15.1, regarding *trin.*

20. W. Green, *Praefatio*, xiii–xv. See also W. Green, "A Fourth Century Manuscript of Saint Augustine?," 191–197; according to this article, Lowe states that the author's name is written by a much later hand, perhaps in the seventh century (192 n. 1), but Green argues in his *Praefatio* that there is no reason to doubt the inscription; why, after all, would a later reader or librarian add it (xv)? Mutzenbecher, "Codex Leningrad Q.v.I.3 (Corbie)," concludes that the signature (Ag***inus) is a later addition because of its characteristic style (431–432), and that the inscription itself is most likely late as well (438–439). Gorman, "The Diffusion of the Manuscripts of Saint Augustine's 'De doctrina christiana' in the Early Middle Ages," 12–13, supports W. Green's hypothesis.

21. Mutzenbecher, "Codex Leningrad Q.v.I.3 (Corbie)," 406–450, esp. 440–442. Schäublin, "Zum Text von Augustin," 173–181, discusses several text-critical problems associated with it.

22. Steinhauser, "Codex Leningradensis Q.v.I.3," 41.

23. See *conf.* 8.1–2.

24. Toom, *Thought Clothed with Sound*, 19–64.

25. Jackson, "Semantics and Hermeneutics."

26. Pollmann, *Doctrina Christiana*.

27. Harrison, *Rethinking Augustine's Early Theology*, esp. 280–287, argues that Augustine—"A Proto-Anti-Pelagian"—lays the way for his anti-Pelagian stance even before becoming a bishop. Cf. Wetzel, "Pelagius Anticipated," 121–132, who argues that Augustine begins in *Simpl.* to express himself similarly to his anti-Pelagian views, though with some differences. For the view that *Simpl.* is Pelagian, see Burns, *The Development of Augustine's Doctrine of Operative Grace*, 8, 112.

28. *retr.* 2.3.

29. Translations of *agon.* are adapted from FC 2, 315–353.

30. Cf. *util. cred.*

31. If Harrison is correct—that Augustine's theology changed in 386 rather than 396—then arguments for a drastic change in theology between the two compositional periods of *De doctrina* are even less convincing (*Rethinking Augustine's Early Theology*).

32. He had, of course, composed other works before becoming bishop.

33. *De doctrina* and *cat. rud.* have much in common at this point, but space precludes further discussion.

34. Though Pollmann, *Doctrina Christiana*, 72, splits the research into two primary positions—arguments for the education of all Christians versus arguments for the education of the clergy—what follows assumes that the situation is slightly more complicated. Because Eugene Kevane's typology still seems remarkably accurate, the subsequent discussion will follow

the order given in "Augustine's *De Doctrina Christiana*," 103–112; the differences will be most apparent in the literature after 1966.

35. Pollmann also categorizes *De doctrina* as a hermeneutics, but her construal is closer to the view I propose here (that *De doctrina* is an *expanded* hermeneutics) and is not to be confused with one like Toom's.

36. For the opposite focus, i.e., only treating the fourth book, see Enos et al., *The Rhetoric of Saint Augustine of Hippo*.

37. Toom, *Thought Clothed with Sound*, 16–17. Cf. Portalié, *A Guide to the Thought of Saint Augustine*, 60 (page citations are to the reprint edition); Sieben, "Die 'Res' der Bibel," 90 n. 75.

38. Toom, *Thought Clothed with Sound*, 236.

39. See also Grech, "Hermeneutical Principles of Saint Augustine in *Teaching Christianity*," 80–94; Schildgen, "Augustine's Answer to Jacques Derrida," 383–397. It is perhaps one of the difficulties of bringing Augustine to bear on contemporary debates that his work can become fragmented.

40. By framing the issue like this, I consciously depart from Schleiermacher's statement that hermeneutics is the inversion of rhetoric and, therefore, its opposite: "The belonging together of hermeneutics and rhetoric consists in the fact that every act of understanding is the inversion of a speech-act, during which the thought which was the basis of the speech must become conscious" (*Hermeneutics and Criticism*, 7). See also Ricoeur, "Rhetoric—Poetics—Hermeneutics," 60–72. I am not negating the insight that understanding speech is in some way the opposite process, but I am suggesting that Augustine goes one step further by making rhetoric come after interpretation and not just before.

41. A point made also by Toom, *Thought Clothed with Sound*, 244.

42. Hill, "*De Doctrina Christiana*," 443–446.

43. Ibid., 444; Hill, "Translator's Note to *Teaching Christianity*," 95.

44. Hill, "*De Doctrina Christiana*," 445.

45. Moreau, "Lecture du 'De doctrina christiana,'" 254–255, also stresses—without citing Hill—the discussion between Augustine and Aurelius and arrives at similar conclusions. See her later "Introduction to *La Doctrine Chrétienne*," where she disagrees with Hill on the use of *ep.* 41, but agrees that Augustine was dealing with a specific, urgent pastoral need: preparing clergy in the ministry of the word (26).

46. Hill, "*De Doctrina Christiana*," 445.

47. *Non enim, etiam si possint haec a tardioribus tandem aliquando perdisci, nos ea tanti pendimus ut eis discendis iam maturas vel etiam graves hominum aetates velimus impendi. Satis est ut adulescentulorum ista sit cura, nec ipsorum omnium quos utilitati ecclesiasticae cupimus erudiri, sed eorum quos nondum magis urgens et huic rei sine dubio praeponenda necessitas occupavit.*

I use Hill's translation to emphasize his argument. It fits the context well: Augustine means adolescents in the church, versus elder ministers who should not leave aside their ecclesial duties to learn how to be better rhetors. See, however, Kevane, "Augustine's *De Doctrina Christiana*," 100–101.

48. Hill, "*De Doctrina Christiana*," 446.

49. Ibid., 446.

50. Press, "Subject and Structure," 106 n. 21, citing *doctr. chr.* Prol. 1, 2.7.10, 2.39.58, 2.41.62, 3.37.56; cf. 1.22.21, 1.24.30. For a fuller treatment, see Press, "Content and Argument," 165–167.

51. Press, "Content and Argument," 166–167.

52. Schäublin, "*De doctrina christiana*," 54.

53. So NPNF and Green. It should be noted that I use "pulpit" aware that there was likely no pulpit in a North African church in the fourth and fifth centuries. Perhaps it is a bit of sleight-of-hand, covering over this historical fact in translation, but—and this is the key point—it renders to our modern minds an accurate (though anachronistic) image.

54. So Robertson and Hill.

55. Kevane, "Augustine's *De Doctrina Christiana*," 100 n. 14. Some examples: *spir. et litt.*, written in response to Marcellinus, or *cat. rud.*, written for Deogratias, or, and more importantly as it is also a handbook of sorts, *ench.*, written for Laurentius.

56. Hill, "*De Doctrina Christiana*," 444.

57. See chapter 3.

58. Pollmann, *Doctrina Christiana*, 73–75.

59. Press, "Content and Argument," 167–168; Press, "Subject and Structure," 118–119. For a list of those who hold the view against which he reacts, see "Content and Argument," 167 n. 4. For an emphasis on *De doctrina*'s rhetorical background, see Eden, *Hermeneutics and the Rhetorical Tradition*, 56.

60. Namely, Kevane, "Augustine's *De Doctrina Christiana*"; Verheijen, "Le De Doctrina Christiana de saint Augustin," 10–20. See Press, "Subject and Structure," 103–107. Pollmann, *Doctrina Christiana*, 89–104, starts with "*tractatio [scripturarum]*," which, as she demonstrates, is molded by Augustine through the ancient genre of "*doctrina*," i.e., the technical textbook for the expert.

61. Press, "Subject and Structure," 107. Cf. Chin, "The Grammarian's Spoils," 167–183. Pollmann, *Doctrina Christiana*, throughout highlights the rhetorical background of the work while emphasizing that it is a hermeneutics.

62. See also Prol. 9; 1.1.1; 4.1.1.

63. Eden, *Hermeneutics and the Rhetorical Tradition*, 53–63, traces the common analogies of reading and the journey home, of the literary work

read and a tapestry, the concept of *context* as a remedy to obscurity, and especially the rhetorical terms *scriptum*, *verba*, and *aequitas*.

64. Press, "Subject and Structure," 112. For his full treatment of the classical tradition, see 107–112.

65. Ibid., 117.

66. Ibid., 122. Eden, *Hermeneutics and the Rhetorical Tradition*, 56, though without the comparison to Augustine's contemporary context, also draws attention to his indebtedness to the earlier rhetorical school of Cicero. Also, see Eden, "The Rhetorical Tradition and Augustinian Hermeneutics," 45–63.

67. For more on Augustine's use of, and departure from, Cicero, see Primmer, "The Function of the *genera dicendi* in *De doctrina christiana* 4," 68–86 (esp. 75–82). The following selections are my additions to Press's argument. He does not reference them.

68. *Nam cum per artem rhetoricam et vera suadeantur et falsa, quis audeat dicere adversus mendacium in defensoribus suis inermem debere consistere veritatem, ut videlicet illi qui res falsas persuadere conantur, noverint auditorem vel benevolum vel intentum vel docilem proemio facere, isti autem non noverint.* Cf. Cicero, *Orat.*, 122. One can note that this is exactly what Augustine does in the prologue.

69. Cf. *Cresc.* 1.1.2–1.3.3.

70. See *Orat.* 43–61, where Cicero downplays the necessity of *inventio* and ordering (*conlocare*). The very fact an orator is called *orator* and not *inventor* demonstrates, he says, the primary quality of importance (61).

71. Press, "Subject and Structure," 120–122.

72. Ibid., 121.

73. Ibid., 122.

74. Again, one need only compare Cicero's emphasis on being called *rhetor* as opposed to *inventor* (*Orat.* 61).

75. Press, "Subject and Structure," 120.

76. Press, "*Doctrina* in Augustine's *De Doctrina Christiana*," 98–120, in fact, thinks *De doctrina* was written with two audiences in mind: the secular readers and the churchly ones. More will be said about the audience below.

77. It does not help Press's case that Augustine focuses only on two of the five aspects of the traditional formulation of rhetoric (*inventio* and *elocutio*, not *dispositio*, *memoria*, or *actio*); I owe this point to Pollmann, *Doctrina Christiana*, 228–229.

78. Press, "Subject and Structure," 120–121.

79. Augustine himself describes the rhetoric he taught in *conf.* 9.2.2: "And it gave me pleasure in your sight not to retire loudly, but quietly to remove the service of my tongue from the marketplace of talkativeness

[*nundinis loquacitatis*], lest more boys, who did not meditate on your law or your peace, but on lying insanities and the warfare of the courts [*bella forensia*], should purchase from my mouth weapons for their madness." The people learning the rhetoric were boys (*pueri*) who were being trained for the law courts. For Augustine, in *conf.*, it is the social location—the law courts—that encouraged lying and warfare; these law courts went in direct opposition to the law of God.

80. A point Pollmann suggests has not been taken seriously enough in earlier discussions (*Doctrina Christiana*, 228).

81. As there are in all patristic interpretive practice. See Young, "The Rhetorical Schools and Their Influence on Patristic Exegesis," 182–199. Pollmann, *Doctrina Christiana*, highlights the work's debt to rhetoric throughout.

82. Press, "Subject and Structure," 106 n. 21.

83. Marrou, *Saint Augustin et la fin de la culture antique*, 381; see also, 332 n. 1. One might find this statement exceptional in light of a good bit of Book 4 (see below). Kevane objects to Marrou's inattention to "the practical pastoral purpose" Augustine had in mind ("Augustine's *De Doctrina Christiana*," 120 n. 111, cf. 128).

84. Marrou, *Saint Augustin et la fin de la culture antique*, 331–332. See also 413, where Marrou states that *De doctrina* is not only the fundamental charter of Christian culture ("la charte fondamentale de la culture chrétienne"), but it is also—curiously—a glimpse into the history of the decline of classical culture.

85. Kevane, "Augustine's *De Doctrina Christiana*," 121. Combès and Farges agree: "Introduction to *La Doctrine Chrétienne*," 155, but Moreau, "Introduction to *La Doctrine Chrétienne*," 24–26, thinks Augustine had clergy in mind, though that does not negate that the work could have formulated a culture.

86. Kevane's article predates Press's.

87. Kevane, "Augustine's *De Doctrina Christiana*," 122–133. See, however, Press, "Subject and Structure," 101–106, where he argues that, although it makes initial sense to begin with *doctrina*, two scholars (Kevane and Verheijen) have nonetheless attempted it and arrived at different conclusions.

88. Kevane, "Paideia and Anti-Paideia," 153–180, also makes this argument in his discussion on the prologue. There, he focuses on the third class of critic, those who espouse what he calls an "anti-intellectualism" (178–179). Press, "Subject and Structure," 102–103, seems to suggest that Kevane thinks *paideia* has a single meaning, but actually, Kevane's view is not that distant from Press's. Press, "*Doctrina* in Augustine's *De Doctrina Christiana*," 100, does go further and suggest that *doctrina* is used to speak

to both pagans and Christians, but it seems Kevane does allow for a comprehensive, though perhaps slightly more narrow, definition of *paideia*, and hence, of *doctrina* ("Augustine's *De Doctrina Christiana*," 124–133).

89. Kevane, "Augustine's *De Doctrina Christiana*," 131.

90. Ibid., 131.

91. Ibid., 132. Pollmann, *Doctrina Christiana*, 217, emphasizes the continuity between grammar and rhetoric in the classical system; the former was taught as a preparation for the latter.

92. Verheijen, "Le De Doctrina Christiana de saint Augustin," 10–20, suggests that only 2.19.29–42.63 can be called a "fundamental charter for a Christian culture," while the rest is a textbook of hermeneutics and Christian expression.

93. Kevane, "Paideia and Anti-Paideia," 160–167, the technical vocabulary is *praecepta, tractare, studiosi, tradere, legere, litterae, discere*, and they "give his treatise an academic tone and a pedagogical purpose from the outset" (160).

94. Kevane, "Augustine's *De Doctrina Christiana*," 132–133. For more on *De doctrina*'s influence into the Middle Ages, see R. Green, "Introduction to *On Christian Teaching*," xix–xxiii, and the volume dedicated to the question of the work's reception, English, *Reading and Wisdom*.

95. Cf. Pollmann, *Doctrina Christiana*, 104–108.

96. Kevane, "Augustine's *De Doctrina Christiana*," 120.

97. Kevane, "Paideia and Anti-Paideia," 173. Simonetti, "Introduction to *L'Istruzione Cristiano*," xii–xiii, suggests a similar scenario.

98. Press, "Subject and Structure," 103–104, does, however, critique Kevane's philology.

99. Harrison, "De doctrina christiana," 122–123, is surely correct to state that the relationship between pagan culture and Christianity is the "subtext" to *De doctrina* and the Fathers in general, but that is different from Augustine offering a self-consciously opposing culture.

100. Kevane, "Augustine's *De Doctrina Christiana*," 130 n. 150.

101. Pollmann, *Doctrina Christiana*, 228–229. See also Pollmann, "Augustine's Hermeneutics as a Universal Discipline!?," 206–231.

102. Pollmann, *Doctrina Christiana*, 215–216; see also 243–244: not even Book 4 can be called a "Christian rhetoric" because it does not adequately cover everything a rhetoric should.

103. Ibid., 89–104. Moreau, "Introduction to *La Doctrine Chrétienne*," 40–41, points out that *De doctrina* is not as impersonal as a textbook often is; Augustine himself emerges time and again from the pages of the work.

104. Pollmann, *Doctrina Christiana*, 98.

105. Ibid., 104: "Auch hat DC keine primär theologisch-dogmatische Zielsetzung, wenngleich in DC 1 dogmatische Reflexionen in die Fixierung

des hermeneutischen Normenhorizontes integriert sind." Pollmann is here comparing *De doctrina* to Origen's *De principiis.*

106. Pollmann, *Doctrina Christiana,* 246, 249.

107. Ibid., 69–75.

108. Ibid., 74.

## 2. *De doctrina christiana:* Eclecticism in Action

1. There was some disagreement over the dating of the prologue, but on the basis of manuscript evidence, such as the Leningrad Codex, and Augustine's statement in 4.1.1 that he wrote the prologue with the initial parts, it is hard to doubt that it was written in the earlier period of composition. See further Duchrow, "Zum Prolog," 165–172, who argues for a late date, as does Opelt, "Doctrina und Doctrina Christiana," 7. Duchrow also posits a change in ideas between the prologue and Books 1 and 2, a view taken on by Mayer, "Res per signa," 100–112, who argues that the prologue is early and that a change in ideas is indefensible. Duchrow, in a later work, admits that his position concerning the dating might be wrong, though he thinks the bulk of his argument remains correct (*Sprachverständnis und Biblisches Hören,* 207 n. 91).

2. For discussion concerning the meaning of *doctrina,* see Kevane, "Augustine's *De Doctrina Christiana,*" 122–133; Press, "*Doctrina* in Augustine's *De Doctrina Christiana,*" 98–120.

3. Markus, "St. Augustine on Signs," 60–83. Markus argues that Augustine is the first to integrate a theory of language into that of sign. Jackson, "The Theory of Signs in St. Augustine's *De Doctrina Christiana,*" 92–147 (136), however, argues that Augustine's originality lies not in his integration (and consequent invention of semiotics) but in his application of the theory to the Bible. See also Duchrow, *Sprachverständnis und Biblisches Hören,* 50–51.

4. Bochet, "Le cercle herméneutique," 16–21, argues that Augustine reverses the discussion of signs and things for theological reasons, specifically, that Christ is the key to scripture.

5. Vessey, "The Great Conference," 69, goes so far as to say that *De doctrina* "[loses] itself in semiotics."

6. R. Williams, "Language, Reality, and Desire," 138.

7. Jackson, "The Theory of Signs in St. Augustine's *De Doctrina Christiana,*" 92.

8. By "terminological distinction," I am not suggesting that Augustine considers signs to be mimetic; they are referential. See further Pollmann, *Doctrina Christiana,* 184–191.

9. R. Williams, "Language, Reality, and Desire," incorrectly conflates the distinction of *signum-res* with that of *uti-frui*. When he states that the *uti-frui* distinction "pervades" the whole of *De doctrina*, he has overstated his case (139).

10. For more on this distinction, see O'Donovan, "*Usus* and *Fruitio* in Augustine," 361–397. O'Donovan suggests that *De doctrina* represents Augustine's exploration of the instrumental and ontological uses of the *uti-frui* pair. See also Burnaby, *Amor Dei*, 104–110; Canning, "The Unity of Love for God and Neighbour," 38–121 (esp. 46–47).

11. It should be noted that there are two classes of things, not three, as some translations of 1.3.3 suggest: *Res ergo aliae sunt quibus fruendum est, aliae quibus utendum, aliae quae fruuntur et utuntur.* Robertson and Gavigan mistranslate the last clause as passive: "Some things are to be enjoyed, others to be used, and there are others which are to be enjoyed and used." As Jackson, "Semantics and Hermeneutics," 70, argues, both grammar and context go against this translation. It should be: "There are some things which must be enjoyed, some which must be used, and others which enjoy and use." The final clause is a subset of the second. For more on this, see Jackson, "Semantics and Hermeneutics," 72.

12. For further discussion on this point, see Pollmann, *Doctrina Christiana*, 143–147.

13. Jackson, "Semantics and Hermeneutics," 72.

14. On the basis of the entirety of 1.22.20–21, I am not as convinced as O'Donovan, "*Usus* and *Fruitio* in Augustine," 389, that Augustine feels his *uti-frui* pairing is "simply a mistake." Augustine may not gloss *uti* as a mode of love in his first definition (1.4.4), but he is clear that it is a form of love in 1.22.21, a love directed toward the love of God (*frui*).

15. For Augustine, all scripture relates to faith, hope, and love (1.37.41–40.44). Faith and hope concern the *res* of scripture, while love concerns the relation to those things. Pollmann, "Hermeneutical Presuppositions," 427, suggests that Augustine is even more radical in *De doctrina* than elsewhere because he narrows the content of the Bible to love of God and love of neighbor from the triad of faith, hope, and love. Augustine surely states that every interpretation of scripture relates to faith, hope, and love (1.40.44), while then showing that, in the end, love alone remains. Thus, Pollmann is correct to note the ethical thrust of *De doctrina*, but it must be made clear that, for Augustine, love is an empty concept without the contents of faith. They are inseparable.

16. Ayres, "Augustine on the Rule of Faith," 37–38, is right to note the coordination of the *regula fidei* with the move to God, a move I highlight by pointing to the coordination of the two rules of faith and of love. Likewise,

A. Williams, *The Divine Sense*, 143–189, helpfully points out the insepara-bility of knowledge and love in Augustine.

17. Numerous articles and chapters have been written about Augus-tine's sign theory in general, all of which deal with *doctr. chr.* at some point. See, e.g., Ando, "Augustine on Language," 45–78; Ayers, "Language Theory and Analysis in Augustine," 1–12; Harrison, *Beauty and Revelation*, 55–96.

18. I here follow Engels, "La doctrine du signe chez saint Augustin," 366–373, translating *signa data* as "given" instead of "conventional" because the distinction between *signa data* and *signa naturalia* is the will that brings about the sign. See also Jackson, "The Theory of Signs in St. Augustine's *De Doctrina Christiana*," 96–97, who argues that Markus goes too far when he states that the sign giver gives the sign its significance. In *De doctrina* "given" refers to the occurrence, not to the significance of the sign. See further Markus, "St. Augustine on Signs," 72–75. Markus agrees with Jack-son's argument in a later article: "Signs, Communication, and Communi-ties," 107 n. 7. See also the discussion in the notes to BA 11/2 (483–495): "intentional signs" (*signes intentionnels*) is another good translation.

19. Thus, I am not convinced by Byassee, *Praise Seeking Understanding*, 61, who argues (referencing a Ph.D. dissertation by Michael Cameron) that Augustine's allegorical approach in *De doctrina* correlates a "temporal sign" with an "atemporal thing," or that the *signa* of scripture here point to "the *res* of eternal, dis-embodied meaning." I do, however, think Byassee (62 n. 20) is correct to insist on the necessity of reading *en. Ps.* and not simply *doctr. chr.* for a full understanding of Augustine's exegesis.

20. For example, Marrou, *Saint Augustin et la fin de la culture antique*, 331–540; Kevane, "Augustine's *De Doctrina Christiana*," 97–133.

21. Verheijen, "Le De Doctrina Christiana de saint Augustin," 10–20.

22. One can also compare Augustine's discussions of the disciplines in *ord.*, where he has a much more positive view of their capacity: one can ascend through them to God (2.14.16). In *doctr. chr.* 2.39.58, Augustine states exactly the opposite: the disciplines are incapable of leading to the blessed life. Pollmann, *Doctrina Christiana*, also points this out and draws attention to Augustine's integration of the arts into his hermeneutical proj-ect as an optional, auxiliary concern (192–195).

23. Moreau, "Lecture du 'De doctrina christiana,'" 261–262, points out that the section has "every appearance" of a digression, though it cannot simply be written off as such; the whole passage has a scope that fits com-fortably where Augustine has placed it.

24. Sieben, "Die 'Res' der Bibel," 84, suggests that *totum istum locum* refers to the quotation from Rom. 1:21–23 just preceding. Whether the

subsequent discussion is predicated on Augustine's understanding of Romans 1 or not, "topic" does justice both to the previous quotation as well as the following consideration of the different kinds of learning.

25. Augustine suggests some uses of astronomy (2.29.46), e.g., fixing the annual celebration of the Passion, but he writes it off as mostly useless. Still, he spends a few sentences on it in a manner comparable to a footnote in a modern book. Moreau, "Introduction to *La Doctrine Chrétienne*," 21, points out that Augustine composed orally, which means one could think of the work as a series of lectures to an audience; as with any good lecturer, he gives examples, detailed remarks, and even repetitions.

26. Verheijen, "Le De Doctrina Christiana de saint Augustin," 16–17, is forced to play down these citations as moments where Augustine shows, in the middle of a digression, that he has not forgotten he is composing a hermeneutics. It seems a more simple explanation is better: this discussion is not a digression but a serious part of his hermeneutical treatise, providing tools for understanding what God says through the words of scripture. Such a reading leaves Augustine's clear structure intact.

27. "Of the prophetic significance of the spoiling of the Egyptians . . . I remember to have set down what occurred to me at the time in my book entitled *De doctrina christiana*; to the effect that the gold and silver and garments of the Egyptians typified certain branches of learning [*doctrinae*] which may be profitably learned or taught among the Gentiles" (*c. Faust.* 22.91, NPNF 1/4 [adapted]).

28. R. Green, "Augustine's *De doctrina Christiana*," 104, suggests that the image of spoiling the Egyptians applies only to those who have already received a secular education, a point provocative though perhaps not entirely persuasive.

29. For a discussion of the oral nature of ancient reading and its influence on Augustine, see Leinhard, "Reading the Bible and Learning to Read," 10–14.

30. Barton, *Biblical Criticism*, 100–101.

31. Toom, *Thought Clothed with Sound*, 220–222.

32. Teske, "Criteria for Figurative Interpretation," 109–122, calls the criterion in *De doctrina* the "maximizing rule for biblical interpretation" in comparison to the "absurdity criterion" that he once thought Augustine utilized in *Gn. adv. Man.* He argues that Augustine espoused an absurdity criterion, though he did not in fact use it. The criterion is "maximizing" because it treats both faith and love. I have chosen "*caritas* criterion" because this is Augustine's stated criterion: a passage's relation to love. As he expounds in *ench.*, love is the relational aspect of faith and hope. Faith and hope are not themselves without love, which will endure eternally, long after faith is replaced by sight and hope replaced by true happiness (see also

*doctr. chr.* 1.38.42). For more on *caritas* as a hermeneutical criterion outside of *doctr. chr.* and Augustine, see Pollmann, *Doctrina Christiana*, 135–147.

33. Not much is known about Tyconius's personal life. He was an educated, North African lay member of the Donatist Church. According to Augustine (*ep.* 93.43), Parmenian, the Donatist bishop, censured Tyconius, demonstrating that he fit neither with the Donatists nor with the Catholics. Augustine himself puzzles over the fact that Tyconius did not move to the Catholic party when he wrote so vigorously against the Donatists (*doctr. chr.* 3.30.42). For more on potential reasons for Tyconius remaining with the Donatists, see Chadwick, "Tyconius and Augustine," 49–55. For more on Tyconius in general, see Frend, *The Donatist Church*, 201–207.

34. On *LR*, see especially Bright, *The Book of Rules of Tyconius*; Kannengiesser and Bright, *A Conflict of Christian Hermeneutics in Roman Africa*, whose two primary articles have been expanded and reprinted in Bright, *Augustine and the Bible*; Pollmann, *Doctrina Christiana*, 32–65.

35. For the two strongest arguments that Augustine misunderstood Tyconius, see Bright, "The Preponderating Influence of Augustine," 109–228; Kannengiesser, "Augustine and Tyconius," 149–177.

36. For the text of *LR*, see Burkitt, *The Book of Rules of Tyconius*; for English translation, see Babcock, *Tyconius: The Book of Rules*.

37. *Ep.* 249. The fact that Augustine recommends *LR* for its ecclesiology, when coupled with his discussion of Tyconius's seventh rule (3.37.55), suggests that Augustine did not fail to grasp what Tyconius was saying. Instead, it seems more likely that Augustine wanted to provide an appropriate context in which to read *LR* and gain the most from it. For arguments that Augustine does not misunderstand Tyconius, see Pollmann, *Doctrina Christiana*, 212–215; Colish, "Augustine's Use and Abuse of Tyconius," 42–48.

38. R. Green, "Introduction to *On Christian Teaching*," xxii; Hagendahl, *Augustine and the Latin Classics*, 568; Monfasani, "The *De doctrina christiana* and Renaissance Rhetoric," 173.

39. Enos et al., eds., *The Rhetoric of St. Augustine of Hippo*. The translation, by Sullivan, is older, dating to 1930, and the Latin is her revision of the text in PL 34.

40. Baldwin, "Saint Augustine on Preaching," 187–203, argues that *De doctrina* "begins rhetoric anew" by going back to Cicero (187). Press, "Subject and Structure," 99–124, argues similarly. Fortin, "Augustine and the Problem of Christian Rhetoric," 219–233, argues in contrast that Augustine subverts Cicero. Marrou, *Saint Augustin et la fin de la culture antique*, 519–521, thinks Augustine shows no originality and is in fact an example of the decline of classical culture. Hagendahl, *Augustine and the Latin Classics*, 558–569, agrees that Augustine simply uses Cicero: "[Augustine's

instruction] follows . . . Cicero's views and directions so closely, often even in the minutest particulars, that it cannot make a substantial claim to novelty and originality in the doctrinal system, at most to a slight modification on this or that point" (567), but he admits that Augustine's project is one of "elimination and concentration," which it seems would suggest some amount of change (cf. Pollmann, *Doctrina Christiana*, 228–241).

41. Primmer, "The Function of the *genera dicendi* in *De doctrina christiana* 4," 68–86 (69).

42. Cicero, *Orat.* 69. For Latin and English text, see Hubbell, *Orator*. Cicero has *probare* ("to demonstrate") in place of *docere*. The two terms are almost synonymous. I owe my translation of *flectere* to Primmer, "The Function of the *genera dicendi* in *De doctrina christiana* 4," 75.

43. I should note here something about my use of gendered pronouns. I am arguing that *De doctrina* was originally primarily intended for ministers, which in Augustine's time would have been male. For that reason (and to avoid wordiness), I utilize the masculine pronoun when translating *De doctrina*. But because—as I will argue—there are theological reasons for widening this audience (already apparent even in Augustine), while keeping the narrow focus on the pulpit and the sermon, I will utilize male and female pronouns when talking about the application of the ideas to the present. For more on the situation of females in North Africa with respect to the clergy in the fourth and fifth centuries, see Miles, "Patriarchy as Political Theology," 55–70.

44. Primmer, "The Function of the *genera dicendi* in *De doctrina christiana* 4," 75.

45. Harrison, "The Rhetoric of Scripture and Preaching," 222.

46. *Orat.* 236, "But the eloquent orator (*eloquentia*) who ought to win not merely approval, *but admiration and shouts of applause*, if it may be, should so excel in all things that he would be ashamed to have anything else awaited with greater anticipation or heard with greater pleasure" (emphasis added).

47. Harrison, "De Doctrina Christiana," 129.

48. Fortin, "Augustine and the Problem of Christian Rhetoric," 221, argues that Augustine's notion of rhetoric "resembles that of Cicero in outward appearance more than in inner substance"; he argues, furthermore, that when Augustine sounds the most like Cicero is the point at which he is the furthest from him (223). For similar conclusions, see R. Green, "Augustine's *De doctrina Christiana*," 106; Foster, "Eloquentia Nostra (DDC IV,VI,100)," 459–494.

49. Simonetti, "Introduction to *L'Istruzione Cristiano*," xxxix, points out that Augustine does not quote Cicero but Cyprian and Ambrose, a move that emphasizes the Christian culture at the expense of the classical one.

50. This is the title of Pollmann's translation in the *Universal Bibliothek* series (Stuttgart: Reclam, 2002), but see her reflections (260–261). In *Doctrina Christiana*, 107, and in "Doctrina christiana (De-)," 552, she glosses the title thus: "über die christlich gebotene Methode der Wissensaneignung und -vermittling" (107), "on the appropriate Christian method of acquiring and relaying knowledge" (I slightly modify the translation by Van Fleteren, "Toward an Understanding of Augustine's Hermeneutic," 126). Simonetti's translation, *L'Istruzione Cristiana*, also has resonances with "Christian Education."

51. The earlier edition, *BA* 11, includes *doctr. chr.* with *cat. rud.*, in a volume entitled "*Le Magistère Chrétien*," "Christian Teaching." The newer edition has separated the two works, and *De doctrina* is in *BA* 11/2; in its introduction, Moreau emphasizes that "*doctrina*" has a larger semantic range than "*doctrine*," and she stresses that this range must be kept in mind, though the volume retains the traditional French title.

52. Harrison, "De Doctrina Christiana," 121, suggests "On Christian Teaching and Learning." While this catches the active and passive registers of *doctrina*, it still suggests a more programmatic treatise than the evidence allows. *De doctrina* is not about learning per se, but about understanding what the Bible says and sharing *that* with others.

53. Press, "Content and Argument," 165–182, is probably the most thorough outline of the text, while Jackson, "Semantics and Hermeneutics," 35–36, follows the rhetorical structure and Pollmann, *Doctrina Christiana*, 90, highlights its coherent, systematic organization, allowing for a more succinct outline than Press's. I have attempted to navigate a middle way, similar to Pollmann, *Christliche Bildung*, 264–267. The numbers in square brackets refer to sections, and in some instances, the numbers cannot be precise; Book 1, for instance, cannot be broken into such definite units because the *regula fidei* section has several discussions about proper love, in spite of my outline's suggestion that the *regula dilectionis* is confined to a specific location, where it is perhaps dealt with more fully, though not exhaustively.

54. There is a tension in the text at this point. Augustine's title shows he conceives of the entirety of the work as concerning "teaching" in some regard, though he locates "teaching" here beneath the *modus inveniendi* before he subdivides it into signs and things. No such statement exists at the start of Book 4, but the final sentence demonstrates that Augustine thinks he has been talking about "teaching" even throughout the fourth book (4.31.64).

55. Concerning the outline of Book 4, I am indebted particularly to Primmer, "The Function of the *genera dicendi* in De doctrina christiana 4," 74–75. See also the Appendix to Enos, *The Rhetoric of Saint Augustine of Hippo*, 330–332.

56. He does not, however, think God reveals himself in the same way in philosophy as in scripture.

### 3. Theological Hermeneutics: *A priori* or *a posteriori?*

1. Schleiermacher, *Hermeneutics and Criticism*, 22; for a description of this decisive shift in hermeneutics, see Grondin, *Introduction to Philosophical Hermeneutics*, 64–74.

2. This is not to contest Zimmermann's claim that theological hermeneutics has, throughout history, had concerns that are similar to philosophical hermeneutics (*Recovering Theological Hermeneutics*).

3. Gadamer, *Truth and Method*, xxvii (page numbers to the reprint edition); Ricoeur describes the shift with Heidegger and Gadamer as "radicalisation" in his essay "The Task of Hermeneutics," 43–62 (44, 53). See also Heidegger, *Being and Time*, 188–210.

4. Gadamer, *Truth and Method*, 254.

5. Grondin, *Introduction to Philosophical Hermeneutics*, xv.

6. Ibid., xiv, 32–39, passim; Gadamer, *Truth and Method*, 418–427.

7. For an argument of the usefulness of hermeneutics in a distinctly theological mode, see Watson, "Hermeneutics and the Doctrine of Scripture," 118–143.

8. See, e.g., Tracy, *The Analogical Imagination*, 101, 103–107: "The fact is that an insistence upon the hermeneutical understanding of philosophy and theology is not a search for that 'middle ground' beloved by 'moderates' but an articulation of the only ground upon which any one of us stands: the ground of real finitude and radical historicity in all hermeneutical understanding" (103); Jeanrond, *Theological Hermeneutics*, for his depiction of Augustine, see 22–26; cf. 181: "The different focus of theological thinking, i.e., God's revelation in this universe, from that of other disciplines of human knowledge does not only not justify a different interpretation theory, rather it demands the application of general hermeneutics both in order to point out this different focus and precisely because of the fact that we have been able to proclaim in our human language God's presence in our human world and history."

9. Webster, *Word and Church*, 47–48.

10. Again, referring to Augustine as speaking about "hermeneutics in general" might sound anachronistic, but he is writing a hermeneutics, and he does have comments about the hermeneutical treatise itself.

11. Thiselton, *New Horizons in Hermeneutics*, 5; see also 6–8, 410–470.

12. Thiselton, "Resituating Hermeneutics in the Twenty-First Century"; cf. Thiselton, "A Retrospective Reappraisal of Part VII," where he

does insist that he does not want philosophy to shape theology; still, philosophical hermeneutics serves as a safeguard for the benefit of theology (802).

13. Cf. Tracy, *Blessed Rage for Order*, 77: "To interpret well must now mean that we attend to and use the hermeneutics of both retrieval and suspicion"; Jeanrond, *Theological Hermeneutics*, 10, who addresses the need for "adequate criteria" for interpretation.

14. It should be noted here that an appeal to general hermeneutics to protect scriptural interpretation does not preclude actual interpretation of the text. Thiselton has, after all, published commentaries on 1 Corinthians (*The First Epistle to the Corinthians*).

15. For example, Bartholomew, "Uncharted Waters," 1–39; Jeanrond, "After Hermeneutics," 85–102.

16. See, e.g., Watson, *Text, Church and World*, 46–59; Jenson, "Hermeneutics and the Life of the Church," 89–105.

17. For a recent example, see Paddison, "Scriptural Reading and Revelation," 433–448; Paddison, *Scripture*, esp. 7–9.

18. C. Wood, *The Formation of Christian Understanding*, 53–54.

19. Ibid., 19.

20. Ibid., 9; cf. Watson, "The Scope of Hermeneutics," 65.

21. Cf. Watson, "The Scope of Hermeneutics," 69: "A general (that is, philosophical) hermeneutics would seek to establish the conditions presupposed in any interpretative act, but its abstraction from local issues would restrict its usefulness in practice"; See also Webster, *Word and Church*, 47–86.

22. For example, Jeanrond, *Theological Hermeneutics*, 44–45; Frei, *The Eclipse of the Biblical Narrative*, 283; Thiselton, *New Horizons in Hermeneutics*, 205–206.

23. By utilizing the terms "general" and "local," such theologians tacitly admit they are under the umbrella of general hermeneutics, even while attempting to step out from under it.

24. See Frei, "The 'Literal Reading' of Biblical Narrative in the Christian Tradition," 130–131.

25. See, respectively, Watson, "The Scope of Hermeneutics," 71; Thiselton, "A Retrospective Reappraisal of Part VII," 802.

26. D. Wood, "The Place of Theology in Theological Hermeneutics," 156–171, makes a similar case, suggesting theological hermeneutics should become more theological.

27. To emphasize, I deploy these terms as a metaphor to explain a conceptual move made by theologians; it is not terminology a theologian would necessarily use to describe him- or herself.

28. Gadamer, "Autobiographical Reflections," 3–38 (20).

29. See Gadamer, *Truth and Method*.

30. Throughout the chapter, I do not use "abstract" pejoratively. Instead, I use it to highlight the theoretical nature of an *a priori* hermeneutics: it seeks to move to a place disconnected from practice in order to think theoretically about interpretation. The concrete practice of (safeguarded) interpretation only comes later.

31. Tracy serves as a good example, though he does state in a later essay that he does not intend his notion of the classic to serve as a "foundationalist" use of hermeneutics ("On Reading the Scriptures Theologically," 59 n. 16). It seems, however, that he misreads himself. See, e.g., *Analogical Imagination*, 233–247. *A priori* refers to the way Tracy uses his general hermeneutics. If his notion of the classic were indeed "clarificatory" ("On Reading the Scriptures Theologically," 59 n. 16), then it would be an example of an *a posteriori* hermeneutics, making use of a general hermeneutical idea analogically to aid an already existing practice. Another example is Schneiders, *The Revelatory Text*.

32. Cf. Frei, "Theology and Interpretation of Narrative," 113.

33. A good example of this model would be Watson, *Text, Church and World*, where he discusses contemporary issues facing biblical interpretation, such as historical and feminist concerns with the biblical texts, and then he proceeds to suggest ways to interpret the texts that are causing problems. Throughout the book, Watson engages with scripture, showing that his hermeneutics is an answer to a problem, rather than a solution created in abstraction from the issue. Also see Fowl, *Engaging Scripture*.

34. Jeanrond, "Hermeneutics and Christian Praxis," 174–188; Jeanrond, "After Hermeneutics"; Jeanrond, "Criteria for New Biblical Theologies," 233–249; Jeanrond, *Text and Interpretation*; Jeanrond, *Theological Hermeneutics*.

35. Jeanrond, *Text and Interpretation*, xvii.

36. Jeanrond, *Theological Hermeneutics*, 8.

37. Ibid., 7.

38. Jeanrond, "Hermeneutics and Christian Praxis," 181.

39. See the discussions in *Text and Interpretation*, 64–72, and *Theological Hermeneutics*, 114–116. One can see such a viewpoint in practice in Jeanrond, *A Theology of Love*: "In this chapter I shall explore some of the biblical voices on love *and assess their potential* for a theology of love today" (25, emphasis added).

40. Jeanrond, "Criteria for New Biblical Theologies"; Räisänen, *Beyond New Testament Theology*.

41. Jeanrond, *Text and Interpretation*, 129, 132; cf. id., *Theological Hermeneutics*, 182.

42. Jeanrond, *Text and Interpretation*, xvi.

43. Ibid., xvi.

44. Cf. Tracy, *Blessed Rage for Order*, 73.

45. Jeanrond, *Text and Interpretation*, 3; cf. Jeanrond, "Hermeneutics and Christian Praxis," 174.

46. Jeanrond, "After Hermeneutics," 92.

47. See chapter 1 of *Text and Interpretation* for Jeanrond's formulation on the basis of Gadamer and Ricoeur. He addresses Tracy in chapter 3 as a theological application of the aforementioned theory.

48. Jeanrond, *Text and Interpretation*, 68; they are "dimensions" and not "steps" because they occur simultaneously. Cf. Ricoeur, "What Is a Text?," 145–164, where he addresses the unnecessary opposition between understanding and explanation.

49. Jeanrond, *Theological Hermeneutics*, 113–116; cf. Ricoeur, "The Hermeneutical Function of Distanciation," 131–144.

50. For a fuller account, see *Text and Interpretation*, 94–119; *Theological Hermeneutics*, 78–119.

51. Jeanrond, "Criteria for New Biblical Theologies," 241.

52. Cf. Jeanrond, "Hermeneutics and Christian Praxis," 181.

53. Fowl argues against Jeanrond that the biblical texts do not require a theological reading (*Engaging*, 29–30). But compare Jeanrond, *Text and Interpretation*, 127.

54. Jeanrond, *Text and Interpretation*, 129–153; Tracy, *Analogical Imagination*, 99–229; Tracy, *Plurality and Ambiguity*, 12–27.

55. Jeanrond, *Text and Interpretation*, 142; cf. Jeanrond, *Theological Hermeneutics*, 160–161.

56. Jeanrond, *Text and Interpretation*, 132, 129.

57. Jeanrond, *Theological Hermeneutics*, 181.

58. Jeanrond, *Theological Hermeneutics*, 22. Vanhoozer, *Is There a Meaning in This Text?*, 117–118, comes to the same conclusion. See, however, Young's blurring of the lines between the typical depictions of Antiochene and Alexandrian interpretation: Young, *Biblical Exegesis and the Formation of Christian Culture*, 296–299; Young, "Alexandrian and Antiochene Exegesis," 334–354.

59. Jeanrond, *Theological Hermeneutics*, 25, cf. 100.

60. Ibid., 25; Jeanrond, "Hermeneutics and Christian Praxis," 180–181.

61. Jeanrond, *Theological Hermeneutics*, 130.

62. Markus, "Signs, Communication, and Communities," 98. For information concerning the Stoic and Epicurean background to Augustine's theory, see Markus, "Augustine on Signs," 60–65. Ticciati, like Markus, refers to Augustine's formulation as a "tryadic relation" in comparison to the "dyadic relation" found in Saussure's semiotics ("The Castration of Signs," 165, 178 n. 17).

63. Cf. *trin.* 15.18–20.

64. Markus, "Signs, Communication, and Communities," 103.

65. R. Williams, "Language, Reality, and Desire," 141.

66. Ibid., 140.

67. McCurry, "Towards a Poetics of Theological Creativity," 415–433, refers to Williams's reading as "inflected interpretive performance" (429).

68. R. Williams, "Language, Reality, and Desire," 147.

69. Ibid., 142.

70. Williams is not alone in reading the semiotics of *De doctrina* in support of a contemporary notion of deferral; see Ferretter, "The Trace of the Trinity," 256–267. Not everyone reads Augustine as a modern: Young, "Augustine's Hermeneutics and Postmodern Criticism," 54; Louth, "Augustine on Language," 151–158. Augustine's language theory has even been used to refute Derrida: Schildgen, "Augustine's Answer to Jacques Derrida," 383–397.

71. Babcock, "*Caritas* and Signification," 146–147.

72. This is a standard observation since Istace, "Le livre premier du 'De doctrina christiana,'" 289–330; Sieben, "Die 'Res' der Bibel," 74–80.

73. He states similar things throughout his works, but never exactly like this: *trin.* 7.7; *en. Ps.* 68.5, 109.12–13; *Io. ev. tr.* 39.1–5.

74. For a discussion on Augustine's use of this analogy, see Toom, "The Potential of a Condemned Analogy," 205–213.

75. *Pace* Jordan, "Words and Word," 187–188. Jordan is not alone, however; see, e.g., Dawson, "Sign Theory, Allegorical Reading, and the Motions of the Soul."

76. Pollmann, *Doctrina Christiana*, 178, also points out that the discussion of the λόγος ἐνδιάθετος and λόγος προφορικός is not used in a linguistic or hermeneutical context but in a theological one.

77. Jeanrond, *Theological Hermeneutics*, 25.

78. This sentence is an allusion to John 1:3, 14 (Vulgate), but the language is also reminiscent of what has now become known as the Nicene Creed, especially when taken with the final sentence of the section.

79. It would also probably be going too far to state that christology is foundational to Augustine's hermeneutics, as Toom does (*Thought Clothed with Sound*, 205–245). As I argue here, I would hesitate to say his sign theory is created around the sign of Christ's humanity (244). Instead, looking for a single basis for Augustine's hermeneutics might be a contemporary concern, one that does not pay enough attention to Augustine's own looser practice. I am, however, sympathetic to the argument that the incarnation recapitulates the double-love command (Bochet, "Le cercle herméneutique," 16–21). The theological idea of the incarnation affects the

theological rationale for reading scripture, but it is not the basis of Augustine's sign theory.

80. A better place to go for a theoretical discussion of signs and things might be Augustine's earlier work, *mag.*, where the focus is on how and whether signs communicate/teach things (see Stock, *Augustine the Reader*, 145–162, for a commentary). Both *doctr. chr.* and *trin.* seem less concerned with how signs work and more concerned with using signs that do in fact work to help explain other phenomena. That is not to say semiotic theory cannot be extrapolated from Augustine's discussions. Cameron, "The Christological Substructure of Augustine's Figurative Exegesis," 74–103, argues that *De doctrina* represents a shift from the sign theory of *mag.*

81. Cf. 2.14.20, where Augustine warns against a desire to appear learned by focusing too much on signs and not enough on things.

82. See further Yeago, "The New Testament and the Nicene Dogma," 87–100; Young, "The 'Mind' of Scripture," 125–141.

83. His appeal to scripture and his first rule in 2.9.14 (to be familiar with all of the books of scripture) demonstrate the *a posteriori* character of his theory, even when appealing to the *regula fidei*.

84. An example of Augustine following his own rule can be seen in *ep.* 166, where he struggles in his letter to Jerome to reconcile his thoughts about unbaptized infants—ideas he firmly believed were taught in scripture—with his ideas of a merciful God (see especially 6.16–9.28). Throughout, he seeks not to depart from scriptural teaching, though it pains him to state that unbaptized children cannot enter heaven. This is not to excuse his tentative doctrine of some form of "limbo," but it does show him following his own rules.

85. R. Williams also brings this point out in "Language, Reality, and Desire," 142–143, though he connects it with semiotics, rather than with scripture itself.

86. See further Greene-McCreight, *Ad Litteram*, 9–10.

87. I use "synchronic" and "diachronic" to refer to reading the canon together as opposed to focusing on the individual books; this is in contrast to R. Williams's interesting and provocative definitions in "The Discipline of Scripture," 45–48.

88. Young, "The 'Mind' of Scripture," 131: "For Augustine the heart of scripture lies in the double-command—to love God and love your neighbor. But if we read the first book of *De Doctrina* we soon discover that that implies reading the scriptures in terms of doctrine of the Trinity and the overarching narrative of fall and redemption, into which the readers themselves are drawn."

89. See Van Fleteren, "St. Augustine, Neoplatonism, and the Liberal Arts," 14–24 (esp. 20–23); Burns, "Delighting the Spirit," 186–189. I would be reticent, however, to claim that Augustine's Neoplatonic language necessarily makes him a Neoplatonist. For a sympathetic argument, see A. Williams, *The Divine Sense*, 8–18, 236–239. One need only compare the language of ascent in *doctr. chr.* to that in *ord.* 2.9.26 to note just how different his later appeal to such language is.

90. Cf. *s. dom. m.* 1.4.11, where Augustine suggests that Isa. 11:2–3 corresponds with the Beatitudes as a progression but in reverse order; *sermo* 347, which deals at length with the passage.

91. I have translated from the Vulgate, which follows the LXX closely.

92. Thus, I must disagree slightly with Pecknold, *Transforming Postliberal Theology*, 139 n. 231, and Bright, "Augustine and the Ethics of Reading the Bible," 55–64. Both argue that all seven stages are phases of scriptural reading, an interpretation a close reading does not fully support.

93. See *Io. ev. tr.* 18.11, where he also utilizes the imagery of weak eyes and light.

94. Burns suggests Augustine does not name the sixth stage *intellectus* because of his focus on the third stage as "knowledge" ("Delighting the Spirit," 187).

95. For a concrete description of ongoing interpretive practice, see Kuruvilla, *Text to Praxis*.

96. For a recent work that seeks to combine philosophical hermeneutics (specifically using Gadamer) and the ecclesial community, see Westphal, *Whose Community? Which Intepretation?*

97. See further Torrance, *Divine Meaning*, 10.

98. For other arguments in this direction, see Frei, "Theology and Interpretation," 112–113; Webster, *Word and Church*, 57–58.

99. For more on theology not overriding the text, see Kelsey, *Proving Doctrine*, 199–200; Torrance, *Divine Meaning*, 32–39.

100. Jeanrond, "Hermeneutics and Christian Praxis," 182; see also Jeanrond, "After Hermeneutics," 179; Jeanrond, "Criteria," 249.

101. Examples abound of Augustine appealing to the *regula fidei* precisely by appealing to scripture: e.g., *Gn. litt.* 2.6.10–14; *trin.* 1; *Io. ev. tr.* 18.

102. Jeanrond, "After Hermeneutics," 88; Jeanrond, "Hermeneutics and Christian Praxis," 181; Jeanrond, *Theological Hermeneutics*, 167–180.

103. Compare Ayres's discussion of the importance of a theological understanding of the soul and its importance for scriptural interpretation: "The Soul and the Reading of Scripture," 173–190.

104. See also the discussion of Aquinas in Levering, *Participatory Biblical Exegesis*, 131–139.

105. Though I have discussed Augustine, contemporary interpreters, such as Frei or Watson, could also be analyzed with similar results.

## 4. Community, Hermeneutics, Rhetoric

1. The possessive, "our God," is yet another indication of the ecclesial nature of this work.

2. See especially Pollmann, *Doctrina Christiana*, 108–121; W. Green, *Praefatio*, ix–xiii.

3. Mayer, "Res per signa," argues that the *signa-res* distinction structures even the prologue (100–112), a view supported by Pollmann, *Doctrina Christiana*, 113, on the basis of Augustine's use of the metaphor of the finger in a linguistic context in *mag.* 3.5 and 10.34.

4. *Et illi ergo et isti me reprehendere desinant et lumen oculorum divinitus sibi praeberi deprecentur.*

5. This supports Peter Brunner's argument that the concern is with "thorough" charismatics, not with charismatic ideas per se ("Charismatische und methodische Schriftauslegung," 59–69, 85–103 [87]).

6. Vessey, "The Great Conference," 52–73, hypothesizes that the prologue is a correction directed at interpreters too intent on charismatic interpretation, while it is a defense against Jerome's professional discipline of biblical interpretation (58).

7. Though I highlight a particular group of people within the church— ministers—I would hesitate to insist on specific opponents, as some do, e.g., Vessey, "The Great Conference," 52–73; Kannengiesser, "Augustine and Tyconius"; Duchrow, "Zum Prolog."

8. Brunner, "Charismatische und methodische Schriftauslegung," 59–69, 85–103; Duchrow, "Zum Prolog"; Mayer, "Res per signa." Mayer suggests no specific opponent need be in Augustine's view because the African Church since Tertullian had numerous groups of charismatics (108). In numerous articles, Kannengiesser contends that Tyconius is the target in view here, in fact the target of the entirety of *De doctrina*, e.g., "Local Setting and Motivation of *De Doctrina Christiana*," 331–339; "Augustine and Tyconius," 149–177. Two immediate objections can be offered: first, Tyconius is not against rules, as *LR* demonstrates. Indeed, even if Tyconius were a rigorous charismatic in *LR*, it is obvious—even on Kannengiesser's own terms—that Augustine at least understood Tyconius to be offering a set of rules like *De doctrina*. Second, Augustine's arguments are of a more general nature, arguing with a hypothetical, unnamed group of people. Perhaps the portion composed in 396/7 could reasonably be vague, but

why is Augustine not *more* critical of Tyconius when he finally includes his rules in 426/7? For further comments on the nature of the opponents, with which I mostly agree, see Press, "Tyconius in Augustine's De doctrina Christiana," 62–66.

9. Pollmann, *Doctrina Christiana*, also glosses the double-love command as comprising both "vertical" and "horizontal" relationships (123). As I do here, she notes it also makes an appearance in the prologue (89, 110–113).

10. Again, I would hesitate to point to a specific group of ministers in the church. Press, "Tyconius in Augustine's De doctrina Christiana," 64, suggests that Augustine has in mind those people throughout the church who—from the beginning—viewed education as a pagan entity.

11. Kevane, "Paideia and Anti-Paideia," 170.

12. Brunner, "Charismatische und methodische Schriftauslegung," 89–99, also stresses the local nature of Augustine's concerns and his subsequent examples: he worries about the breakdown of the church. It also becomes difficult to agree with Kannengiesser that Augustine has Tyconius in mind here (see, e.g., "Local Setting and Motivation"), as Augustine appreciates Tyconius's ecclesiology (*ep.* 249).

13. Opelt, "Doctrina und Doctrina Christiana," 14, points out the connection between pride and illumination in the prologue and Augustine's focus in 2.13.20 on pride in scholarship. Pride is a danger both when appealing to divine illumination and to human disciplines.

14. *Pace* Kevane, "Paideia and Anti-Paideia."

15. Pollmann, *Doctrina Christiana*, 248, emphasizes the necessity of coupling the anthropology of *doctr. chr.* with that of Augustine's later anti-Pelagian works. The view here is exceptionally positive and balances what is sometimes seen as a one-sidedness in his later works (cf. Brown, *Augustine of Hippo*, 441–481).

16. One might suggest that this is a perfect example of the kind of person Augustine has in mind when writing *De doctrina*: someone who can explain to others what scripture means, even in its obscure sections.

17. Rather than positing with Mayer, "Res per signa," 100–112, that the *signa-res* distinction runs throughout even the prologue, it would be better to point out this continual appeal to the twofold love of God and neighbor. Even if Augustine does not quote the double-love command here, it certainly structures the horizontal and vertical relationships he describes.

18. Prol. 8, I have substituted plural verbs for the singular. Compare Augustine's discussion of the *magister intus* in *mag.* 11.38–14.46. He does not negate interior illumination in *De doctrina*, but he does go further than in the earlier dialogue regarding exterior teaching.

19. One can compare this sentiment to 4.28.62, where Augustine discusses those who cannot prepare their own sermons but read ones prepared by others.

20. Cf. *doctr. chr.* 1.11.11.

21. See *doctr. chr.* 1.18.17, where the church's roles of comforter and place of salvation come to the fore.

22. Pollmann, *Doctrina Christiana*, 121–147, also argues that *caritas* is both the beginning and end of Augustine's hermeneutics, the "normative horizon" (*Normenhorizont*).

23. Cf. *pecc. mer.* 1.27.50 (concerning Hebrews).

24. It perhaps should be stressed that the Roman Catholic Church as it exists today did not exist in Augustine's time, though it can be stressed equally that Augustine certainly thought of the Church as a unity. One need only compare his criticisms against the Donatists (e.g., *agon.* 29.31).

25. Green's and Hill's translation of *meruerunt* as a passive verb slightly obscures this point.

26. For two different viewpoints on the development of the canon, see von Campenhausen, *The Formation of the Christian Bible*, and Trobisch, *The First Edition of the New Testament*.

27. As La Bonnardière states: "It is liturgical usage which distinguishes canonical books" ("The Canon of Sacred Scripture," 35).

28. As an aside, it seems appropriate to suggest that the contemporary church would do well to heed this kind of attention to scripture before reading it aloud: grasping the sense of the passage and how the argument goes is not enough because one must also be prepared to inflect the passage correctly and help the congregation understand it. A reader—whether of the Old Testament, Epistle, or Gospel—has a responsibility to bring the words to life.

29. Cf. *spir. et litt.*

30. Why the terminology changes from Jesus and Paul to the early church and Augustine is a separate matter.

31. Augustine's canonical list does not correspond to traditional canonical ordering. Daniel and Ezekiel are reversed when compared to the traditional LXX ordering. In addition, the New Testament list has several oddities: Acts is placed between James and before Revelation, while Colossians comes after the two letters to the Thessalonians and before the two to Timothy, and James is after Jude rather than before the letters of Peter. It is unclear whether Augustine had a different order before him or if these changes are aberrations. Therefore, not much can be concluded from them. For more on canonical ordering in the first centuries of the church, see Trobisch, *The First Edition of the New Testament*, 24–38.

32. Cf. *retr.* 2.4.2.

33. Cf. *conf.* 12.18.27.

34. Cf. *conf.* 13.13.14, where Paul is no longer the one speaking, but Christ through him.

35. Press does not discuss the section on the canon in any significant manner (see "Content and Argument," 173), while Kevane fails to address it. By focusing myopically on *De doctrina's* general background or subsequent effects, they fail to note specific passages that, when taken together, cumulatively support a modified version of Hill's thesis.

36. Pollmann, *Doctrina Christiana*, 121–147, discusses Book 1 in terms of *caritas* as the "normative horizon" of Augustine's hermeneutics. Such a stress on the *regula dilectionis* and the ethical dimension runs the risk of overemphasizing ethics at the expense of a theological understanding of the *regula fidei*. Pollmann does point to the "dogmatic restriction" on Augustine's hermeneutics ("Augustine's Hermeneutics as a Universal Discipline!?," 213–214). As the following discussion will demonstrate, Augustine refers to Book 1 as the *regula fidei*, which is coupled with the *regula dilectionis*. There are two *regulae*, not one. The *regula dilectionis* does have some priority, and *caritas* is the *telos* of scripture, but never apart from the *regula fidei*.

37. Certainly for Augustine faith will pass away, but only in the eschaton, when we see with our eyes what we love (1.39.43).

38. Cf. *ench.* 2.8; 31.117.

39. The discussion in this section concerns passages that, when punctuated incorrectly, would go against the *regula fidei* (his example is John 1:1–2), those that do not really matter as far as the *regula* is concerned but whose context dictates the punctuation (his example is Phil. 1:22–24), or instances where neither dictates a certain punctuation (his example is 2 Cor. 7:1–2).

40. See Young, "The 'Mind' of Scripture," 125–141; Eden, *Hermeneutics and the Rhetorical Tradition*, 19, where she argues that, for ancient interpreters, intentionality was aligned with the wholeness of the work.

41. Paddison, *Scripture*, is a good example of a work seeking to undermine typical "competitive understandings of divine and human agency in relation to Scripture" (32).

42. In Book 3, Augustine seems to operate with an opposition between love and its opposite, lust. This may help to understand the importance of the *regula dilectionis* for interpreting such passages as those concerning the patriarch's marital practices.

43. This was an important issue for Augustine, e.g., *conf.* 3.7.12–14; *nupt. et conc.* 1.9.8–10.9.

44. It is interesting, though, that Augustine takes time to argue that the Patriarchs were not in fact sinning even by the standards of his own day. They were not lustful, just practical. He actually feels the need to show that they were moral even by the standards of his own day, with the one exception of actually having multiple wives.

45. Cf. *cat. rud.* 4.8 and its combination of the double-love command with the record of Christ (either as predicted in the Old Testament or witnessed in the New).

46. Neither Press nor Kevane note the importance of the two *regulae* because of their commitments to tracing the influences of the rhetorical system and the ancient *paideia*. By failing to note the importance of these two rules, the precise ecclesial nature of the work is missed. The *regula dilectionis* requires action, which requires others, putting the emphasis on the community.

47. Cf. Hagendahl, *Augustine and the Latin Classics*, 566: "The prevailing opinion that the fourth book was to all intents and purposes written for the instruction of the clergy remains unquestionable."

48. Cavadini, "The Sweetness of the Word," 165, calls it "the dynamics of conversion."

49. Harrison, "Rhetoric of Scripture and Preaching," 217–220.

50. Cf. *Orat.* 122.

51. As with "pulpit," I am performing a bit of a sleight-of-hand with my translation of *sermo*; a *sermo* in Augustine's day was not exactly the same thing as a "sermon" in our day. This passage shows, however, that Augustine's use of the word is in line with my own.

52. To see Augustine approach a topic from numerous different ways to teach his congregation, one need only look at some of his sermons on John.

53. For more on the Ciceronian background to *doctr. chr.* 4 and Augustine's break from it, see Primmer, "The Function of the *genera dicendi* in *De doctrina christiana* 4," 68–86, and Pollmann, *Doctrina Christiana*, 215–216, 228–241.

54. Pollmann plays down the use of the Pastorals and ministerial language (e.g., *sacerdos* and *episcopus*), stating that such language comes from Augustine's use of biblical citations (*Doctrina Christiana*, 73–74), but as I argue here, the use of these biblical passages and their vocabulary is precisely the point.

55. A comparison between this quotation and the prologue demonstrates yet again the fundamental continuity of *De doctrina*.

56. I have brought out the ecclesial aspect of *populum* here, while other translators translate it as "whether in public or in private," which seems to

mask the location Augustine stresses and goes against the use of *populum* elsewhere in Book 4. See the end of 4.18.37, where Augustine discusses a sermon before a congregation, just after referring to a "teacher in the church giving a sermon" (*doctor in ecclesia facit inde sermonem*); cf. 4.29.62, 4.30.63.

57. Pollmann, *Doctrina Christiana*, 69–75; cf. Pollmann, "Augustine's Hermeneutics as a Universal Discipline!?," 219, where she appeals to the same passage. As will become evident, I agree that the work has a universalizing direction. I only disagree over where it comes into play.

58. Again, Augustine suggests as much in *ep.* 2*.3 (*Ad Firmum*), where he rebukes Firmus for simply enjoying *civ.* and not submitting to the cleansing waters of baptism.

59. The subsequent chapter discusses this section more fully.

60. The following derives from *doctr. chr.* 4.22.51–26.58.

61. One can note that this section calls to mind the discussion in the prologue, where Augustine states that, by writing, he does no more than a person who delivers a sermon.

62. In spite of his comment in 1.39.43 that suggests otherwise. Brunner, "Charismatische und methodische Schriftauslegung," 102–103, actually uses the prologue to argue against Augustine's statement regarding the dispensability of the Bible, suggesting Augustine contradicts himself and should have kept to the ideas of the prologue ("to humans through humans"). See the discussion in the subsequent chapter.

63. I would like to thank Angus Paddison for sharing a paper that helped my thinking on this topic ("The Living Authority of Scripture"). He seeks to develop a "Trinitarian account of authority," and this move locates scripture's authority "in the triune fellowship revealed to creation in history *which the church is privileged to participate in*" (emphasis his).

### 5. *De doctrina christiana* and the Theological Interpretation of Scripture

1. Treier, *Introducing Theological Interpretation*, 14, 201.

2. Ibid., 18–19.

3. For example, Childs, *Biblical Theology of the Old and New Testaments*; Childs, *The Struggle to Understand Isaiah*; Seitz, *Figured Out*. Fowl, *Theological Interpretation of Scripture*, 82–84, suggests the title "Theological Approaches to the Old Testament," under which one might also place Moberly, *The Bible, Theology, and Faith*.

4. For example, Kelsey, *Proving Doctrine*; Frei, *The Identity of Jesus Christ*; Lindbeck, *The Nature of Doctrine*.

5. Hauerwas, *Unleashing the Scripture*; Fowl, *Engaging Scripture*.

6. For example, Watson, *Text, Church and World*; Watson, *Agape, Eros, Gender*.

7. Treier, *Introducing Theological Interpretation*, 20–36, treats these different viewpoints. For a particularly good meditation on exegesis from a Roman Catholic perspective, see Levering, *Participatory Biblical Exegesis*.

8. Treier, *Introducing Theological Interpretation*, 79–100.

9. While one could also make an argument for Kevin Vanhoozer, it seems that Fowl's construal of the community and the terminology he uses put him in closer proximity to Augustine's program than Vanhoozer is.

10. Though he appeals to Augustine on several occasions, Fowl does not claim to be Augustinian in a strict sense of the term.

11. C. Wood, *The Formation of Christian Understanding*, 43; Watson, *Text, Church and World*, 3–6.

12. For example, Webster, *Holy Scripture*, 42–67; though see Gavin D'Costa's argument that Webster's theology of the church could be strengthened: "Revelation, Scripture, and Tradition," 337–350; Frei, "Literal Reading."

13. See especially Watson, *Text, Church and World*, 1–17, 46–59; Turner and Green, "New Testament Commentary and Systematic Theology," 1–22; Reno, "Series Preface," 9–14.

14. "Interpretive communities" comes from Fish, *Is There a Text in This Class?* I use it as shorthand for those who emphasize the necessity of the ecclesial community for biblical interpretation. For some who espouse such a viewpoint, see Hauerwas, *Unleashing the Scripture*, 19–28; Fowl and Jones, *Reading in Communion*, 29–55 (all citations to the reprint edition); Kelsey, *Proving Doctrine*, 158–181.

15. I here focus on the typical flow of the debate. Treier highlights the need to look beyond this two-sided debate to the global community, especially to the "global south" (*Introducing Theological Interpretation*, 157–186). There are other options, such as liberation theologies, where reading with the poor and the oppressed is more decisive than reading with the church. For an example of the direction liberation theologies are currently moving, see Althaus-Reid, Petrella, and Susin, *Another Possible World*.

16. Immediately, one thinks of Krister Stendahl's famous article "Biblical Theology, Contemporary," 418–431. See also Childs, *Biblical Theology*, 80–90.

17. For example, Frei (tacitly) dispenses with biblical-critical pursuits in *The Identity of Jesus Christ*, 51–201; Hauerwas, *Matthew*, 20–21.

18. For example, Lindbeck, "Scripture, Consensus and Community," 201–222, where historical criticism gives a "basically negative contribution" to theology by limiting its options for reading a text (210–211); Watson, *Text and Truth*, 6–9.

19. Frei, "Literal Reading," 117–152, esp. 139–149. For a discussion of Frei's notion of the literal sense, see Dawson, *Christian Figural Reading*, 141–185.

20. Frei, "Literal Reading," 144.

21. See also Frei, "Theology and the Interpretation of Narrative," 94–115.

22. See Greene-McCreight, "Literal Sense," 455–456. Greene-McCreight distinguishes "literal sense" from "plain sense" (the former applies to verbal meaning, the latter to the interplay between that verbal meaning and the ruled reading of the community); Tanner, "Theology and the Plain Sense," 59–78.

23. Jenson, "Hermeneutics and the Life of the Church," 98. See also Jenson, *Canon and Creed*.

24. Cf. Hall, "Reading the Bible from within Our Traditions," 88–107, who argues that the canon and the rule of faith arose together in the context of the church.

25. Moberly, "Biblical Criticism and Religious Belief," 71–100, esp. 86–88, makes a similar statement when critiquing Barton: "If one is not to bring any theological presuppositions to the study of the Bible, I await to learn from Barton on what grounds he recognizes diverse ancient texts as still constituting a Bible today" (86).

26. Such narratives are common. Frei, *Eclipse of the Biblical Narrative* is the premier example. See, however, Barton's critique of them (*Biblical Criticism*, 117–136).

27. For the corrosiveness of theology on biblical interpretation, see Barton, *Biblical Criticism*, 137–186; Räisänen, *Beyond New Testament Theology*, 151–188; Barr, *The Concept of Biblical Theology*, 189–208, 605–607. For the benefit, see Bockmuehl, *Seeing the Word*, 75–99; Moberly, *Bible, Theology, and Faith*, 1–44; Watson, *Text, Church and World*, 7–14.

28. "Nine Theses on the Interpretation of Scripture," 1–5 (3). Hays also insists on the necessity of the ecclesial community in "Reading the Bible with Eyes of Faith," 5–21.

29. Barton, *Biblical Criticism*, 185–186. Though he does well to show that theological interpreters often develop a "straw man" falsely labeled "biblical criticism" that they then proceed to tear down, one might wonder whether he does the same to theological interpreters, describing them all as reader response critics. See Moberly's criticisms, which follow a similar line of argument, "Biblical Criticism," esp. 76–85.

30. Barton, *Biblical Criticism*, 164: "One cannot establish what the Bible means if one insists on reading it as necessarily conforming to what one already believes to be true—*which is what a theological reading amounts to*" (emphasis added).

31. Vischer, *The Pentateuch*.

32. See especially Hauerwas, *Unleashing the Scripture*, 15–44; Hauerwas, *Matthew*, 18–21. Hauerwas is especially indebted to Fish. For a good, more complete analysis of Hauerwas's engagement with scripture, see Sarisky, *Scriptural Interpretation*.

33. Hauerwas, *Unleashing the Scripture*, 36.

34. Hauerwas, *Matthew*, 27. I should stress that Hauerwas is correct—on some level—to insist that what the text means is sometimes less important than how the community—in the power of the Spirit—acts on it. Still, what the text means, as I will argue, is of utmost theological importance. Vanhoozer, *First Theology*, 275–308, suggests using the term "natural sense" to describe the normative sense of scripture that can hold together text and community.

35. Hauerwas, *Matthew*, 18.

36. Ibid., 18.

37. See further *Pro Ecclesia* 17, no. 1 (Winter 2008), 13–34. All three reviews, including the generally positive one by Mangina, comment on the way that Hauerwas at times fails to pay attention to Matthew (Mangina, "Hidden from the Wise, Revealed to Infants," 13–19; Bockmuehl, "Ruminative Overlay," 20–28; Johnson, "Matthew or Stanley?," 29–34).

38. Hauerwas, *Matthew*, 137–145.

39. Ibid., 145 (emphasis added).

40. Cf. Hauerwas, *Unleashing the Scripture*, 42: "A sermon is scriptural when it inscribes a community into an ongoing Christian narrative."

41. Watson, *Text and Truth*.

42. Fowl, *Engaging Scripture*, 13–21.

43. Ibid., 19, 56–75. See also Fowl, "The Ethics of Interpretation," 379–398; Fowl, "Texts Don't Have Ideologies," 15–34. In these essays, Fowl follows Stout, "What Is the Meaning of a Text?," 1–12.

44. For the notion of "interpretive interests," see Fowl and Jones, *Reading in Communion*, 15; Fowl, "Ethics of Interpretation," 385–388; Fowl, *Engaging Scripture*, 57–58.

45. Fowl, "Introduction to *The Theological Interpretation of Scripture*," xiii.

46. Fowl, *Engaging Scripture*, 22.

47. Fowl, *Philippians*, 5.

48. Fowl, "Further Thoughts on Theological Interpretation," 125–126.

49. Fowl, "Scripture," 353.

50. Fowl, *Theological Interpretation*, 14.

51. Spinks, *The Bible and the Crisis of Meaning*, 42.

52. This focus on God speaking through the Bible is a more recent aspect in Fowl's work. His distaste for general hermeneutical theory, on the other hand, is constant.

53. Cf. Barton, *Biblical Criticism*, 159: "Assimilating any text, the Bible included, is a two-stage operation. The first stage is a perception of the text's meaning; the second, an evaluation of that meaning in relation to what one already believes to be the case. . . . This cannot be collapsed into a single process, in which meaning is perceived and evaluated at one and the same time and by the same operation."

54. For another argument in this direction, see Reno, "Biblical Theology and Theological Exegesis," 385–408.

55. Fowl, *Philippians*, 224.

56. Fowl, "Scripture," 355.

57. For example, Webster, *Word and Church*, 9–46. It should be noted that Webster's ontology of scripture has many points in common with the view espoused here.

58. See especially Fowl, "Scripture," 346–351.

59. Ibid., 346.

60. Ayres and Fowl, "(Mis)Reading the Face of God," 513–528.

61. Fowl, "Scripture," 347.

62. Fowl, *Theological Interpretation*, 7.

63. He here follows Webster, *Holy Scripture*.

64. Fowl, "Scripture," 348. See also Fowl, *Theological Interpretation*, 1–12.

65. Fowl, "Scripture," 348.

66. Ibid., 353.

67. Fowl does utilize the term *"telos"* in a book review, but "use" nonetheless describes his program better: Fowl, "Review of *Seeing the Word*," 517. In his recent book (*Theological Interpretation*), Fowl does speak in language similar to that which I use against him here: "Scripture is holy because of its divinely willed role in making believers holy" (12). The primary difference, as I will highlight, is whether or not this description can and should be applied to scripture in connection to its internal structure, that is, its connection to the communicative intent within its pages.

68. Fowl, "Scripture," 351.

69. Hill translates the pronouns referring to *sapientia* literally as "she." By doing so, he introduces the problem of gender into a section where it is absent in the Latin, although *sapientia* is a feminine noun. Rather than being "delightful" or "faithful" as Rebecca Harden Weaver claims, it is actually unfaithful to the sense of Augustine's text ("Reading the Signs," 33 n. 13). See also Augustine's comments on gender in Greek and Latin in *trin.* 12.5.5.

70. Cf. *Io. ev. tr.* 2, esp. 15–16.

71. Sieben, "Die 'Res' der Bibel," 76–80, demonstrates that Matt. 22:37–40, which is quoted here, structures the second main section of

*De doctrina* 1 (22.20–34.38). Matt. 22:37–40 is "die christliche *Telos-formel*."

72. *Ille autem iuste et sancte vivit qui rerum integer aestimator est. Ipse est autem qui ordinatam habet dilectionem.* Augustine continues: "He neither loves what should not be loved, nor does he fail to love what should be loved, nor does he love more what he ought to love less, nor does he love equally what should be loved either less or more." Green's unnecessary addition of "*aut minus diligat quod amplius diligendum est*" has no textual basis, as he admits.

73. Quoted above.

74. In context, *quibus* and *machinis*, both plural, still refer to scripture, which is also plural here, *scripturis*.

75. See, e.g., Fowl, *Engaging Scripture*, 35–40: The view that thinks the biblical text "has" a meaning (i.e., that there is something internal to the text apart from its use) "is theoretically mistaken in thinking of meanings as properties of texts, and theologically mistaken in locating the bases of coherent and faithful Christian faith and practice in the text of the Bible interpreted in isolation from Christian doctrines and ecclesial practices" (40); Fowl, "The Role of Authorial Intention," 78–82.

76. Fowl, *Engaging Scripture*, 36–37.

77. Ibid., 206.

78. Ibid., 63.

79. Fowl, "Virtue," suggests that *De doctrina* has the clearest statement of "virtue through interpretation."

80. Fowl, "Scripture," 355.

81. Though earlier than his later, more nuanced position, it is fair to say that Fowl still holds to the majority of what he wrote in *Engaging Scripture*, as he refers back to it on numerous occasions; e.g., "Further Thoughts," 127 n. 3, *Philippians*, 207 n. 3.

82. For the material used here, see Fowl, *Engaging Scripture*, 62–96. One cannot help but notice how similar Fowl's appeal to the community to prevent interpretive anarchy is to Fish, *Is There a Text in This Class?*, 303–321. Fowl himself references Fish on a few occasions (e.g., *Engaging Scripture*, 73 n. 26; "Authorial Intention," 76 n. 10).

83. Fowl, *Engaging Scripture*, 81, 83.

84. Ibid., 87.

85. As Seitz does, citing an imprecision in Fowl's definition of "virtue" (*Figured Out*, 28–29).

86. Fowl, *Theological Interpretation*, 52.

87. Fowl, *Theological Interpretation*, 54–75, gives the practices he thinks are important for guiding Christians to their end. Once more, his concern

is to keep the ecclesial community primary, rather than becoming too dependent on hermeneutical theory.

88. Fowl, *Engaging Scripture*, 199. It is difficult to reconcile this focus on interpreters who have gone with Fowl's interpretation of Acts 15 (119–127).

89. Ibid., 200.

90. Spinks, *The Bible and the Crisis of Meaning*, 66, reaches a similar conclusion.

91. Fowl, *Engaging Scripture*, 116.

92. In *Theological Interpretation*, Fowl does have a discussion of the Spirit's providential role in the construction of the canon (11–12), but, once more, he downplays the importance of a priority being placed on the communicative intent of the biblical authors (48).

93. Fowl, "Scripture," 358. As he pointed out in a personal interview, Fowl's focus on the divided church is crucial to his program. As I will argue, Augustine's construal would actually allow the reading of scripture to heal that division; it is difficult to see how this would come about on Fowl's model.

94. Cf. *ench.* 8; here, Augustine discusses how faith, hope, and love fit together. Faith is belief in all things of the past, present, and future; hope concerns only good things in the future; both concern things we cannot see. Love is how one relates to the proper objects of faith and hope. One has to have faith to love and to hope. He concludes: "Hence, there is neither love without hope, nor hope without love, and neither one of them without faith."

95. See especially Augustine's views on grace in the anti-Pelagian writings.

96. Cf. *Io. ev. tr.* 46, esp. 5–6, where Augustine discusses God teaching through those who are actually false teachers, with reference to Matt. 23:2–3 as well as Phil. 1:15–18. Fowl would disagree with his interpretation of Phil. 1:18, arguing that the passage does not express a preference for preaching with selfish motives over no preaching at all; instead, "this phrase is an expression of faith in God's providential oversight of the gospel's progress" (*Philippians*, 42). Fowl's reading seems to be an example of drawing the distinction too firmly. The passage may well be about both: preaching with selfish motives is better than no preaching at all *and* motives are not really the issue because of God's providential oversight.

97. It is telling that, in *Reading in Communion*, Fowl and Jones play down the strength of scripture's ability to critique the community's action. In the end, they are left appealing to the need for a prophetic voice from within the community (103–104). Augustine would agree, but he would ascribe to scripture itself the prophetic voice, though, again, when interpreted.

98. Though it might appear that Fowl has moved away from his critique of "meaning" when reading such articles as "Authorial Intention," it is evident that his earlier criticisms do still bear weight with him: "Scripture," 353.

99. Fowl, "Authorial Intention," 80.

100. Ibid., 81.

101. Ibid., 81–82.

102. Ibid., 78–79.

103. For more on authorial intention and its relationship to scriptural interpretation, see Wolterstorff, *Divine Discourse*, 130–182; Vanhoozer, *Is There a Meaning in This Text?*, 218–280; Watson, *Text and Truth*, 98–106.

104. Cf. *Philippians*; after discussing whether Phil. 2:7 can be interpreted in light of Chalcedonian christology, Fowl states: "The question is not whether Paul thought this way himself. Rather, the question is whether one uses the historical-critical, sociological, philosophical, or Christian theological categories for ordering that diversity [found in scripture]" (96).

105. Fowl, "The Importance of a Multivoiced Literal Sense of Scripture," 37.

106. Fowl, *Theological Interpretation*, 50.

107. Ibid., 44–53. I do think Fowl is correct to note the difference between "communicative intention" and "communicative motive," and I think here, he is close to theological interpreters like Watson and Vanhoozer, as he himself states.

108. The last clause is *ne consuetudine deviandi etiam in transversum aut perversum ire cogatur*. Green mixes the metaphor by translating it "in case the habit of deviating should force him to go astray or even adrift."

109. I would be remiss if I failed to point to Augustine's thoughts about authorial intention and the multiplicity of meanings in *conf.* 12.24.

110. The reference to "member" (*membrum*) could be an allusion Paul's continual metaphor of the church as the body of Christ (e.g., 1 Cor. 12:12–27). Green picks this up in his translation, though he does not footnote it as an allusion.

111. This statement should not be confused with R. Williams's position ("Language, Reality, and Desire"). For Augustine, the only things that become signs are those referred to by the signs of scripture. He is not discussing reality in general.

112. Moberly's notion of the implicit metaphorical register of certain Old Testament texts is reminiscent of this idea: *The Bible, Theology, and Faith*, 128–131, 229–230.

113. One can also note that he later discusses the need to recognize that certain practices are not considered wrong at all times (3.12.19–14.22). The way to apply them, however, is by paying attention to them as *signa*.

114. *Quod cum apparuerit, verba quibus continetur aut a similibus rebus ducta invenientur aut ab aliqua vicinitate adtingentibus.* This sentence alone demonstrates that TeSelle is off the mark when he states that *De doctrina* has a "rather free-wheeling approach to the biblical texts": "Engaging Scripture: Patristic Interpretation of the Bible," 33.

115. Cf. *conf.* 13.24.36, where he discusses the literal level of Genesis 1 and his metaphorical interpretation of it.

116. Augustine goes on in 3.28.39 to warn against creating meanings that cannot be found elsewhere in scripture. His flexibility here has canonical limits.

117. The translation was for the Gentiles' benefit (2.25.22).

118. Fowl, *Engaging Scripture*, 127.

119. Ibid., 127.

120. Ibid., 126.

121. See, e.g., Fowl, "Literal Sense," 40; Fowl, *Theological Interpretation*, 50.

122. Certainly, Augustine could use the weight of his authority when he felt it was necessary, as the history of the Donatist controversy suggests (though how much force he actually had to use is debatable). For accounts, see esp. Lancel, *Saint Augustine*, 287–304; Brown, *Augustine of Hippo*, 230–239, 334–336.

123. Levering, *Participatory Biblical Exegesis*, 130, also notes such a trend in Fowl.

124. Fowl, "Scripture," 355.

125. Ibid., 357. Cf. Fowl, "Further Thoughts," 128.

126. Rom. 5:5. See, e.g., *spir. et. litt.* 6.4; *gr. et pecc. or.* 1.9.10; *gr. et lib. arb.* 18.39; *Gn. litt.* 4.9.16.

127. See Levering, *Participatory Biblical Exegesis*, 123–131. It seems that he and Augustine are in agreement when Levering—after critiquing Fowl—states: "Put another way, God's revelatory *doctrina* succeeds in expressing itself in and through the texts composed by the inspired authors, in the Holy Spirit, of Scripture. These texts possess that meaning in themselves, but not on their own, since they always participate in and mediate God the Trinity's teaching" (131).

128. Interestingly, of prime importance for the supposed opponents is the elevation of purity of heart above human knowledge (Duchrow, "Zum Prolog," 165–172; Pollmann, *Doctrina Christiana*, 76–84).

129. It should be noted in passing that this focus on the human authors is an instance of Augustine avoiding the docetism potentially associated with ecclesial readings that worries Jeanrond.

130. Fowl, "Further Thoughts," 130 (emphasis added).

131. The reader should bear in mind my argument in the second chapter. This statement is not meant to underwrite any kind of foundational hermeneutical theology.

132. By "biblical theology," I do not have in mind those who see theology as corrosive, as, say, Barr does. Rather, I refer to those who, like Childs, seek to attend to what the text says in its historical context and only secondarily make the move to the contemporary context. On this definition, one might also include N. T. Wright's notions of "critical realism" and theology as the fifth act of a play. See, e.g., Wright, *The New Testament and the People of God*; Wright, *Scripture and the Authority of God*.

133. Childs, "Toward Recovering Theological Exegesis," 22.

134. Childs does not claim that the Old Testament has an "independent" voice per se: "The dialogical move of biblical theological reflection which is being suggested is from the partial grasp of fragmentary reality found in both testaments to the full reality which the Christian church confesses to have found in Jesus Christ, in the *combined witness* of the two testaments" (*Biblical Theology*, 85, emphasis added). But Watson seems to be on the mark when he critiques Childs's lack of a christological center: "The main problem lies in the assumption that the decision to include the Jewish scriptures in the Christian canon without alteration gives the Old Testament a relatively autonomous status in relation to the New" (*Text and Truth*, 209–216 [212]).

135. Fowl also discusses Childs in *Engaging Scripture*, 24–28.

136. Childs, "Toward Recovering Theological Exegesis," 23–25; cf. Childs, "Speech-Act Theory and Biblical Interpretation," 384–388: "An initial problem in applying the double-agency theory in this larger hermeneutical role of divine discourse is that it remains, at best, an imaginative philosophical construct. *There is no convincing evidence* such a move was ever operative in the actual interpretation of the Bible" (385, emphasis added); this article reviews Wolterstorff's *Divine Discourse*. But see Lindbeck, "Postcritical Canonical Interpretation," 26–51.

137. Childs, "Toward Recovering Theological Exegesis," 23.

138. Ibid., 24.

139. Ibid., 25.

140. Ibid., 24.

141. Childs does state that the church is always present in interpretation, but he means something fundamentally different from Fowl or Augustine because of his continual insistence on the Old Testament's "discrete voice": "The Sensus Literalis of Scripture," 80–93; "On Reclaiming the Bible for Christian Theology," 1–17.

142. Cf. Barth, CD 1/2, 727–736.

143. For discussion concerning the appeal to general hermeneutics, arguing that it underwrites a certain foundational anthropology, see Webster, *Word and Church*, 58–65.

144. The final clause: *sed quantum quisque veniens existimare potuerit, plus perveniens inventurus est.*

### Conclusion

1. Ayres, "On the Practice and Teaching of Christian Doctrine," 88, who references Barnes, "Rereading Augustine's Theology of the Trinity," 150.

2. Really, this point is nothing more than a call for theologians to read well, but, especially in the case of Augustine, it bears repeating. Examples of misreading Augustine abound, not least in his doctrine of the Trinity. See, e.g., Gunton, *The Promise of Trinitarian Theology*, 30–55. (I choose Gunton precisely because of the strength of his theological proposals, in spite of his imprecise account of Augustine's theology.) For a recent, nuanced account of Augustine's trinitarian theology, see Ayres, *Augustine and the Trinity*.

3. Again, the distinction between the point of view I express here and Pollmann, *Doctrina Christiana*, 69–75, is small. Pollmann highlights the universalizing tendency while downplaying the focus on ministers, and I want to stress the focus on ministers before generalizing.

4. I would suggest that this second thesis is an extension of Ayres's supplement to Barnes's criteria. Ayres suggests that theologians "need to develop the same sense of attention to the dead as they consider it appropriate to show towards the living" ("On the Practice and Teaching of Christian Doctrine," 88); putting the past theologian into close dialogue with present ones is a practical way of accomplishing this goal.

5. Webster, *Holy Scripture*, 17.

6. For more on the "critique of ideology" see Ricoeur, *Hermeneutics and the Human Sciences*, 87–100.

7. Ibid., 94.

8. See, e.g., Derrida, *Of Grammatology*.

9. Again, for such a viewpoint, see Schleiermacher, *Hermeneutics and Criticism*, 7.

10. And indeed in theological education. How much time do we spend teaching students how to understand concepts and texts, and how little on expressing what they have learned in writing and in dialogue with their peers?

11. For a survey of recent theological hermeneutics, none of which seems to discuss a rhetorical turn, see Treier, "Theological Hermeneutics, Contemporary," 787–793. There are notable exceptions. For instance,

Webster's *Holy Scripture*, 131–133; there are discussions of how interpretation fits in the church, and how interpretation leads to fellowship with God, though the actual *practice* of communicating understanding with others and its rationale is lacking. Another good example, this time even with reflection on practice, is Paddison, *Scripture*, esp. 93–121.

12. Ayres, "The Soul and the Reading of Scripture," 189.

13. For a helpful discussion, with appeal to Basil of Caesarea, of the relationship between "hermeneutical space and time" and how this relationship is coordinated by a theology of scripture, the reader, the church, and the act of reading scripture in time, see Sarisky, *A Theological Account of Scriptural Interpretation*.

14. Jenson, *Systematic Theology*, 2:171.

15. Webster, *Word and Church*, 46.

16. Sarisky, *Scriptural Interpretation*, 179, makes a similar point in reference to the theology of Hauerwas.

17. I owe the terminology of scripture's center to Watson, *Text and Truth*, 121–123, who in turn takes it from Barth, CD III/1, 24.

18. Barth, CD II/2, 389.

19. Dawson, *Christian Figural Reading and the Fashioning of Identity*, 15.

20. As helpful as Wright's "Five-Act Model" is (*The New Testament and the People of God*; *Scripture and the Authority of God*, 121–127), a weakness is that it does not seem to allow for any kind of figural or allegorical reading of the Old Testament. Certainly, as Wright would do, one should point out the narrative flow in which the Achan storyline fits, but in light of God's purposes for scripture (assuming the foregoing Augustinian suggestions are correct), a slightly more flexible approach should be allowed to stand alongside Wright's. In personal communication, Wright stated that his primary concern in these books is with what makes scripture authoritative. A figural reading, he suggests, is more "homiletical" and not "load-bearing" for doctrinal discussions. Such a distinction, I think, can be helpful, though it should not be overemphasized.

21. The interpretation that follows would be more akin to what Byassee calls "allegory" as opposed to what he sees as Augustine's "Christological literalism" in his interpretation of the Psalms (*Praise Seeking Understanding*, 205–219, 223–233).

22. For a helpful meditation on reading scripture in the broken church, see Radner, *Hope amongst the Fragments*.

23. The idea of sin as a force impeding creation's proper course comes from Gunton, *The Promise of Trinitarian Theology*, 178–192.

24. Watson, *Text and Truth*, 182 (emphasis original).

25. 2 Tim. 1:14. Whether Paul wrote the letter or not, the interpretation remains the same.

26. Jenson, *Canon and Creed*, 41.

27. Two notable contributions that follow this line are Davis and Hays, *The Art of Reading Scripture*, and Green and Turner, *Between Two Horizons*. Ayres, "The Soul and the Reading of Scripture," treats Davis and Hays, so I will here discuss the article in Green and Turner's volume.

28. Hall, "Reading the Bible from within Our Traditions," 104.

29. Hall, "Reading the Bible from within Our Traditions," does discuss how this theological understanding affects the "faith and practice" of the church (106), but what I mean to stress here is that it is not enough to say this in passing; one must make it explicit. In fact, if we follow Augustine, the "practice" of love can norm reading in a more forceful way than "faith" does.

30. Barth, CD II/1, 274.

31. One can note that I have dropped "hope" from my equation. As Augustine implies again and again, faith and hope are extremely similar, one being about how both good and bad things are and were, the other about how only good things will be (*ench.* 8).

32. It should be noted that "biblical criticism" is no more a monolithic entity than "theological interpretation," but it still remains the case that some proponents of theological interpretation often downplay the usefulness of biblical criticism. In light of Augustine, it is not necessary to dismiss it out of hand.

33. Byassee, *Praise Seeking Understanding*, 146.

34. One can note that Augustine's view need not imply that the author had in mind a relationship between Christ and the church, or even between YHWH and Israel. His *signa-res* distinction is useful on this score.

35. "The Way of the Cross," in *The Book of Occasional Services 1994* (New York: Church Publishing, 1995), 71.

36. For similar reflections, see Byassee, *Praise Seeking Understanding*, 261–268.

37. I utilize the structure of the Scottish Liturgy 1970 (The General Synod of the Scottish Episcopal Church) but others would reveal similar points.

38. Though this description of a sermon is likely idealistic, that does not make it any less true. Perhaps a better integration of courses on exegesis and homiletics would make it a reality.

39. One can also note the way the readings represent God speaking to the church while in the psalm the church speaks to God.

# Bibliography

ANCIENT TEXTS

I here provide critical editions as well as translations consulted (in square brackets).

## Works by Augustine

*Confessiones.* CCL 27, ed. Lucas Verheijen (1981). [*Confessions.* Translated by R. S. Pine-Coffin. London: Penguin, 1961.]

*Contra duas epistulas Pelagianorum.* CSEL 60, 421–570, ed. Karl F. Urba and Joseph Zycha (1913). [*Against Two Letters of the Pelagians.* Translated by Robert E. Wallis. NPNF 1/5, 373–434. Christian Literature, 1887. Reprint, Peabody, Mass.: Hendrickson, 2004.]

*Contra epistulam manichaei quam vocant fundamenti.* CSEL 25, 191–248, ed. Joseph Zycha (1891). [*Against the Epistle of Manichaeus Called Fundamental.* Translated by Richard Stothert. NPNF 1/4, 125–150. Christian Literature, 1887. Reprint, Peabody, Mass.: Hendrickson, 2004.]

*Contra Faustum.* CSEL 25, 249–797, ed. Joseph Zycha (1891). [*Reply to Faustus the Manichaean.* Translated by Richard Stothert. NPNF 1/4, 151–345. Christian Literature, 1887. Reprint, Peabody, Mass.: Hendrickson, 2004.]

*De agone christiano.* CSEL 41, 99–138, ed. Joseph Zycha (1900). [*The Christian Combat.* Translated by Robert P. Russell. FC 2/4, 307–353. New York: Fathers of the Church, 1947.]

*De catechizandis rudibus.* CCL 46, 115–178, ed. J. B. Bauer (1969). [*On Catechizing of the Uninstructed.* Translated by S. D. F. Salmond. NPNF 1/3, 277–314. Christian Literature, 1887. Reprint, Peabody, Mass.: Hendrickson, 2004.]

*De civitate dei.* CCL 47–48, ed. Bernard Dombart and Alphonso Kalb (1955). [*City of God.* Translated by Marcus Dods. NPNF 1/2, 1–511. Christian Literature, 1887. Reprint, Peabody, Mass.: Hendrickson, 2004.]

*De diversis quaestionibus ad Simplicianum.* CCL 44, 5–91, ed. Almut Mutzenbecher (1970). [*To Simplician Book 1.* In *Augustine: Earlier Writings.* Edited and translated by John H. S. Burleigh. LCC 6, 376–406. London: SCM, 1953.]

*De doctrina christiana.* Oxford Early Christian Texts, ed. and trans. R. P. H. Green (1995); CSEL 80, ed. William M. Green (1963); CCL 32, ed. Joseph Martin (1962); BA 11, ed. and trans. G. Combès and J. Farges (1949); *L'Istruzione Cristiana,* ed. and trans. Manlio Simonetti (Fondazione Lorenzo Valla, 1994); BA 11/2, introduction and trans. Madeleine Moreau, notes by Isabelle Bochet and Goulven Madec (1997). [*On Christian Teaching.* Translated by R. P. H. Green. Oxford: Oxford University Press, 1997; *Teaching Christianity.* Translated by Edmund Hill. WSA I/11. New York: New City, 1996; *On Christian Doctrine.* Translated by D. W. Robertson. Library of Liberal Arts. New Jersey: Prentice Hall, 1958; *Christian Instruction.* Translated by John J. Gavigan. FC 2/4, 1–235. New York: Fathers of the Church, 1947; *Christian Doctrine.* Translated by J. F. Shaw. NPNF 1/2, 513–597. Christian Literature, 1887. Reprint, Peabody, Mass.: Hendrickson, 2004; *Die christliche Bildung.* Translated by Karla Pollmann. Universal-Bibliothek. Stuttgart: Reclam, 2002; *S. Aureli Augustini Hipponiensis Episcopi De Doctrina Christiana, Liber Quartus: A Commentary with a Revised Text, Introduction and Translation.* Translated by (Sister) Thérèse Sullivan. In *The Rhetoric of Saint Augustine of Hippo:* De Doctrina Christiana *and the Search for a Distinctly Christian Rhetoric,* ed. Richard Leo Enos et al., 33–183. Studies in Rhetoric and Religion 7. Waco, Tex.: Baylor University Press, 2008.]

*De Genesi ad litteram.* CSEL 28, 1–435, ed. Joseph Zycha (1894). [*The Literal Meaning of Genesis.* Translated by Edmund Hill. WSA I/13, 153–506. New York: New City, 2002.]

*De Genesi ad litteram imperfectus liber unus.* CSEL 28, 459–503, ed. Joseph Zycha (1894). [*Unfinished Literal Commentary on Genesis.* Translated by Edmund Hill. WSA I/13, 103–151. New York: New City, 2002.]

*De Genesi adversus Manichaeos.* CSEL 91, ed. Dorothea Weber (1998). [*On Genesis: A Refutation of the Manichees.* Translated by Edmund Hill. WSA I/13, 23–102. New York: New City, 2002.]

*De gratia Christi et de peccato originali.* CSEL 42, 125–206, ed. Karl F. Urba and Joseph Zycha (1902). [*On the Grace of Christ, and on Original Sin.*

Translated by Peter Holmes. NPNF 1/5, 213–255. Christian Literature, 1887. Reprint, Peabody, Mass.: Hendrickson, 2004.]

*De gratia et libero arbitrio.* Patrologia Latina 44, 881–912, ed. Jacques-Paul Migne (1861). [*On Grace and Free Will.* Translated by Robert E. Wallis. NPNF 1/5, 435–465. Christian Literature, 1887. Reprint, Peabody, Mass.: Hendrickson, 2004.]

*De magistro.* CCL 29, 139–203, ed. K.-D. Daur (1970). [*The Teacher.* Translated by John H. S. Burleigh. LCC 6, 64–101. London: SCM, 1953.]

*De natura et gratia.* CSEL 60, 231–300, ed. Karl F. Urba and Joseph Zycha (1913). [*On Nature and Grace.* Translated by Peter Holmes. NPNF 1/5, 115–151. Christian Literature, 1887. Reprint, Peabody, Mass.: Hendrickson, 2004.]

*De nuptiis et concupiscentia.* CSEL 42, 211–319, ed. Karl F. Urba and Joseph Zycha (1902). [*On Marriage and Concupiscence.* Translated by Peter Holmes. NPNF 1/5, 259–308. Christian Literature, 1887. Reprint, Peabody, Mass.: Hendrickson, 2004.]

*De ordine.* CCL 29, 87–137, ed. W. M. Green (1970). [*Divine Providence and the Problem of Evil.* Translated by Robert P. Russell. FC 5/1, 227–332. New York: Cima, 1948.]

*De peccatorum meritis et remissione et de baptismo parvulorum.* CSEL 60, 1–152, ed. Karl F. Urba and Joseph Zycha (1913). [*On the Merits and Remission of Sins, and on the Baptism of Infants.* Translated by Peter Holmes. NPNF 1/5, 15–78. Christian Literature, 1887. Reprint, Peabody, Mass.: Hendrickson, 2004.]

*De spiritu et littera.* CSEL 60, 153–230, ed. Karl F. Urba and Joseph Zycha (1913). [*The Spirit and the Letter.* Translated by John Burnaby. LCC 8, 195–250. London: SCM, 1955.]

*De trinitate.* CCL 50, ed. W. J. Mountain (1968). [*The Trinity.* Translated by Edmund Hill. WSA I/5. New York: New City, 1991; *On the Holy Trinity.* Translated by Arthur West Haddan. NPNF 1/3, 1–228. Christian Literature, 1887. Reprint, Peabody, Mass.: Hendrickson, 2004.]

*De utilitate credendi.* CSEL 25, 1–48, ed. Joseph Zycha (1891). [*On the Profit of Believing.* Translated by C. L. Cornish. NPNF 1/3, 345–366. Christian Literature, 1887. Reprint, Peabody, Mass.: Hendrickson, 2004.]

*Enarrationes in Psalmos.* CCL 38–40, ed. D. E. Dekkers and J. Fraipont (1956). [*Expositions on the Book of Psalms* (partial). Translated by A. Cleveland Coxe. NPNF 1/8. Christian Literature, 1887. Reprint, Peabody, Mass.: Hendrickson, 2004.]

*Enchiridion ad Laurentum de fide spe et caritate.* CCL 46, 21–114, ed. E. Evans (1969). [*Faith, Hope and Charity.* Translated by Bernard M. Peebles. FC

2/4, 355–472. New York: Fathers of the Church, 1947; *The Enchiridion.* Translated by J. F. Shaw. NPNF 1/3, 229–276. Christian Literature, 1887. Reprint, Peabody, Mass.: Hendrickson, 2004.]

*Epistulae.* CSEL 34, 44, 57, ed. A. Goldbacher (1895–1923). [*The Letters of St. Augustin.* Translated by J. G. Cunningham. NPNF 1/1, 209–593. Christian Literature, 1887. Reprint, Peabody, Mass.: Hendrickson, 2004.]

*Epistulae* (Divjak). CSEL 88, ed. J. Divjak (1981). [*Letters 1\*–29\*.* Translated by Robert B. Eno. FC 81. Washington, D.C.: The Catholic University of America Press, 1989.]

*Epistulae ad Romanos inchoata expositio liber unus.* CSEL 84, 145–181, ed. J. Divjak (1971). [*Unfinished Commentary on the Epistle to the Romans.* In *Augustine on Romans,* ed. and trans. Paula Fredriksen Landes, 52–89. Chico, Cal.: Scholars Press, 1982.]

*Retractiones.* CCL 57, ed. Almut Mutzenbecher (1984). [*The Retractions.* Translated by Mary Inez Bogan. FC 60. Washington, D.C.: The Catholic University of America Press, 1968.]

*Tractatus in Iohannis evangelium.* CCL 36, ed. D. R. Willems (1954). [*Tractates on the Gospel of John.* Translated by John Gibb and James Innes. NPNF 1/7, 1–452. Christian Literature, 1887. Reprint, Peabody, Mass.: Hendrickson, 2004.]

Works by Others

Athanasius. *Contra Gentes* and *De Incarnatione,* ed. and trans. Robert W. Thomson. Oxford Early Christian Texts. Oxford: Clarendon, 1971.

Cicero. *Orator.* Loeb Classical Library 342, trans. H. M. Hubbell. London: William Heinemann, 1939.

Origen. *De principiis.* Sources Chrétiennes 252, 253, 268, 269, 312, ed. and trans. Henri Crouzel and Manlio Simonetti (1978–1984). [*On First Principles.* Translated by G. W. Butterworth. London: SPCK, 1936.]

Tyconius. *The Book of Rules of Tyconius,* ed. F. C. Burkitt. Vol. 3, Texts and Studies: Contributions to Biblical and Patristic Literature, ed. J. Armitage Robinson. Cambridge: Cambridge University Press, 1895. [*Tyconius: The Book of Rules.* Translated by William S. Babcock. Texts and Translations 31. Atlanta: Scholars, 1989.]

SECONDARY SOURCES

Althaus-Reid, Marcella Maria, Ivan Petrella, and Luiz Carlos Susin, eds. *Another Possible World.* Reclaiming Liberation Theology. London: SCM, 2007.

Andrews, James A. "Abbreviations of Aug.'s works, with dates of composition and Aug.'s discussion in *retractiones*." In *The Oxford Guide to the Historical Reception of Augustine*, ed. Karla Pollmann et al. Oxford: Oxford University Press, forthcoming.

Ando, Clifford. "Augustine on Language." *Revue des Études Augustiniennes* 40 (1994): 45–78.

Arnold, Duane W. H., and Pamela Bright, eds. *De Doctrina Christiana: A Classic of Western Culture*. Notre Dame: University of Notre Dame Press, 1995.

Ayers, Robert H. "Language Theory and Analysis in Augustine." *Scottish Journal of Theology* 29 (1976): 1–12.

Ayres, Lewis. "On the Practice and Teaching of Christian Doctrine." *Gregorianum* 80 (1999): 33–94.

———. *Nicaea and Its Legacy: An Approach to Fourth-Century Trinitarian Theology*. Oxford: Oxford University Press, 2004.

———. "Augustine on the Rule of Faith: Rhetoric, Christology, and the Foundation of Christian Thinking." *Augustinian Studies* 36 (2005): 22–49.

———. "The Soul and the Reading of Scripture: A Note on Henri De Lubac." *Scottish Journal of Theology* 61 (2008): 173–190.

———. *Augustine and the Trinity*. Cambridge: Cambridge University Press, 2010.

Ayres, Lewis, and Stephen E. Fowl. "(Mis)Reading the Face of God: The Interpretation of the Bible in the Church." *Theological Studies* 60 (1999): 513–528.

Babcock, William S. "*Caritas* and Signification in *De Doctrina Christiana* 1–3." In *De Doctrina Christiana: A Classic of Western Culture*, ed. Duane W. H. Arnold and Pamela Bright, 145–163. Notre Dame: University of Notre Dame Press, 1995.

Baldwin, Charles Sears. "St. Augustine on Preaching (*De Doctrina Christiana*, IV)." In *The Rhetoric of Saint Augustine of Hippo: De Doctrina Christiana and the Search for a Distinctly Christian Rhetoric*, ed. Richard Leo Enos et al., 187–203. Studies in Rhetoric and Religion 7. Waco, Tex.: Baylor University Press, 2008.

Barnes, Michel René. "Rereading Augustine's Theology of the Trinity." In *The Trinity: An Interdisciplinary Symposium on the Trinity*, ed. Stephen T. Davis, Daniel Kendall, S.J., and Gerald O'Collins, S.J., 145–176. Oxford: Oxford University Press, 1999.

Barr, James. *The Concept of Biblical Theology: An Old Testament Perspective*. Minneapolis: Fortress, 1999.

Barth, Karl. *The Epistle to the Romans*, 6th ed. Translated by Edwyn C. Hoskyns. London: Oxford University Press, 1933.

————. *The Doctrine of the Word of God*, Part 2. Translated by G. T. Thomson and Harold Knight. Vol. 1, *Church Dogmatics*, ed. G. W. Bromiley and T. F. Torrance. Edinburgh: T&T Clark, 1956.

————. *The Doctrine of Creation*, Part 1. Translated by J. W. Edwards et al. Vol. 3, *Church Dogmatics*, ed. G. W. Bromiley and T. F. Torrance. Edinburgh: T&T Clark, 1958.

Bartholomew, Craig G. "Uncharted Waters: Philosophy, Theology and the Crisis in Biblical Interpretation." In *Renewing Biblical Interpretation*, ed. Craig Bartholomew, Colin Greene, and Karl Möller, 1–39. Carlisle: Paternoster, 2000.

Barton, John. *The Nature of Biblical Criticism*. Louisville: Westminster John Knox, 2007.

Bochet, Isabelle. "Le cercle herméneutique dans le *De doctrina christiana* d'Augustin." *Studia Patristica* 33, ed. Elizabeth A. Livingstone (1997): 16–21.

Bockmuehl, Markus. *Seeing the Word: Refocusing New Testament Study*. Studies in Theological Interpretation. Grand Rapids: Baker, 2006.

————. "Ruminative Overlay: Matthew's Hauerwas." *Pro Ecclesia* 17, no. 1 (2008): 20–28.

Bonner, Gerald. *Freedom and Necessity: St. Augustine's Teaching on Divine Power and Human Freedom*. Washington, D.C.: The Catholic University of America Press, 2007.

Bright, Pamela. *The Book of Rules of Tyconius: Its Purpose and Inner Logic*. Vol. 2, Christianity and Judaism in Antiquity, ed. Charles Kannengiesser. Notre Dame: University of Notre Dame Press, 1988.

————. "'The Preponderating Influence of Augustine': A Study of the Epitomes of the *Book of Rules* of the Donatist Tyconius." In *Augustine and the Bible*, ed. and trans. Pamela Bright, 109–128. Notre Dame: University of Notre Dame Press, 1999. [Expanded from: "Tyconius and His Interpreters: A Study of the Epitomes of the *Book of Rules*." In *A Conflict of Christian Hermeneutics in Roman Africa: Tyconius and Augustine*, Charles Kannengiesser and Pamela Bright, 23–39. Protocol of the Fifty-Eighth Colloquy: 16 October 1988, ed. Wilhelm Wuellner. Center for Hermeneutical Studies in Hellenistic and Modern Culture. Berkeley: Center for Hermeneutical Studies, 1989.]

————. "Augustine and the Ethics of Reading the Bible." In *The Reception and Interpretation of the Bible in Late Antiquity: Proceedings of the Montréal Colloquium in Honour of Charles Kannengiesser, 11–13 October 2006*, ed. Lorenzo DiTommaso and Lucian Turcescu, 55–64. Vol. 6, Bible and Ancient Christianity. Leiden: Brill, 2008.

Bright, Pamela, ed. and trans. *Augustine and the Bible*. Notre Dame: University of Notre Dame Press, 1999.

Brock, Brian. *Singing the Ethos of God: On the Place of Christian Ethics in Scripture.* Cambridge: Eerdmans, 2007.

Brown, Peter. *Augustine of Hippo: A Biography.* London: Faber & Faber, 1967. [New edition with epilogue: London: Faber & Faber, 2000.]

Brunner, Peter. "Charismatische und methodische Schriftauslegung nach Augustins Prolog zu De doctrina christiana." *Kerygma und Dogma* 1 (1955): 59–69, 85–103.

Burnaby, John. *Amor Dei: A Study of the Religion of St. Augustine.* London: Hodder & Stoughton, 1938.

Burnett, Richard E. *Karl Barth's Theological Exegesis: The Hermeneutical Principles of the* Römerbrief *Period.* Grand Rapids: Eerdmans, 2004.

Burns, J. Patout. *The Development of Augustine's Doctrine of Operative Grace.* Paris: Études Augustiniennes, 1980.

———. "Delighting the Spirit: Augustine's Practice of Figurative Interpretation." In *De Doctrina Christiana: A Classic of Western Culture,* ed. Duane W. H. Arnold and Pamela Bright, 183–194. Notre Dame: University of Notre Dame Press, 1995.

Byassee, Jason, *Praise Seeking Understanding: Reading the Psalms with Augustine.* Grand Rapids: Eerdmans, 2007.

Cameron, Michael. "The Christological Substructure of Augustine's Figurative Exegesis." In *Augustine and the Bible,* ed. and trans. Pamela Bright, 74–103. Notre Dame: University of Notre Dame Press, 1999.

Canning, R. "The Unity of Love for God and Neighbour." *Augustiniana* 37 (1987): 38–121.

Cavadini, John C. "The Sweetness of the Word: Salvation and Rhetoric in Augustine's *De doctrina christiana.*" In *De Doctrina Christiana: A Classic of Western Culture,* ed. Duane W. H. Arnold and Pamela Bright, 164–181. Notre Dame: University of Notre Dame Press, 1995.

Chadwick, Henry. "Tyconius and Augustine." In *A Conflict of Christian Hermeneutics in Roman Africa: Tyconius and Augustine,* Charles Kannengiesser and Pamela Bright, 49–55. Protocol of the Fifty-Eighth Colloquy: 16 October 1988, ed. Wilhelm Wuellner. Center for Hermeneutical Studies in Hellenistic and Modern Culture. Berkeley: Center for Hermeneutical Studies, 1989.

Childs, Brevard S. "The Sensus Literalis of Scripture: An Ancient and Modern Problem." In *Beiträge zur Alttestamentlichen Theologie: Festschrift für Walther Zimmerli zum 70. Geburtstag,* ed. Herbert Donner, Robert Hanhard, and Rudolf Smend, 80–93. Göttingen: Vandenhoeck & Ruprecht, 1977.

———. *Biblical Theology of the Old and New Testaments: Theological Reflection on the Christian Bible.* Minneapolis: Fortress, 1992.

————. "On Reclaiming the Bible for Christian Theology." In *Reclaiming the Bible for the Church*, ed. Carl E. Braaten and Robert W. Jenson, 1–17. Edinburgh: T&T Clark, 1995.

————. "Toward Recovering Theological Exegesis." *Pro Ecclesia* 6 (1997): 16–26.

————. *The Struggle to Understand Isaiah as Christian Scripture*. Cambridge: Eerdmans, 2004.

————. "Speech-Act Theory and Biblical Interpretation." *Scottish Journal of Theology* 58 (2005): 375–392.

Chin, Catherine M. "The Grammarian's Spoils: *De Doctrina Christiana* and the Contexts of Literary Education." In *Augustine and the Disciplines: From Cassiciacum to* Confessions, ed. Karla Pollmann and Mark Vessey, 167–183. Oxford: Oxford University Press, 2005.

Colish, Marcia L. "Augustine's Use and Abuse of Tyconius." In *A Conflict of Christian Hermeneutics in Roman Africa: Tyconius and Augustine*, Charles Kannengiesser and Pamela Bright, 42–48. Protocol of the Fifty-Eighth Colloquy: 16 October 1988, ed. Wilhelm Wuellner. Center for Hermeneutical Studies in Hellenistic and Modern Culture. Berkeley: Center for Hermeneutical Studies, 1989.

Combès, G., and J. Farges. Introduction to *La Doctrine Chrétienne*. BA 11, 151–606. Paris: Desclée de Brouwer et Cie, 1949.

Daly, Brian E. "Is Patristic Exegesis Still Usable? Reflections on Early Christian Interpretation of the Psalms." *Communio* 29 (2002): 185–216.

Davis, Ellen F., and Richard B. Hays, eds. *The Art of Reading Scripture*. Grand Rapids: Eerdmans, 2003.

Dawson, David. "Sign Theory, Allegorical Reading, and the Motions of the Soul in *De Doctrina Christiana*." In *De Doctrina Christiana: A Classic of Western Culture*, ed. Duane W. H. Arnold and Pamela Bright, 123–141. Notre Dame: University of Notre Dame Press, 1995.

————. *Christian Figural Reading and the Fashioning of Identity*. Berkeley: University of California Press, 2002.

D'Costa, Gavin. "Revelation, Scripture, and Tradition: Some Comments on John Webster's Conception of 'Holy Scripture.'" *International Journal of Systematic Theology* 6 (2004): 337–350.

Derrida, Jacques. *Of Grammatology*. Translated by Gayatri Chakravorty Spivak. Baltimore: Johns Hopkins University Press, 1997.

Drobner, Hubertus R. "Studying Augustine: An Overview of Recent Research." In *Augustine and His Critics: Essays in Honour of Gerald Bonner*, ed. Robert Dodaro and George Lawless, 18–34. London: Routledge, 2000.

Duchrow, Ulrich. "Zum Prolog von Augustins De Doctrina Christiana." *Vigiliae christianae* 17 (1963): 165–172.

———. *Sprachverständnis und Biblisches Hören bei Augustin.* Tübingen: J. C. B. Mohr, 1965.

Eagleton, Terry. *Literary Theory: An Introduction,* 2nd ed. Oxford: Blackwell, 1996.

Eden, Kathy. "The Rhetorical Tradition and Augustinian Hermeneutics in *De doctrina christiana.*" *Rhetorica* 8 (1990): 45–63.

———. *Hermeneutics and the Rhetorical Tradition: Chapters in the Legacy and Its Humanist Reception.* Yale Studies in Hermeneutics. London: Yale University Press, 1997.

Engels, J. "La doctrine du signe chez saint Augustin." *Studia Patristica* 6, ed. F. L. Cross, 366–373. Berlin: Akademie, 1962.

English, Edward D., ed. *Reading and Wisdom: The* De doctrina christiana *of Augustine in the Middle Ages.* London: Notre Dame Press, 1995.

Enos, Richard Leo, et al., eds. *The Rhetoric of Saint Augustine of Hippo:* De Doctrina Christiana *and the Search for a Distinctly Christian Rhetoric.* Studies in Rhetoric and Religion 7. Waco, Tex.: Baylor University Press, 2008.

Ferretter, Luke. "The Trace of the Trinity: Christ and Difference in Saint Augustine's Theory of Language." *Literature and Theology* 12, no. 3 (1998): 256–267.

Fish, Stanley. *Is There a Text in This Class? The Authority of Interpretive Communities.* Cambridge, Mass.: Harvard University Press, 1980.

Fortin, Ernest L. "Augustine and the Problem of Christian Rhetoric." In *The Rhetoric of Saint Augustine of Hippo:* De Doctrina Christiana *and the Search for a Distinctly Christian Rhetoric,* ed. Richard Leo Enos et al., 219–233. Studies in Rhetoric and Religion 7. Waco, Tex.: Baylor University Press, 2008.

Foster, David. "Eloquentia Nostra (DDC IV,VI,100): A Study of the Place of Classical Rhetoric in Augustine's *De doctrina christiana* Book Four." *Augustinianum* 36, no. 2 (1996): 459–494.

Fowl, Stephen E. "The Ethics of Interpretation, or What's Left Over after the Elimination of Meaning." In *The Bible in Three Dimensions: Essays in Celebration of Forty Years of Biblical Studies in the University of Sheffield,* ed. David J. A. Clines, Stephen E. Fowl, Stanley E. Porter, 379–398. Journal for the Study of the Old Testament Supplement Series 87. Sheffield: Sheffield Academic, 1990.

———. "The New Testament, Theology, and Ethics." In *Hearing the New Testament: Strategies for Interpretation,* ed. Joel B. Green, 394–410. Grand Rapids: Eerdmans, 1995.

———. "Texts Don't Have Ideologies." *Biblical Interpretation* 3, no. 1 (1995): 15–34.

———. Introduction to *The Theological Interpretation of Scripture: Classic and Contemporary Readings*, ed. Stephen E. Fowl. Oxford: Blackwell, 1997.

———. *Engaging Scripture*. Challenges in Contemporary Theology. Oxford: Blackwell, 1998.

———. "The Role of Authorial Intention in the Theological Interpretation of Scripture." In *Between Two Horizons: Spanning New Testament Studies and Systematic Theology*, ed. Joel B. Green and Max Turner, 71–87. Grand Rapids: Eerdmans, 2000.

———. *Philippians*. The Two Horizons New Testament Commentary. Grand Rapids: Eerdmans, 2005.

———. "Virtue." In *Dictionary for Theological Interpretation of the Bible*, ed. Kevin J. Vanhoozer, 837–839. London: SPCK, 2005.

———. "Further Thoughts on Theological Interpretation." In *Reading Scripture with the Church: Toward a Hermeneutic for Theological Interpretation*, by A. K. M Adam et al., 125–130. Grand Rapids: Baker, 2006.

———. "The Importance of a Multivoiced Literal Sense of Scripture." In *Reading Scripture with the Church: Toward a Hermeneutic for Theological Interpretation*, by A. K. M Adam et al., 35–50. Grand Rapids: Baker, 2006.

———. "Scripture." In *The Oxford Handbook of Systematic Theology*, ed. John Webster, Kathryn Tanner, and Iain Torrance, 345–361. Oxford: Oxford University Press, 2007.

———. Review of *Seeing the Word*, by Markus Bockmuehl. *Modern Theology* 24 (2008): 516–518.

———. *Theological Interpretation of Scripture*. Cascade Companions. Eugene: Cascade, 2009.

Fowl, Stephen E., and L. Gregory Jones. *Reading in Communion*. Grand Rapids: Eerdmans, 1991. Reprint, Eugene: Wipf and Stock, 1998.

Frei, Hans W. *The Eclipse of the Biblical Narrative*. London: Yale University Press, 1974.

———. "The 'Literal Reading' of Biblical Narrative in the Christian Tradition: Does It Stretch or Will It Break?" In *Theology and Narrative: Selected Essays*, ed. George Hunsinger and William C. Placher, 117–152. Oxford: Oxford University Press, 1993.

———. "Theology and Interpretation of Narrative: Some Hermeneutical Considerations." In *Theology and Narrative: Selected Essays*, ed. George Hunsinger and William C. Placher, 94–116. Oxford: Oxford University Press, 1993.

———. *The Identity of Jesus Christ: The Hermeneutical Bases of Dogmatic Theology.* Eugene: Wipf and Stock, 1997.

Frend, W. H. C. *The Donatist Church: A Movement of Protest in Roman North Africa.* Oxford: Clarendon, 1952.

Gadamer, Hans-Georg. *Truth and Method.* Translated by Garrett Barden and John Cumming. New York: Crossroads, 1989. Reprint, London: Continuum, 2003.

———. "Autobiographical Reflections." In *The Gadamer Reader: A Bouquet of the Later Writings,* ed. and trans. Richard E. Palmer, 3–38. Topics in Historical Philosophy. Evanston: Northwestern University Press, 2007.

Gorman, Michael M. "The Diffusion of the Manuscripts of Saint Augustine's 'De doctrina christiana' in the Early Middle Ages." *Revue Bénédictine* 95 (1985): 11–24.

Grech, Prosper. "Hermeneutical Principles of Saint Augustine in *Teaching Christianity.*" In Introduction to *Teaching Christianity (De Doctrina Christiana),* by Augustine, 80–94. Translated by Edmund Hill. Part 1, Vol. 11, The Works of Saint Augustine: A Translation for the Twenty-First Century, ed. John E. Rotelle. New York: New City, 1996.

Green, Joel B., and Max Turner, eds. *Between Two Horizons: Spanning New Testament Studies and Systematic Theology.* Grand Rapids: Eerdmans, 2000.

———. *The Two Horizons New Testament Commentary.* Grand Rapids: Eerdmans, 2005–2007.

Green, Roger P. H. "Augustine's *De doctrina Christiana*: Some Clarifications." *Res Publica Litterarum* 15 (1992): 99–108.

———. Introduction to *De doctrina christiana,* by Augustine. Oxford Early Christian Texts. Oxford: Clarendon, 1995.

———. Introduction to *On Christian Teaching,* by Augustine. Oxford World's Classics. Oxford: Oxford University Press, 1997.

Green, William M. "A Fourth Century Manuscript of Saint Augustine?" *Revue Bénédictine* 69 (1959): 191–197.

———. "Textual Notes on Augustine's 'De doctrina christiana.'" *Revue des Études Augustiniennes* 8 (1962): 225–231.

———. *Praefatio* to *De doctrina christiana.* CSEL 80 (1963), vii–xxix.

Greene-McCreight, Kathryn E. *Ad Litteram: How Augustine, Calvin, and Barth Read the 'Plain Sense' of Genesis 1–3.* New York: Peter Lang, 1999.

———. "Literal Sense." In *Dictionary for Theological Interpretation of the Bible,* ed. Kevin J. Vanhoozer, 455–456. London: SPCK, 2005.

Grondin, Jean. *Introduction to Philosophical Hermeneutics.* Translated and edited by Joel Weinsheimer. London: Yale University Press, 1994.

Gunton, Colin E. *The Promise of Trinitarian Theology*, 2nd ed. Edinburgh: T&T Clark, 1997.

Hagendahl, Harald. *Augustine and the Latin Classics*. Studia Graeca et Latina 20. Göteborg: Almquist & Wiksell, 1967.

Hall, Robert W. "Reading the Bible from within Our Traditions: The 'Rule of Faith' in Theological Hermeneutics." In *Between Two Horizons: Spanning New Testament Studies and Systematic Theology*, ed. Joel B. Green and Max Turner, 88–107. Grand Rapids: Eerdmans, 2000.

Harrison, Carol. *Beauty and Revelation in the Thought of Saint Augustine*. Oxford: Clarendon, 1992.

———. "The Rhetoric of Scripture and Preaching: Classical Decadence or Christian Aesthetic?" In *Augustine and His Critics: Essays in Honour of Gerald Bonner*, ed. Robert Dodaro and George Lawless, 214–230. London: Routledge, 2000.

———. "De Doctrina Christiana." *New Blackfriars* 87, no. 1008 (2006): 121–131.

———. *Rethinking Augustine's Early Theology: An Argument for Continuity*. Oxford: Oxford University Press, 2006.

Hauerwas, Stanley. *Unleashing the Scripture: Freeing the Bible from Captivity to America*. Nashville: Abingdon, 1993.

———. *Matthew*. Brazos Theological Commentary on the Bible. Grand Rapids: Brazos, 2006.

Hays, Richard B. "Reading the Bible with Eyes of Faith: The Practice of Theological Exegesis." *Journal of Theological Interpretation* 1, no. 1 (2007): 5–21.

Heidegger, Martin. *Being and Time*. Translated by John Macquarrie and Edward Robinson. New York: HarperOne, 1962.

Hill, Edmund. "*De Doctrina Christiana*: A Suggestion." *Studia Patristica* 6, ed. F. L. Cross, 443–446. Berlin: Akademie, 1962.

———. Translator's Note to *Teaching Christianity* (*De Doctrina Christiana*), by Augustine, 95–97. Part 1, Vol. 11, The Works of Saint Augustine: A Translation for the Twenty-First Century, ed. John E. Rotelle. New York: New City, 1996.

Istace, Gilbert, "Le livre premier du '*De doctrina christiana*' de Saint Augustin." *Ephemerides Theologicae Lovanienses* 32 (1956): 289–330.

Jackson, B. Darrell. "Semantics and Hermeneutics in Saint Augustine's *De doctrina christiana*." Ph.D. diss., Yale University, 1967.

———. "The Theory of Signs in St. Augustine's *De Doctrina Christiana*." In *Augustine: A Collection of Critical Essays*, ed. R. A. Markus, 92–147. Garden City: Anchor, 1972. [= *Revue des Études Augustiniennes* 15 (1969): 9–49].

Jacobs, Alan. *A Theology of Reading: The Hermeneutics of Love*. Radical Traditions. Boulder: Westview, 2001.

Jeanrond, Werner G. "Hermeneutics and Christian Praxis: Some Reflections on the History of Hermeneutics." *Literature and Theology* 2 (1988): 174–188.

———. *Text and Interpretation as Categories of Theological Thinking.* Translated by Thomas J. Wilson. Eugene: Wipf and Stock, 1988.

———. "After Hermeneutics: The Relationship Between Theology and Biblical Studies." In *The Open Text: New Directions for Biblical Studies?*, ed. Francis Watson, 85–102. London: SCM, 1993.

———. *Theological Hermeneutics: Development and Significance.* London: SCM, 1994.

———. "Criteria for New Biblical Theologies." *The Journal of Religion* 76 (1996): 233–249.

———. *A Theology of Love.* London: T&T Clark, 2010.

Jenson, Robert W. "Hermeneutics and the Life of the Church." In *Reclaiming the Bible for the Church*, ed. Carl E. Braaten and Robert W. Jenson, 89–105. Edinburgh: T&T Clark, 1995.

———. *Systematic Theology*, 2 vols. Oxford: Oxford University Press, 1997–1999.

———. *Canon and Creed.* Interpretation. Louisville: Westminster John Knox, 2010.

Johnson, Luke Timothy. "Matthew or Stanley? Pick One." *Pro Ecclesia* 17, no. 1 (2008): 29–34.

Jordan, Mark D. "Words and Word: Incarnation and Signification in Augustine's *De doctrina christiana.*" *Augustinian Studies* 11 (1980): 177–196.

Kannengiesser, Charles. "Local Setting and Motivation of *De Doctrina Christiana.*" In *Augustine: Presbyter Factus Sum*, ed. Earl C. Muller, Joseph T. Lienhard, and Roland J. Teske, 331–339. New York: Peter Lang, 1993.

———. "The Interrupted *De doctrina christiana.*" In *De Doctrina Christiana: A Classic of Western Culture*, ed. Duane W. H. Arnold and Pamela Bright, 3–13. Notre Dame: University of Notre Dame Press, 1995.

———. "Tyconius crux interpretorum: A Response to Karla Pollmann." *Augustinian Studies* 29 (1998): 99–108.

———. "Augustine and Tyconius: A Conflict of Christian Hermeneutics in Roman Africa." In *Augustine and the Bible*, ed. and trans. Pamela Bright, 149–177. Notre Dame: University of Notre Dame Press, 1999. [Expanded from: "Augustine and Tyconius: A Conflict of Christian Hermeneutics in Roman Africa." In *A Conflict of Christian Hermeneutics in Roman Africa: Tyconius and Augustine*, Charles Kannengiesser and Pamela Bright, 1–22. Protocol of the Fifty-Eighth Colloquy: 16 October 1988, ed. Wilhelm Wuellner. Center for Hermeneutical Studies in Hellenistic and Modern Culture. Berkeley: Center for Hermeneutical Studies, 1989.]

Kannengiesser, Charles, and Pamela Bright. *A Conflict of Christian Herme-neutics in Roman Africa: Tyconius and Augustine*. Protocol of the Fifty-Eighth Colloquy: 16 October 1988, ed. Wilhelm Wuellner. Center for Hermeneutical Studies in Hellenistic and Modern Culture. Berkeley: Center for Hermeneutical Studies, 1989.

Kelsey, David H. *Proving Doctrine: The Uses of Scripture in Modern Theology*. Harrisburg: Trinity, 1999.

Kevane, Eugene. "Augustine's *De Doctrina Christiana*: A Treatise on Chris-tian Education." *Recherches Augustiniennes* 4 (1966): 97–133.

———. "Paideia and Anti-Paideia: The *Prooemium* of St. Augustine's *De Doctrina Christiana*." *Augustinian Studies* 1 (1970): 153–180.

Kugler, Robert A. "Tyconius's *Mystic Rules* and the Rules of Augustine." In *Augustine and the Bible*, ed. and trans. Pamela Bright, 129–148. Notre Dame: University of Notre Dame Press, 1999.

Kuruvilla, Abraham. *Text to Praxis: Hermeneutics and Homiletics in Dialogue*. Library of New Testament Studies 374. London: T&T Clark, 2009.

La Bonnardière, Anne-Marie. "The Canon of Sacred Scripture." In *Augus-tine and the Bible*, ed. and trans. Pamela Bright, 26–41. Notre Dame: University of Notre Dame Press, 1999.

La Bonnardière, Anne-Marie, ed. *Saint Augustine et la Bible*. Bible et tous les temps. Paris: Beauchesne, 1986.

Lancel, Serge. *Saint Augustine*. Translated by Antonia Nevill. London: SCM, 2002.

Leinhard, Joseph T. "Reading the Bible and Learning to Read: The Influ-ence of Education on St. Augustine's Exegesis." *Augustinian Studies* 27 (1996): 7–25.

Lettieri, Gaetano. *L'Altro Agostino: Ermeneutica e retorica della grazia dalla crisi alla metamorfosi del De doctrina christiana*. Brescia: Morcelliana, 2001.

Levering, Matthew. *Participatory Biblical Exegesis: A Theology of Biblical Interpretation*. Notre Dame: University of Notre Dame Press, 2008.

Lindbeck, George A. *The Nature of Doctrine: Religion and Theology in a Post-liberal Age*. Philadelphia: Westminster, 1984.

———. "Postcritical Canonical Interpretation: Three Modes of Retrieval." In *Theological Exegesis: Essays in Honor of Brevard S. Childs*, ed. Chris-topher Seitz and Kathryn Greene-McCreight, 26–51. Grand Rapids: Eerdmans, 1999.

———. "Scripture, Consensus and Community." In *The Church in a Post-liberal Age*, ed. James J. Buckley, 201–222. Radical Traditions. London: SCM, 2002.

Louth, Andrew. "Augustine on Language." *Journal of Literature and Theology* 3 (1989): 151–158.

Mangina, Joseph L. "Hidden from the Wise, Revealed to Infants: Stanley Hauerwas's Commentary on Matthew." *Pro Ecclesia* 17, no. 1 (2008): 13–19.

Markus, R.A. "St. Augustine on Signs." In *Sacred and Secular: Studies on Augustine and Latin Christianity*, 60–83. Aldershot: Variorum, 1994.

———. "Signs, Communication, and Communities in Augustine's *De Doctrina Christiana*." In *De Doctrina Christiana: A Classic of Western Culture*, ed. Duane W.H. Arnold and Pamela Bright, 97–109. Notre Dame: University of Notre Dame Press, 1995.

Marrou, Henri-Irénée. *Saint Augustin et la fin de la culture antique*. Paris, 1938.

Martin, Joseph. *Praefatio* to *De doctrina christiana libri quattuor*. CCL 32 (1962), vii–xxxvii.

Mayer, Cornelius. "'Res per signa': Der Grundgedanke des Prologs in Augustins Schrift *De doctrina christiana* und das Problem seiner Datierung." *Revue des Études Augustiniennes* 20 (1974): 100–112.

McCurry, Jeffrey. "Towards a Poetics of Theological Creativity: Rowan Williams Reads Augustine's *De doctrina* after Derrida." *Modern Theology* 23 (2007): 415–433.

Miles, Margaret R. "Patriarchy as Political Theology: The Establishment of North African Christianity." In *Rereading Historical Theology: Before, During, and After Augustine*, 55–70. Eugene: Cascade, 2008.

Moberly, R.W.L. *The Bible, Theology, and Faith: A Study of Abraham and Jesus*. Cambridge Studies in Christian Doctrine. Cambridge: Cambridge University Press, 2000.

———. "Biblical Criticism and Religious Belief." *Journal of Theological Interpretation* 2 (2008): 71–100.

———. Review of *The Bible and the Crisis of Meaning: Debates on the Theological Interpretation of Scripture* by D. Christopher Spinks. *Journal of Theological Studies* 59 (2008): 710–712.

Monfasani, John. "The *De doctrina christiana* and Renaissance Rhetoric." In *Reading and Wisdom: The De doctrina christiana of Augustine in the Middle Ages*, ed. Edward D. English, 172–188. London: Notre Dame Press, 1995.

Moreau, Madeleine. "Lecture du 'De doctrina christiana.'" In *Saint Augustine et la Bible*, ed. Anne-Marie la Bonnardière, 253–285. Bible et tous les temps. Paris: Beauchesne, 1986.

———. Introduction to *La Doctrine Chrétienne*. Oeuvres de Saint Augustine. *Bibliothèque Augustinienne* 11/2, 9–50. Paris: Institut d'Études Augustiniennes, 1997.

Murphy, James J. "St. Augustine and the Debate about a Christian Rhetoric." In *The Rhetoric of Saint Augustine of Hippo:* De Doctrina Christiana *and the Search for a Distinctly Christian Rhetoric*, ed. Richard Leo Enos et al., 205–218. Studies in Rhetoric and Religion 7. Waco, Tex.: Baylor University Press, 2008.

Mutzenbecher, Almut. "Codex Leningrad Q.v.I.3 (Corbie): Ein Beitrag zu seiner Beschreibung." *Sacris Erudiri* 18 (1967–68): 435–437.

O'Donovan, Oliver. "*Usus* and *Fruitio* in Augustine, *De Doctrina Christiana* I.*" Journal of Theological Studies* 33 (1982): 361–397.

Opelt, Ilona. "Doctrina und Doctrina Christiana." *Der altsprachliche Unterricht* 9 (1966): 5–22.

O'Regan, Cyril. "*De Doctrina Christiana* and Modern Hermeneutics." In *De Doctrina Christiana: A Classic of Western Culture*, ed. Duane W. H. Arnold and Pamela Bright, 217–243. Notre Dame: University of Notre Dame Press, 1995.

Paddison, Angus. *Theological Hermeneutics and 1 Thessalonians.* Society for New Testament Studies Monograph Series 133. Cambridge: Cambridge University Press, 2005.

———. "Scriptural Reading and Revelation: A Contribution to Local Hermeneutics." *International Journal of Systematic Theology* 8 (2006): 433–448.

———. *Scripture: A Very Theological Proposal.* London: T&T Clark, 2009.

———. "The Living Authority of Scripture." Paper presented to the Society of the Study of Theology, April 2011.

Pagels, Elaine. *Adam, Eve, and the Serpent.* London: Weidenfeld & Nicolson, 1988.

Patte, Daniel, and Eugene TeSelle, eds. *Engaging Augustine on Romans: Self, Context, and Theology in Interpretation.* Romans through History and Cultures Series. Harrisburg: Trinity, 2002.

Pecknold, C. C. *Transforming Postliberal Theology: George Lindbeck, Pragmatism and Scripture.* London: T&T Clark, 2005.

Plumer, Eric. "*Expositio epistulae ad Galatas.*" In *The Oxford Guide to the Historical Reception of Augustine*, ed. Karla Pollmann et al. Oxford: Oxford University Press, forthcoming.

Pollmann, Karla. *Doctrina Christiana: Untersuchungen zu den Anfängen der christlichen Hermeneutik unter besonderer Berücksichtigung von Augustinus, De doctrina christiana.* Paradosis 41. Freiburg, Switzerland: Universitätsverlag Freiburg Switzerland, 1996.

———. "Doctrina christiana (De-)." In Vol. 2, *Augustinus-Lexikon*, ed. Cornelius Mayer. Basel: Schwabe, 1996.

———. "To Write by Advancing in Knowledge and to Advance by Writing." *Augustinian Studies* 29, no. 2 (1998): 131–137.

————. "Hermeneutical Presuppositions." In *Augustine Through the Ages: An Encyclopedia*, ed. Allan D. Fitzgerald, 426–429. Cambridge: Eerdmans, 1999.

————. *Augustinus: Die christliche Bildung (De doctrina Christiana)*. Universal-Bibliothek. Stuttgart: Reclam, 2002.

————. "Augustine's Hermeneutics as a Universal Discipline!?" In *Augustine and the Disciplines: From Cassiciacum to* Confessions, ed. Karla Pollmann and Mark Vessey, 206–231. Oxford: Oxford University Press, 2005.

Pollmann, Karla, and Mark Vessey, eds. *Augustine and the Disciplines: From Cassiciacum to* Confessions. Oxford: Oxford University Press, 2005.

Portalié, Eugene. *A Guide to the Thought of Saint Augustine*. Translated by Ralph J. Bastian. Chicago: Henry Regnery Company, 1960. Reprint, Westport: Greenwood, 1975.

Press, Gerald A. "The Subject and Structure of Augustine's De Doctrina Christiana." *Augustinian Studies* 11 (1980): 99–124.

————. "The Content and Argument of Augustine's *De Doctrina Christiana*." *Augustiniana* 31 (1981): 165–182.

————. "*Doctrina* in Augustine's *De Doctrina Christiana*." *Philosophy and Rhetoric* 17, no. 2 (1984): 98–120.

————. "Tyconius in Augustine's De doctrina Christiana." In *A Conflict of Christian Hermeneutics in Roman Africa: Tyconius and Augustine*, Charles Kannengiesser and Pamela Bright, 62–66. Protocol of the Fifty-Eighth Colloquy: 16 October 1988, ed. Wilhelm Wuellner. Center for Hermeneutical Studies in Hellenistic and Modern Culture. Berkeley: Center for Hermeneutical Studies, 1989.

Primmer, Adolf. "The Function of the *genera dicendi* in *De doctrina christiana* 4." In *De Doctrina Christiana: A Classic of Western Culture*, ed. Duane W. H. Arnold and Pamela Bright, 68–86. Notre Dame: University of Notre Dame Press, 1995.

Radner, Ephraim. *Hope amongst the Fragments: The Broken Church and Its Engagement of Scripture*. Grand Rapids: Brazos, 2004.

Rae, Murray A. *History and Hermeneutics*. London: T&T Clark, 2005.

Räisänen, Heikki. *Beyond New Testament Theology*, 2nd ed. London: SCM, 2000.

Reno, R. R. "Biblical Theology and Theological Exegesis." In Vol. 5, *Out of Egypt: Biblical Theology and Biblical Interpretation*, ed. Craig Bartholomew et al., 385–408. Bletchley: Paternoster, 2004.

————. Series Preface to the Brazos Theological Commentary on the Bible. In *Matthew* by Stanley Hauerwas, 9–14. Grand Rapids: Brazos, 2006.

Reno, R. R., ed. *Brazos Theological Commentary on the Bible.* Grand Rapids: Brazos, 2005–2009.

Ricoeur, Paul. "The Hermeneutical Function of Distanciation." In *Hermeneutics and the Human Sciences*, ed. John B. Thompson, 131–144. Cambridge: Cambridge University Press, 1981.

———. "The Task of Hermeneutics." In *Hermeneutics and the Human Sciences*, ed. John B. Thompson, 43–62. Cambridge: Cambridge University Press, 1981.

———. "What Is a Text? Explanation and Understanding." In *Hermeneutics and the Human Sciences*, ed. John B. Thompson, 145–164. Cambridge: Cambridge University Press, 1981.

———. "Rhetoric—Poetics—Hermeneutics." Translated by Robert Harvey. In *Rhetoric and Hermeneutics in Our Time: A Reader*, ed. Walter Jost and Michael J. Hyde, 60–72. New Haven: Yale University Press, 1997.

Rowe, C. Kavin, and Richard B. Hays. "Biblical Studies." In *The Oxford Handbook of Systematic Theology*, ed. John Webster, Kathryn Tanner, and Iain Torrance, 435–455. Oxford: Oxford University Press, 2007.

Sarisky, Darren. *Scriptural Interpretation: A Theological Account.* Oxford: Blackwell, forthcoming.

Schäublin, Christoph. "Zum Text von Augustin, De doctrina Christiana." *Wiener Studien* N. F. 8 (1974): 173–181.

———. "*De doctrina christiana*: A Classic of Western Culture?" In *De Doctrina Christiana: A Classic of Western Culture*, ed. Duane W. H. Arnold and Pamela Bright, 47–67. Notre Dame: University of Notre Dame Press, 1995.

Schildgen, Brenda Deen. "Augustine's Answer to Jacques Derrida in the De Doctrina Christiana." *New Literary History* 25 (1994): 383–397.

Schleiermacher, Friedrich. *Hermeneutics and Criticism and Other Writings.* Translated by Andrew Bowie. Cambridge Texts in the History of Philosophy. Cambridge: Cambridge University Press, 1998.

Schneiders, Sandra M. *The Revelatory Text: Interpreting the New Testament as Sacred Scripture*, 2nd ed. Collegeville: Liturgical, 1999.

Scottish Liturgy 1970. The General Synod of the Scottish Episcopal Church.

Seitz, Christopher R. *Figured Out: Typology and Providence in Christian Scripture.* Louisville: Westminster John Knox, 2001.

Sieben, Hermann-Josef. "Die 'Res' der Bibel: Eine Analyse von Augustinus, *De Doctr. Christ.* I–III." *Revue des Études Augustiniennes* 21 (1975): 72–90.

Simonetti, Manlio. Introduction to *L'Istruzione Cristiano.* Fondazione Lorenzo Valla, 1994.

Spinks, Christopher D. *The Bible and the Crisis of Meaning: Debates on the Theological Interpretation of Scripture.* London: T&T Clark, 2007.

Steinhauser, Kenneth B. "Codex Leningradensis Q.v.I.3: Some Unresolved Problems." In *De Doctrina Christiana: A Classic of Western Culture,* ed. Duane W. H. Arnold and Pamela Bright, 33–43. Notre Dame: University of Notre Dame Press, 1995.

Stendahl, Krister. "Biblical Theology, Contemporary." In Vol. 1, *Interpreter's Dictionary of the Bible,* 418–431. New York: Abingdon, 1962.

Stock, Brian. *Augustine the Reader: Meditation, Self-Knowledge, and the Ethics of Interpretation.* London: Belknap, 1996.

Stout, Jeffrey. "What Is the Meaning of a Text?" *New Literary History* 14, no. 1 (1982): 1–12.

Studer, Basil. "Augustinus und Tyconius im Licht der patristichen Exegese." *Augustinian Studies* 29 (1998): 109–117.

Tanner, Kathryn E. "Theology and the Plain Sense." In *Scriptural Authority and Narrative Interpretation,* ed. Garrett Green, 59–78. Philadelphia: Fortress, 1987.

TeSelle, Eugene. *Augustine the Theologian.* London: Burns & Oates, 1970.

———. "Engaging Scripture: Patristic Interpretation of the Bible." In *Engaging Augustine on Romans: Self, Context, and Theology in Interpretation,* ed. Daniel Patte and Eugene TeSelle, 1–62. Harrisburg: Trinity, 2002.

Teske, Roland J. "Criteria for Figurative Interpretation in St. Augustine." In *De Doctrina Christiana: A Classic of Western Culture,* ed. Duane W. H. Arnold and Pamela Bright, 109–122. Notre Dame: University of Notre Dame Press, 1995.

Thiselton, Anthony C. *New Horizons in Hermeneutics: The Theory and Practice of Transforming Biblical Reading.* Grand Rapids: Zondervan, 1992.

———. *The First Epistle to the Corinthians: A Commentary on the Greek Text.* The New International Greek Testament Commentary. Grand Rapids: Eerdmans, 2000.

———. "Resituating Hermeneutics in the Twenty-First Century: A Programmatic Reappraisal." In *Thiselton on Hermeneutics: Collected Works with New Essays,* 33–50. Cambridge: Eerdmans, 2006.

———. "A Retrospective Reappraisal of Part VII: The Contributions of the Five Essays to Hermeneutics, and the Possibility of Theological Hermeneutics." In *Thiselton on Hermeneutics: Collected Works with New Essays,* 793–807. Cambridge: Eerdmans, 2006.

Ticciati, Susannah. "The Castration of Signs: Conversing with Augustine on Creation, Language, and Truth." *Modern Theology* 23 (2007): 161–179.

Toom, Tarmo. *Thought Clothed with Sound: Augustine's Christological Hermeneutics in* De Doctrina Christiana. Vol. 4, International Theological Studies: Contributions of Baptist Scholars, ed. Thorwald Lorenzen. Bern: Peter Lang, 2002.

———. "The Potential of a Condemned Analogy: Augustine on λόγος ἐνδιάθετος and λόγος προφορικός." *The Heythrop Journal* 48, no. 2 (2007): 205–213.

Torrance, Thomas F. *Divine Meaning: Studies in Patristic Hermeneutics.* Edinburgh: T&T Clark, 1995.

Tracy, David. *Blessed Rage for Order: The New Pluralism in Theology.* New York: Seabury, 1975.

———. *The Analogical Imagination: Christian Theology and the Culture of Pluralism.* London: SCM, 1981.

———. *Plurality and Ambiguity: Hermeneutics, Religion, Hope.* London: Harper & Row, 1987.

———. "On Reading the Scriptures Theologically." In *Theology and Dialogue: Essays in Conversation with George Lindbeck,* ed. Bruce D. Marshall, 35–68. Notre Dame: University of Notre Dame Press, 1990.

Treier, Daniel J. "Theological Hermeneutics, Contemporary." In *Dictionary for Theological Interpretation of the Bible,* ed. Kevin J. Vanhoozer, 787–793. London: SPCK, 2005.

———. "Biblical Theology and/or Theological Interpretation of Scripture?" *Scottish Journal of Theology* 61 (2008): 16–31.

———. *Introducing Theological Interpretation of Scripture: Recovering a Christian Practice.* Grand Rapids: Baker, 2008.

Trobisch, David. *The First Edition of the New Testament.* Oxford: Oxford University Press, 2000.

Turner, Max, and Joel B. Green. "New Testament Commentary and Systematic Theology: Strangers or Friends?" In *Between Two Horizons: Spanning New Testament Studies and Systematic Theology,* ed. Joel B. Green and Max Turner, 1–22. Grand Rapids: Eerdmans, 2000.

Van Fleteren, Frederick. "St. Augustine, Neoplatonism, and the Liberal Arts: The Background to *De Doctrina Christiana.*" In *De Doctrina Christiana: A Classic of Western Culture,* ed. Duane W. H. Arnold and Pamela Bright, 14–24. Notre Dame: University of Notre Dame Press, 1995.

———. "Augustine's Principles of Biblical Exegesis, *De doctrina christiana* Aside: Miscellaneous Observations." *Augustinian Studies* 27 (1996): 109–130.

———. "Toward an Understanding of Augustine's Hermeneutic." *Augustinian Studies* 29 (1998): 118–130.

————. "Principles of Augustine's Hermeneutic: An Overview." In *Augustine: Biblical Exegete*, ed. Frederick Van Fleteren and Joseph C. Schnaubelt, 1–32. New York: Peter Lang, 2001.

Vanhoozer, Kevin J. *Is There a Meaning in This Text? The Bible, the Reader, and the Morality of Literary Knowledge.* Grand Rapids: Zondervan, 1998.

————. *First Theology: God, Scripture, and Hermeneutics.* Downers Grove: InterVarsity, 2002.

Vanhoozer, Kevin J., ed. *Dictionary for Theological Interpretation of the Bible.* London: SPCK, 2005.

Verheijen, L. M. J. "Le De Doctrina Christiana de saint Augustin: Un manuel d'herméneutique et d'expression chrétienne avec, en II.19 (29)–42 (63), une 'charte fondamentale pour une culture chrétienne.'" *Augustiniana* 24 (1974): 10–20.

Vessey, Mark. "The Great Conference: Augustine and His Fellow Readers." In *Augustine and the Bible*, ed. and trans. Pamela Bright, 52–73. Notre Dame: University of Notre Dame Press, 1999.

Vischer, Wilhelm. *The Pentateuch.* Translated by A. B. Crabtree. Vol. 1, *The Witness of the Old Testament to Christ.* London: Lutterworth, 1949.

Von Campenhausen, Hans. *The Formation of the Christian Bible.* Translated by J. A. Baker. Philadelphia: Fortress, 1972.

Watson, Francis. *Text, Church and World: Biblical Interpretation in Theological Perspective.* Edinburgh: T&T Clark, 1994.

————. "Bible, Theology and the University: A Response to Philip Davies." *Journal for the Study of the Old Testament* 71 (1996): 3–16.

————. "The Scope of Hermeneutics." In *The Cambridge Companion to Christian Doctrine*, ed. C. E. Gunton, 65–80. Cambridge: Cambridge University Press, 1997.

————. *Text and Truth: Redefining Biblical Theology.* Edinburgh: T&T Clark, 1997.

————. *Agape, Eros, Gender: Towards a Pauline Sexual Ethic.* Cambridge: Cambridge University Press, 2000.

————. "Hermeneutics and the Doctrine of Scripture: Why They Need Each Other." *International Journal of Systematic Theology* 12 (2010): 118–143.

Watson, Gerard. "Saint Augustine's Theory of Language." In *The Rhetoric of Saint Augustine of Hippo: De Doctrina Christiana and the Search for a Distinctly Christian Rhetoric*, ed. Richard Leo Enos et al., 247–265. Studies in Rhetoric and Religion 7. Waco, Tex.: Baylor University Press, 2008.

"The Way of the Cross." In *The Book of Occasional Services 1994*, 56–73. New York: Church Publishing, 1995.

Weaver, Rebecca Harden. "Reading the Signs: Guidance for the Pilgrim Community." *Interpretation* 58, no. 1 (2004): 28–41.

Webster, John. *Word and Church: Essays in Christian Dogmatics*. Edinburgh: T&T Clark, 2001.

———. *Holy Scripture: A Dogmatic Sketch*. Cambridge: Cambridge University Press, 2003.

———. "Karl Barth." In *Reading Romans through the Centuries: From the Early Church to Karl Barth*, ed. Jeffrey P. Greenman and Timothy Larson, 205–223. Grand Rapids: Brazos, 2005.

———. "Theologies of Retrieval." In *The Oxford Handbook of Systematic Theology*, ed. John Webster, Kathryn Tanner, and Iain Torrance, 583–599. Oxford: Oxford University Press, 2007.

Westphal, Merold. *Whose Community? Which Intepretation? Philosophical Hermeneutics for the Church*. The Church and Postmodern Culture, ed. James K. A. Smith. Grand Rapids: Baker, 2009.

Wetzel, James. "Pelagius Anticipated: Grace and Election in Augustine's *Ad Simplicianum*." In *Augustine: From Rhetor to Theologian*, ed. Joanne McWilliam, 121–132. Ontario: Wilfrid Laurier University Press, 1992.

Williams, Anna N. *The Divine Sense: The Intellect in Patristic Theology*. Cambridge: Cambridge University Press, 2007.

Williams, Rowan. "Language, Reality, and Desire in Augustine's *De Doctrina*." *Journal of Literature and Theology* 3, no. 2 (1989): 138–150.

———. "The Discipline of Scripture." In *On Christian Theology*, 44–59. Oxford: Blackwell, 2000.

———. *Why Study the Past? The Quest for the Historical Church*. London: Darton, Longman and Todd, 2005.

Wolterstorff, Nicholas. *Divine Discourse: Philosophical Reflections on the Claim that God Speaks*. Cambridge: Cambridge University Press, 1995.

Wood, Charles M. *The Formation of Christian Understanding: An Essay in Theological Hermeneutics*. Philadelphia: Westminster, 1981.

Wood, Donald. "The Place of Theology in Theological Hermeneutics." *International Journal of Systematic Theology* 4 (2002): 156–171.

Work, Telford. *Living and Active: Scripture in the Economy of Salvation*. Grand Rapids: Eerdmans, 2002.

Wright, N. T. *The New Testament and the People of God*. London: SPCK, 1992.

———. *Scripture and the Authority of God: How to Read the Bible Today*. New York: HarperCollins, 2011.

Yeago, David S. "The New Testament and the Nicene Dogma: A Contribution to the Recovery of Theological Exegesis." In *The Theological Interpretation of Scripture: Classic and Contemporary Readings*, ed. Stephen Fowl, 87–100. Oxford: Blackwell, 1999.

Young, Frances. "The Rhetorical Schools and Their Influence on Patristic Exegesis." In *The Making of Orthodoxy: Essays in Honour of Henry Chadwick*, ed. Rowan Williams, 182–199. Cambridge: Cambridge University Press, 1989.

———. *Biblical Exegesis and the Formation of Christian Culture*. Cambridge: Cambridge University Press, 1997.

———. "Alexandrian and Antiochene Exegesis." In *A History of Biblical Interpretation*. Vol. 1, *The Ancient Period*, ed. Alan J. Hauser and Duane F. Watson, 334–354. Grand Rapids: Eerdmans, 2003.

———. "Augustine's Hermeneutics and Postmodern Criticism." *Interpretation* 58, no. 1 (2004): 42–55.

———. "The 'Mind' of Scripture: Theological Readings of the Bible in the Fathers." *International Journal of Systematic Theology* 7 (2005): 126–141.

Zimmermann, Jens. *Recovering Theological Hermeneutics: An Incarnational-Trinitarian Theory of Interpretation*. Grand Rapids: Baker, 2004.

# Index of Ancient Texts

The following refer to citations and to substantive discussions. I have omitted citations that fall within an overarching discussion. For example, *doct. chr.* 1.4.4 does not appear because the passage is discussed in the section covering book 1.

## Texts by Augustine

# Index of Names and Subjects

JAMES A. ANDREWS

is research associate in the Cambridge Inter-Faith Programme,

Faculty of Divinity, University of Cambridge.